Strength
for the
Journey

Messages of Hope and
Inspiration from God's Word

DAVID RENISON

WESTBOW
PRESS®
A DIVISION OF THOMAS NELSON
& ZONDERVAN

WestBow Press books may be ordered through booksellers or by contacting:

WestBow Press
A Division of Thomas Nelson & Zondervan
1663 Liberty Drive
Bloomington, IN 47403
www.westbowpress.com
844-714-3454

Scripture quotations are taken from the Holy Bible, King James Version.

ISBN: 979-8-3850-1673-0 (sc)
ISBN: 979-8-3850-1672-3 (e)

Library of Congress Control Number: 2024900738

Print information available on the last page.

WestBow Press rev. date: 01/23/2024

Dedication

To the Berean Class

Friends who pursue faithfulness to the Word
of God every Sunday morning!

Contents

Introduction

Spend some time reading messages of hope and inspiration from God's Word! STRENGTH FOR THE JOURNEY broadens the audience of two other widely read publications, WORSHIP THE KING! and LIGHT FOR OUR WAY. All devotionals are prayerfully written and anchored to Biblical (KJV) references.

Whether you have grown in the knowledge of our Lord (2 Peter 3:18) or are a newcomer to the Christian faith, we all live in the progression of becoming more like Jesus. As you read the following pages, I trust you will be strengthened for life's journey.

The Deity of Jesus Christ

JOHN 1:1 DECLARES, "IN THE BEGINNING WAS THE WORD (SPEAKING OF Jesus), and the Word was with God, and the Word was God." Jesus' identity has been confused, denied, and wrongly portrayed for nearly two thousand years. But Scripture teaches that Jesus is God. When Jesus came to the coasts of Philippi, he asked his disciples, saying, "Whom do men say that I, the Son of man, am?" The varied responses He received in Matthew 16:13-16 are still given by many today. Some will say that Jesus is merely a prophet, an honorable man, or a good moral teacher. But believing in the deity of Jesus is essential to our being saved from the wrath of God (Rev. 20:11-15). The apostle Paul said, "Believe on the Lord Jesus Christ, and you shall be saved" (Acts. 16:31). Then, in his first letter to the Corinthians (15:1-4), Paul declares the gospel by which we are saved; how that Christ died for our sins, that he was buried, and that He rose again the third day according to the scriptures. We must believe in the all-sufficiency of Christ as Savior: "Neither is there salvation in any other: for there is none other name under heaven given among men, whereby we must be saved" (Acts 4:12). The fullness of God in Christ is foundational to Biblical Christianity (Col. 2:9). If Jesus is not God and Christ is not risen, our faith is meaningless (1 Cor. 15:14).

After Jesus' disciples told Him the speculations others were making about His identity, He asked a piercing question: "But whom say ye that I am?" Simon Peter answered, "Thou art the Christ, the Son of the living God." The word Christ means "the anointed One." And in identifying Jesus as the Christ, Peter declared the Messiah as God incarnate who came to be the world's Savior. The Bible reveals Christ as the eternal God who took on human flesh to redeem fallen humanity. Jesus did not begin His life in Bethlehem's manger. He has existed

1

from eternity past and will never cease to exist (Col. 1:16, Rev. 1:8). Every attribute of sovereignty and deity is ascribed to Jesus Christ. He is omniscient (all-knowing), omnipotent (all-powerful), and His eternality is revealed in both the Old and New Testaments (Micah 5:2, Isa. 9:6, John 8:58, Heb. 7:3).

Of the sufficiency of Jesus, the Holy Spirit led Apostle Paul to write, "For in him dwelleth all the fullness of the Godhead bodily" (Col. 2:9). This is a mystery that we cannot intellectually understand, and I have grown weary of those who say they can. There are many things we cannot comprehend (Rom. 11:33-34), not the least of which is the manner in which God manifests Himself to us (John 14:23-26, 2 Cor. 13:14). Nevertheless, Bible truths are certain, and they are eternal (Ps. 119:160). My prayer is that we place as much emphasis on verses 30 and 31 of Mark 12 as we do on verse 29. A resolution of the people does not socially determine the doctrine of the Deity of Christ. As there are inherent physical laws, so there are inherent Biblical laws. A majority could vote unanimously to suspend the law of gravity for one hour, but no one in their right mind would jump off the roof to test it. We live by faith (2 Cor. 5:7). How do you explain a man who had once been hungry (Mark 11:12), then fed thousands with a little boy's tiny lunch (John 6), and later proclaimed, "I am the bread of life?" Who does this? How does a man carried in a boat stand to take control of (Mark 5:35-41) - and even walk on - the very sea on which his vessel sailed? How can a man tell a person He is the water of everlasting life (John 4:10-14) and later say, "I thirst" (John 19:28) even as he is dying? How can we understand a man like that? How do we define a man who raised himself from the dead, walked through walls, and ascended into heaven? The answer is, "We can't." But this we know: He is the image of the invisible God (Col. 1:15)!

Christian friend, our journey is one of faith (2 Cor. 5:7), and we must exchange mere intellectual knowledge and understanding for the simplicity of believing. Accepting Jesus as a great moral teacher but not taking His claim to be God is something we cannot do. Why? Because a man who was merely human and said the same things Jesus said would not be a moral man at all (John 8:58, 17:1-21). The choice is ours: to disbelieve or bow at Jesus's feet and call Him Lord! We who teach and preach the gospel must not think of ourselves as public relations agents sent to establish goodwill between Christ and the world. We must not imagine ourselves commissioned to make Christ acceptable to science, big business, the press, sports, or modern entertainment. We are not diplomats. We are ambassadors. Jesus said, "I am the light of the world… if ye believe not that I am he, ye shall die in your sins" (John 8). The physical manifestation of Christ was prophesied seven hundred years before Jesus was born. The Old Testament prophet Isaiah said, "Therefore the Lord himself shall give you a sign; Behold, a virgin shall conceive, and bear a son, and shall call his name Immanuel." His very name means "God with us!"

Someone has said, "The chances of just eight of the three hundred Old Testament prophetical references about Jesus being fulfilled in one person is 1 in 10 to the 17th power." He said, "Imagine the entire state of Texas covered in silver dollars, two feet deep. Only one coin would be marked, and the entire sea of silver dollars would be thoroughly mixed. A blindfolded man would be instructed to travel as far as he wished, but he must pick up the marked coin on his first try." Whether or not this is a good illustration is beyond me. But this I know: Reconciliation with God did not come by man's initiative (2 Pet. 1:21). We have redemption through Christ, for salvation is only of God! In 1 John 4:9-10, we read, "In this was manifested the love of God toward us, because that God sent his only begotten Son into the world, that we might live through him." Jesus is the sacrifice for our sins. His purpose in coming was to seek and save those who are lost (Luke 19:10). And as the substitutionary atonement at Calvary, Jesus freely offers eternal life to all who will turn from feeling secure in the deeds they have done (Isa. 54:6) and trust only in Him (John 14:6, Acts 4:12).

The resurrection of Jesus provided resounding proof of His deity. Not only had He raised others from the dead, but He raised Himself from the dead. Henry Morris said, "The bodily resurrection of Jesus Christ from the dead is the crowning proof of Christianity" (1 Cor. 15:17-19). In John 21:12, we read that, after His resurrection, Jesus made Himself known to the disciples through a miraculous work. Then, in verse 12, He invites them to "Come and dine." How are we answering the invitation? I say this because His call to us should be treated as even more than an invitation. Let me illustrate: Someone once wrote and asked Emily Post, the etiquette expert of another generation, "What is the correct procedure when one is invited to the White House but has a previous engagement?" She replied, "An invitation to dine at the White House is a command, and it automatically cancels any other engagement." So, what do we do when Jesus Christ, God manifest in the flesh, the Creator of all things, the King of kings, the Lord of lords, the Ruler of the universe, and the Savior of souls invites us to grow in relationship with Him? We must consider well the way we answer when He calls.

Shortly after joining the Navy, the recruit asked his officer for a pass so he could attend a wedding. The officer gave him the pass but informed the young man he would have to be back by 7 p.m. Sunday. "You don't understand, sir," said the recruit. "I'm in the wedding." "No, you don't understand," the officer shot back. "You're in the Navy!" If we have been born again, we are not our own (1 Cor. 6:19-20). The apostle Peter says we are a chosen generation, a royal priesthood, a holy nation, a peculiar people; that we should show forth the praises of Him who called us out of darkness into his marvelous light (1 Peter 2:9). In 2 Timothy 2:3-5, Apostle Paul tells us to endure hardness, as a good soldier of Jesus Christ. We dare not entangle ourselves with the affairs of this life in ways - or to the extent - that would displease the One who has enlisted us into His army. Jesus Christ is not valued at all until He is valued above all. There is no such thing as part-time loyalty to Jesus Christ. George MacDonald wrote,

> I said: Let me walk in the field.
> God said: Nay, walk in the town.
> I said: There are no flowers there.
> He said: No flowers, but a crown.
> I cast one look at the fields, then set my face to the town.
> He said: My child, do you yield? Will you leave the
> flowers for the crown? Then into His hand went mine,
> and into my heart came He; and I walk in a light Divine,
> the path I had feared to see."

Who is Jesus? This is the most important question we will ever consider. Why? He is God's only provision for sin (Rom. 5:8). He is the only way to everlasting life in heaven (John 14:6, Acts 4:12). Jesus is infinitely more than a prophet, a good teacher, or a godly man. He is Messiah (John 1:41), King (1 Tim. 6:15), and Priest (Heb. 4:14-16). He is the Savior (Matt. 1:20-21), the Sovereign One (Eph. 1:17-23), the Creator (1 Cor. 8:6), and Sustainer of all things (Heb. 1:1-10). He is our Redeemer (Eph. 1:7). He is the One who deserves our highest honor, loyalty, and praise. We who believe in the atoning blood of Christ and His resurrection are justified by grace; we have been redeemed (Rom. 3:24-25). O, how wonderful it is that our Lord is ready to assume full responsibility for a life wholly yielded to Him.

No Other Gospel

If someone were to ask you, "What is the gospel of the Bible?" how would you respond? The apostle Paul summarizes the answer in Romans 1:16, "… it is the power of God unto salvation to every one that believeth…" The gospel is that Jesus died for our sins, according to the Scripture, that He was buried, and that He raised Himself from the dead (1 Cor. 15:3-4). It is the person and work of Christ, the sin-bearing sacrifice of Jesus and His righteousness that is imputed to those who believe (Matt. 5:48, Rom. 3:22, 2 Cor. 5:21). The New Testament word gospel means "good news," referring to the announcement that Jesus has brought the rule of God to our world through His life, ministry, death, and resurrection (Rom. 1:1-4, 1 Cor. 15:1-4). The heart of the Gospel of Jesus Christ is justification by faith alone, in Christ alone, apart from the works of the law (Eph. 2:1-10). In biblical terms, the good news to be preached to everyone everywhere is "Jesus Christ and him crucified" (1 Cor. 2:2). The gospel is the incarnation of God in Jesus, the long-awaited Messiah of the Old Testament. Not just a man, but God (John 1:1-14). The "gospel of God" is not a message about God. It is a message that belongs to God, is authored by God, and is owned by God. In Romans 1:11-12, Paul writes, "But I certify you, brethren, that the gospel which was preached of me is not after man. For I neither received it of man, neither was I taught it, but by the revelation of Jesus Christ." And because the gospel originates with God himself, it is not ours to edit.

Writing to the churches at Galatia, Apostle Paul expressed his great astonishment that the Galatian Christians, who had come to Jesus with great rejoicing when he brought the gospel message, were now listening to those who were teaching the bondage of observing external rules

(Gal. 1:6-24). They were pouring theological weedkiller on the precious seeds Paul had planted. Their deceptive message was that, in addition to faith in the work of Christ, these Gentiles needed to add observance to old covenant laws. Our nature is to move toward the salvation of self-reliance because it builds our self-worth. But we must rest decisively in God's work, not our own. We were converted through believing, not doing (Rom. 1:17). The Holy Spirit carries us from our first steps of faith until our last breath (Gal. 3:3). Many preach the gospel plus something; perhaps the need for a certain degree of emotional reaction or a measure of religious rules. People are often motivated by guilt to make staggering commitments, which they quickly discover they are unable or unwilling to sustain. Their confidence rests on some performance they have achieved. All of this represents something of my upbringing. Do not put pride in your pedigree (Rom. 2:17-20). A religious heritage brings no bonus points. Don't try to do what only God can do. Salvation is God's business, and the Scriptures declare that no flesh shall be justified by the works of the law (Rom. 3:20, Gal. 2:16-21, 5:4). The great need is to be taught biblically, not just stirred emotionally. Nothing can be in the heart that is not first in the mind. Paul speaks of a transformation of our minds in Romans 12:2. Godly living is not based on emotional surges of Charismatic sensationalism. Deliverance from sin is never found in a program, rule book, religious manipulation, drama, or theatrics. There can be no mixture of grace and human interference. The gospel is a message of grace that convicts us of our sins (Acts 16:30), produces a changed life through true repentance (Acts 26:20), and assures us of God's forgiveness and eternal life in heaven (1 John 1:9).

Some will tie the gospel to miraculous works as validating signs of salvation. Others connect it to the inward power of the messenger. Neither is relative to the gospel of Christ. These mistaken points of view have been the cause of guilt, condemnation, and despair. People have gotten into following religious hunches from pulpits rather than "searching the scriptures daily, whether those things were so" (Acts 17:11). Just because someone is heartfelt in their conviction does not mean they are right. It is possible to be sincerely wrong. Very talented preachers came to the Galatian church with the information they said was vital to Christianity. Nowadays, a distorted message replete with denominational practices and traditions is often disguised as a "higher plateau in God" or "matured faith" (2 Pet. 2:1, Acts 4:12). Legalists are work-driven, not grace-driven, believing they are saved by what they do, experience, or know. The letter to Galatia is in your Bible because Paul couldn't tolerate a diluted gospel. We don't need a place to work; we need someone to work in our place. That "someone" is Jesus Christ. Friends, we are brought into a saving relationship with God because His grace is sufficient. His strength is made perfect in our weakness (1 Cor. 12:9). The cost of your sins is more than you can pay. The gift of your God is more than you can imagine. The righteousness of God is revealed in Scripture (Rom. 1:17). The truth of God effectually works in a believer (1 Thess. 2:13). The salvation of God is given by the Holy Spirit's power and deep conviction (1 Thess. 1:5). Salvation comes from heaven downward, not earth upward (Luke 1:78, James 1:17). Our faith does not stand in men's wisdom but in command of God (1 Cor. 2:1-5). There is no other gospel!

The good tidings of great joy (Luke 2:10) have never been about earning an entrance into God's family. I need not torment myself with the fear that my faith may fail (1 Pet. 1:5). As grace led me to trust in the first place, grace will keep me believing (John 10:28-29, 1 John 5:11-13). The Almighty who saved me first is still there to save me. There is never a point at which I am any less kept than I was the first moment He saved me (John 5:24, Rom. 8:1, 1 Pet. 1:5). We are not allowed to tamper with God's perfect gospel. We read in 1 Timothy 6:3-5, "If any man teach otherwise, and consent not to wholesome words, even the words of our Lord Jesus Christ, and to the doctrine which is according to godliness; He is proud, knowing nothing..." The apostle said, "From such withdraw thyself." We are in the service of the One in whom resides all authority to save from sin (Matt. 28:18). God converted Paul by revealing Himself on the Damascus road (Acts 9:1-19), and this was the beginning of an incredible journey. When once, by the power of God, a lame man instantly rose to his feet (Acts 2-3), Peter took advantage of the moment to preach a deeply convicting message. The apostle preached that Jesus was the promised Messiah and that salvation is found only in Him (Acts 4:12). Peter didn't merely proclaim Jesus as a way of salvation but the *only* way. Many who heard the gospel that day were saved! Jesus said, "I am the way, the truth, and the life; no man cometh unto the Father, but by me" (John 14:6). A true believer is marked by following the scriptures and allowing the Holy Spirit to work. A Christian will manifest the fruit of the Spirit (Gal. 5:21-22) by living according to God's Word. Their eyes are upon the God of the Bible, and they submit to Him without hesitation or reservation.

No matter where we travel, we find the shadow of hopelessness. We see it in the deep lines that furrow troubled brows. We sense it in humanity's search for fulfillment. Jesus said to a despairing world, "I have come that they might have life and that they might have it more abundantly" (John 10:10). The moment one receives Christ is the beginning of a new life. The Holy Spirit helps us cast off the old and put on the new (Eph. 4:22-24). The cross of Christ is the bridge over which all must pass if they would stand in the courts of Heaven (Eph. 2:13-16). Evangelist Billy Graham tells the story of a businessman in Melbourne, Australia, who, having separated from his wife and family, was living with another woman and drinking excessively while his business was deteriorating. "He came one night to our meeting and found Christ as Savior. A sense of release swept his soul. His tormented conscience was eased. His mind was cleared. With tears of joy, he was received once more into his family. He told me later, 'What resolution, religious pretenses, psychiatrists and doctors failed to do, Christ did for me in a few moments.' Then he made a statement I shall never forget. He said, 'To be a Christian is exhilarating!'" The gospel of the Cross is the power that works in us to do God's will, conforming us to the image of His Son (Rom. 8:29).

Carl Medearis said, "I visited a missions school at a large church in Waco, Texas, and decided to try a test in a class-sized proportion. "Tell me," I told the group, "what is the gospel?" A young lady raised her hand. "The free gift of God." "Good," I said. I went to the chalkboard and wrote a gift from God. "Somebody else?" "Freedom from sin," a man near the back called out. "Eternal life," said another. "Keep going," I said. I stayed busy at the chalkboard, listing the items as they came in. Freedom. Righteousness. Moral purity. Grace.

Unconditional love. Healing and deliverance. Redemption. Faith in God. New life. After five minutes, we filled the chalkboard with a list of things we believed were the gospel. "Excellent," I said. "Did we miss anything?" The room was silent for a minute. I could see heads turning. I could hear pages rustling. Everybody seemed to think something significant was missing, but nobody wanted to volunteer to name the missing item. Finally, after the second minute of silence, a girl near the front raised her hand. "How come none of us mentioned Jesus?" "Exactly," I said. We closed the session and went for a break. Point made.

Jesus Christ is the only hope for weary, sin-sick souls. Believers in the first-century church went everywhere preaching the Word (Acts 8:4); their message was the Cross (Acts 2:24-36). The gospel frees us from living by the world's standards because we have found our worth in Christ. The gospel is not a social platform or a self-improvement program. The gospel is not about how to have your best life now. The gospel does not guarantee health or financial success in this life. Some are very winsome in their presentation to satisfy the emotional needs of people who are taken in before they know what they're listening to. The gospel is not sharing our ideas about religion. The gospel is the narrative of who Jesus is and what He did (Acts 2:22-36). Many Christians seem to have lost their confidence in the gospel message. But in his letter to Christians in Rome, Paul presents the gospel as the only remedy for sin (Rom. 6:15-18). The doctrine of grace begins with a proper view of God's holiness and our sinfulness (1 Sam. 2:2, Jer. 17:9). In Philippians chapter three, Paul said he had spent his life trying to accumulate things he assumed would make him acceptable to God. But when he experienced the righteousness of God freely granted to him, he counted "all things but loss for the excellency of the knowledge of Christ Jesus." The apostle wasn't only putting off the burdensome ways of the old life but also putting on the graces of Jesus Christ through the power of the Holy Spirit (Col. 3:1-17). Brothers and sisters, embrace the purity of the gospel message wholeheartedly, for it is the power of God unto salvation to everyone who believes!

Lord Jesus, forgive us for our lack of confidence in the power you have invested in your gospel. That gospel has saved us, and because we have received it, we stand righteous before God. Please give us the courage and the passion to communicate your message in its fullness, for there is no other gospel. We pray this in your name and according to your will. Amen.

Loving the Wounded Among Us

WE WERE CREATED TO BE RELATIONAL (GEN. 2:18). OUR PURPOSE, fulfillment, and life itself flow from a relationship with our Creator. I believe our relationships define us. They represent who we are, whose we are, where we've been, where we are, and where we're going. Our relationship with God is the one that matters most. Jesus said, "I am the vine, ye are the branches… without me, ye can do nothing" (John 15:5). It is from this "vertical" connection that all "horizontal" relationships exist. We are God's masterpiece, made in His image (Gen. 1:27). We are the only creation for whom Jesus was willing to die. And if our alliance with God is broken, it is not because of anything He has done (2 Tim. 2:13). We have turned away from Him, causing injury to ourselves - and possibly others. When 10-year-old Jordan was asked, "How does knowing God's love affect your relationships with people?" He replied, "When somebody is being picked on or has no friends, I cheer them up. If somebody gets hurt, I try to help them and see if they're okay."

In 1983, Chuck Girard was inspired to write the song 'Don't Shoot the Wounded' when a friend said, "The Christian army is the only army that shoots its wounded." The first stanza reads:

> Don't shoot the wounded, they need us more than ever
> They need our love no matter what it is they've done
> Sometimes, we just condemn them,
> And don't take time to hear their story
> Don't shoot the wounded, someday, you might be one.

What a sad commentary. And who among us has not taken a shot, all too ready to aim our firearm of condemnation at someone who is not too different from us? And the shots are usually fired from the high walls we have built to hide our own weaknesses. We do not build fortresses around our strengths... there is no need for that. We only fortify our insecurities.

Many of us have been injured by betrayal, injustice, false accusations, humiliation, abandonment, or rejection – and it feels terrible! We struggle with questions like, "Can God ever use me again? Will Christians ever love me again? Will the church abandon me?" The brutal truth of life is that we all suffer from emotional pain, and it can last for years. Some people long for spiritual healing. Others, because of the pain they have endured, would rather inflict the same on a friend or family member. Perhaps this is happening to you right now. How do we treat a person when we feel the burden of their displeasure through no fault of our own? First, consider these three things: Every Christian will be persecuted (2 Tim. 3:12), those persecuted for righteousness's sake will inherit the kingdom of heaven (Matt. 5:10), and most importantly, the Son of God was wounded for our transgressions (Isa. 53:5). Demonstrate the love of Christ by being attentive to a person with emotional injuries. While the world stresses the importance of independence, the Bible teaches interdependence. Scripture emphasizes community (Rom. 12:4-5). Paul said, "Bear ye one another's burdens, and so fulfill the law of Christ" (Gal. 6:2). God said, "My strength is made perfect in weakness" (2 Cor. 12:9).

Emotional pain can manifest in sadness, anger, anxiety, shame, and guilt. How should we respond to those who "found God lacking" or have left the Christian family because of a bad experience? From those who were hurt by church leaders - to children who grew up in the faith but now reject it - to those who are angry with family members still walking with God, their stories are not something we should dismiss. They deserve our attention. Even if they mistreat us, we are to be Christlike. Quick answers, condemnation, and angry emotional responses serve no one. This only justifies their leaving the Bible-believing fellowship. Instead of being led by our desire to be correct, we can have the mind of Christ and let compassion motivate our actions (1 Cor. 2:16). Jesus always spoke the truth in love (Eph. 4:15). He taught what is doctrinally correct to a person who needed correction. Listening is not the same as approving. Compassion is not the same as compromise. Gentleness is not turning a blind eye to sin. A wounded person's experience does not negate ours nor modify the truth of Jesus Christ. The declarations of those who have turned their backs on God do not change the gospel message. Jesus Christ is still the "good tidings of great joy" to all people (Luke 2:10). Consequently, we should humbly listen, care for, and attend to their wounds as Jesus would. We should ask ourselves, "How can I best demonstrate love? How can I communicate truth in a way that will be heard?" Instead of asking, "How do I give them the right answers?" we ask, "How can I respond in a way that helps them see Jesus?" Many who have walked away seek an excuse to part ways with Jesus, but some hope there is a way back. We can illuminate their path by listening, loving, and sharing the stories we know to be true – ours and that of Jesus Christ.

All of us will be tempted to blame God and others for our conduct or neglect. A relational divide between two individuals often begins with a rejection of God. An injured person is consumed with what has been done to them, and since we live in their sphere of influence, they may cause us to share their discontent. Is this right? No. Is this fair? No. But it's real. From their perspective, they believe they have every right to be angry and unforgiving. Sadly, we become the "collateral damage" of their war with God. So, as believers, what can we do? We ask the Lord to soften their hearts by whatever means necessary. We pray that they will bow in complete surrender to Almighty God. Some parents, spouses, adult children, extended family members, or friends delight in making others conform to their wishes. Therefore, we must set boundaries for ourselves. Accepting responsibility for someone else's misguided resentment doesn't help anyone. There is a difference between supporting someone and trying to fix their problems to make them happy. One you can do. The other you simply cannot. But God can!

Why do people treat us poorly when they have a problem with God? It's mainly because their life is out of control, and it's much too hard to manage without God's loving guidance (John 15:5). Apostle Paul learned that looking at the attacks around him was not his job. His responsibility was to look to a God who was - and is - in the business of healing hearts. Seek God's wisdom, and He will be with you. All of us have experienced turning points in our lives. We have had opportunities to pivot, hit our knees, and fully surrender to God. Sadly, not everyone will kneel at the Cross. Some want to cling tightly to an identity as a victim, believing that they have been wronged in a way that cannot be healed or forgiven. They think this gives them an excuse to nurture their anger and negative feelings about God. Why? Because making excuses is easier than submitting to the Lordship of the Holy Spirit. For them, self-pity is a reliable friend who always gives them a ready audience, and it's difficult to convince them to apply God's sovereign love to their wounds. Therefore, we pray earnestly for them!

The Psalmist David's disappointment with a close friend is apparent in Psalm 55 as he cries out to God for help. He said, "My heart is sore pained within me." Was he being hurt by his enemies? Not at all. Notice what he says, "For it was not an enemy that reproached me; then I could have borne it." The sorrow of his heart was caused by a man with whom he was well acquainted. And of this person, he said, "We took sweet counsel together and walked unto the house of God in company" (v14). When we are hurt, emotions can overwhelm us. Finding ourselves alone and without the joy of the Lord, it becomes easy to lash out at those around us or clench a fist at God. It happens that a storm that leads one man to Jesus Christ drives another away (Acts 27:9-12). What is this drift? It is the decline of faith, doctrine, and practice, the loss of what we once valued most. If you feel you're a target of someone's unwarranted displeasure, love them through prayer and kindness. Jesus said, "Let your light so shine before men, that they may see your good works, and glorify your Father which is heaven" (Matt. 5:16). In Psalm 55, David expresses his confidence in God's help. He says, "As for me, I will call upon God, and the Lord shall save me. Evening, and morning, and at noon, will I pray, and cry aloud: and he shall hear my voice."

The Bible tells us to minister grace to those who will hear (Eph. 4:29), especially those in the household of faith (Gal. 6:10). A church is where we give and receive love and care. It's a local assembly where we grow in our faith and know God. We dare not make a lasting scar on the heart of a sibling and then try to justify our actions. Are we concerned for the well-being of God's children? Do we consider how we may have hurt them, even perhaps long ago? Respect is not gained from what we say but by how we act. People who have walked away from the community of God's people care little about the position we may hold in a local church. They are impressed by the life we live. God's missionary and author Amy Carmichael (1867-1951) wrote, "If I have not compassion on my fellow-servant, even as my Lord had pity on me, then I know nothing of Calvary's love." Christ came to people who were His enemies to make them His friends (Rom. 5:10). It's never too late to apologize and unlock the door to emotional healing.

So, what message should we give our wounded brothers and sisters? Consider your own reasons for joining the family of God. You didn't come to Jesus because you were well-adjusted and secure. You came because you desperately wanted God to give you a new heart— the same with me. Anger, confusion, bitterness, anxiety, or sorrow; whatever negative emotion I may experience is an opportunity to come to Jesus and be made whole. It's an occasion to feel the loving arms of a Heavenly Father who knows me, takes great delight in me, and has the power to restore me. I don't go to church because I am holy. I go to church because I am broken and needy. I need a community of Christians who care for me. I need to hear uplifting songs. I need the reading of Scripture and the preaching of God's Word. I need to be reminded of the cross of Calvary, through which I have a restored relationship with God and the promise of new life. As I kneel at the Cross, divine conviction stirs, and I rededicate my life to God. The gospel is the message of heaven to mankind. There are no words so profound as those in the Bible. There is no blessedness like my fellowship with the Lord and His children. In the household of believers, the Lord renews my spirit. He provides healing. I only have to bring my brokenness, and God takes care of the rest. This is the message we give to the wounded among us.

An Encounter With Jesus

IN LUKE 24:13-35, TWO OF JESUS' DISCIPLES WERE WALKING FROM Jerusalem to the village of Emmaus. The men had just left the holy city and were returning home, sad and confused. Sad because their hope died on a cross and was buried in a tomb; confused because they had heard reports that the grave was found empty by women who said Jesus was alive (v1-12). But since no one had seen Him, they doubted. It's easy for us to imagine their conversation as they walked together that day. No doubt they were trying to make sense of their desperate situation. Don't we all? Their hopes were dashed. Jesus was murdered, and nothing had happened by the third day. They and many other Jews once believed that Jesus would free His people from the tyranny of the Romans, but their faith was shaken when things went wrong. Their belief was based on what they could see and not on the truth Jesus had spoken to them in better days. Oh, we can certainly identify with this scenario. Their disappointment manifested from misinterpreting what Jesus came to Earth to accomplish. Jesus had foretold his death at least three times (Mark 8:31-33, 9:30-32, 10:32-34), but the Greek text declares these men were "slow of heart to believe." It's not that they didn't believe because they intellectually couldn't, but because of troubled hearts. Are you overwrought today? Jesus Christ was the answer to confusion then - and still is today. Bring your burden to the Lord, for He is an immovable, unshakable, faithful fortress (Ps. 18:1-3, Heb. 13:8). He is from past to present to future, your Rock of refuge for every moment!

These men were walking and discussing all the events of the past few days when the resurrected Jesus came alongside them and listened to their conversation. Scripture tells us they were kept from recognizing

Him (v16). It appears the men were debating what was true and why things had happened because Jesus' first reaction was to tell them they were "foolish" and "slow" in their belief. Still unrevealed, Jesus attempted to help their unbelief by telling them that although things look hopeless, they must look no further than Scripture to understand. Later, in their home, Jesus opened their understanding to the truth of His words. And if we ask Him (Rev. 3:20), He will do the same for us! How do you act when your spirit is disturbed, and life seems unfair? What do you do when darkness seems to drown out the promises of God? Never doubt in the night what God gave you in the light. Jesus said, "What I tell you in darkness, that speak ye in light: and what ye hear in the ear, that preach ye upon the housetops" (Matt. 10:27). Jesus doesn't want us to respond to troubling times in misplaced fear, but with confidence in His promises. Today is the day to grow your faith. Be encouraged – and encourage others! Our Lord is in every circumstance, regardless of what we think about the situation. Do not rely on your feelings, but look to God's Word. Life is so much better that way!

There was a time when sadness and confusion prevented me from seeing God's purpose. It was a challenging situation. Yes, I continued walking with the Lord in salvation but was preoccupied with my immediate difficulties. I was like the disciples; "slow of heart to believe." Nevertheless, it was an encounter with Jesus during which I gained a deeper understanding of God. The faithfulness of God was made known to me in the dark, and I am forever grateful. You and I are not so different from the Emmaus disciples. Let God into your house. Allow Him to break bread with you. Believe what He says and allow His words to fill you with hope. Just as Christ was gracious enough to open the disciples' eyes to His resurrection, He is also merciful when we struggle to believe. The experience of the two men on the Emmaus road is powerful. Not only does it serve as one of many post-resurrection appearances of Jesus, but it shows us how we can look to the Bible to see God's plan unfolding.

At an average walking pace from Jerusalem to Emmaus, Jesus taught a two-and-one-half hour Bible study: "Beginning at Moses and all the prophets, he expounded unto them in all the scriptures the things concerning himself" (Luke 24:27). Whatever Old Testament passages

Jesus shared with the travelers, he showed them God's promise to bring salvation to lost sinners and how it was accomplished in his life, death, and resurrection (John 3:16, Rom. 5:8). He wanted them to know that the Bible is true, trustworthy, and consistent. Steve Richardson had lost several close family members to drowning accidents and sickness. Several other private family incidents occurred, and his bride-to-be broke his heart. Jilted, hurt - and very angry - Steve went, alone, to his church to tell the Lord goodbye and leave his faith. In desperation, he knelt and began to talk to the Lord. He said, "Lord, I just stopped here to say goodbye. And I guess, thank you for everything you've done for me in the past." He began naming each thing. An hour later, after being lost in God's presence, Steve came out with a smile and a song:

> Verse 1:
> My steps had led me far away; sometimes, I wondered why. They had taken me down lonely roads beneath the darkened sky. But every time I lost my way, my Lord came to me. He sought me out; He took my hand and said He'd walk with me.

> Chorus:
> Just to walk with Him means everything to me. Just to know He's near, His hand is leading me. Though the world pass me by, go their way, let me be; just to walk with Him means everything to me.

Experiencing loss is never easy, but God walks with us. The two companion disciples left Jerusalem, perhaps feeling there was no longer reason to stay (v13,18). The Bible says they were discussing recent events among themselves (v14-15). There is comfort in talking with other believers about the things that trouble us, especially when experiences are shared. In that sense, the Emmaus Road story presents a timeless and reassuring picture of the church. If you are struggling, ask the Lord to help you find fellowship. When we endure loss, disappointment, or confusion, the body of Christ is there to help us. Our Lord can use His people to bring healing. When the two men associated their sorrow with "the things that happened," Jesus replied, "What sort of things?" (v18-19). He is showing us that helping others involves asking questions so we can understand their needs. The presence of the Lord brings a reassurance that we need to move forward. I am overwhelmed by the power of the Holy Spirit and what He has done in my life.

Zaccheus met the Lord for salvation (Luke 19:1-10). Nicodemus sought Jesus in the middle of the night (John 3:1-21, 19:39). The woman with the issue of blood went to Jesus for healing (Mark 5:25-34). The widow of Nain, whose son died, had an encounter with Jesus, and her son's life was restored (Luke 7:11-17). The Samaritan woman at Jacob's well had a divine appointment with God (John 4:1-42). Jacob had a face-to-face meeting with Jehovah at a place called Peniel (Gen. 32:30). Abraham's encounter with God caused him to go where he did not know (Heb. 11:8). Moses spoke with I AM at the burning bush (Ex. 3:13). King David talked about times in the wilderness when none of his elder brothers was around (1 Sam. 17:34-37). They were beautiful and wonderful times spent with God. When you have an encounter with Jesus and a willing heart, you will never be the same again. Saul, the prosecutor, became Paul the apostle (Acts 9:1-19). Rahab, a former harlot, was changed from the inside out and began a new life with God (Josh. 2:1-14). Peter got a second chance to prove his love for the Lord (Luke 22:54-62, John 21:15-25). The dying thief was delivered from the wrath of God in a moment (Luke 23:39-43). Formerly possessed by Satan's power, a delivered Mary Magdalene was the first to declare the risen Savior (Luke 8:2, Mark 16:9). A blind man met Jesus and received his sight (John 9:35-38). Cornelius humbly submitted to the gospel message (Acts 10). To have God rewrite our stories is the greatest miracle of all! Encounters with Jesus will seldom be what we expect. And sometimes, He will address questions we weren't asking. We might pray for guidance in a specific direction. He reminds us to seek wisdom instead (Matt. 6:33). If we ask Him to take particular sorrows out of our lives, He may tell us to trust and wait patiently (Ps. 27:14). Our Lord wants us to understand He has everything under control (Isa. 45:6-7).

The town of Emmaus represents the place we go to escape the place of our pain and disappointment. Josephus said: "Now Emmaus if it be interpreted, may be rendered 'a warm bath' - for therein is a spring of warm valuable water for healing." Your Emmaus could be whatever you do or wherever you go to ease your sorrow – or your disillusionment with the Lord. God can meet with us in our ordinary places and experiences when life becomes too hard. But sometimes, He meets us in unfamiliar manifestations – and when we least expect Him. Part of the Christian existence is discovering how little we rest on Christ, constantly discovering that we need to place more confidence in Him. We may feel discomfort, but He has promised to be with us (Matt. 28:20). Do not create a false expectation of how the Lord will answer your prayer. Wrong assumptions about how God will move in our lives can cause us to miss His visitation. There are outcomes we wish we could control, but we cannot. Sometimes, human expectations that do not materialize will cause confusion, resentment, and bitterness against God. The Psalmist David prayed, "Create in me a clean heart, O God; and renew a right spirit within me" (Ps. 51:10).

The Holy Spirit is ever-present, and He wants to travel the road of life with you. Do not ignore the truth of who God is or His ability to help you in your time of need. The truth of God's Word is more real than what we feel. Don't fear the darkness; even the tiniest spark of Light will be seen there. With "a right spirit," every encounter with God will lead you into a more meaningful relationship. Ultimately, the Emmaus story is a glorious transformation of two men who did not fully understand the experience. Yet, they became powerful witnesses for Jesus (Luke 24:35). Two grief-stricken friends were not ready, but God made them willing. Their sorrow turned into joy. Death turned into life. Dashed expectations became new possibilities. With eyes open and hearts burning (v30-35), they understood God in ways they had never known. This is the blessing of an encounter with Jesus Christ!

Soli Deo Gloria

THE WRITINGS OF JOHANN SABASTIAN BACH SHAPED THE MUSIC OF HIS day, and they continue to inspire us today. Living in the late 17th and early 18th century, Bach composed several hundred pieces, many of which were written to draw people closer to God. The title of his first published composition is translated as "God is My King." His musical manuscripts reveal something exciting and inspiring. In many of his works, he wrote "JJ" at the top of the page. JJ was an abbreviation for the Latin phrase "Jesu Juva," which, translated into English, means "Jesus, help." Bach didn't write a single note without seeking God's blessing with the prayer, "Jesus, help me." The composer wanted the world to know that God alone would receive glory for anything he accomplished. An even greater contribution might be the three letters written at the end of his sheet music to clarify the purpose of his work: SDG. These letters are the abbreviation of the Latin phrase "*Soli Deo Gloria,*" translated as "To God Alone, the Glory." His music was not written to bring attention to the performers, the conductor, or even the composer. This music was crafted for the glory of God. Every note, chord, and page of music pointed beyond its human creator to the One by whom "all things are created" (Col. 1:16). Soli Deo Gloria captures the essence of Paul's words in 1 Corinthians 10:31, "Whether therefore ye eat, or drink, or whatsoever ye do, do all to the glory of God." Every day presents an opportunity to bring glory to our God. Soli Deo Gloria is not limited to church buildings, religious anthems, and sacred hymns - but to every corner of life.

In 1 Timothy 1:17, Apostle Paul declares the glory of the only One deserving, "Now unto the King eternal, immortal, invisible, the only wise God, to honor and glory forever and ever. Amen." In Isaiah 42:8,

God is speaking, "I am the Lord: that is my name: and my glory will I not give to another, neither my praise to graven images." Jehovah, the great I AM, declares that we should value no opinions, maintain no doctrines, and entertain no thoughts that would disparage the honor of His name. Nor should we ascribe to our wisdom, skill, or power that which He alone can accomplish. God will not allow us to take credit for what He does. King Herod was immediately struck down because he accepted the people's worship instead of giving the glory to God (Acts 12:20-23). In Jeremiah 9:23, we read the words of the Lord, "Let not the wise man glory in his wisdom, neither let the mighty man glory in his might, let not the rich man glory in his riches: but let him glory in this, that he understand and know me, that I am the Lord that exercises lovingkindness, judgment, and righteousness, in the earth: for in these things I delight, saith the Lord."

We love to be recognized, congratulated, honored and validated. But oh, what a deadly sin it is when our eyes shift to ourselves instead of focusing on Jesus. Herod's position of authority did not save him. His royal robes could not keep him alive. In 2 Corinthians 10, Paul rebukes those in the church of Corinth who were boasting about their accomplishments. The human spirit longs for recognition and appreciation. We want others to think highly of us and to praise us for our achievements. And when we take the glory that belongs to God and selfishly make it our own, we steal what rightfully belongs to Him (Acts 14:8-18). Although the phrase *Mother Nature* is popular, it is an incorrect reference to the natural world. Creation came into existence by the will of God (Rev. 4:11). The Almighty spoke into existence the laws of nature, and He alone sustains the universe! When I think about the many times I have desired recognition for my efforts, I thank God for His mercy! The apostle Peter said, "Blessed be the God and Father of our Lord Jesus Christ..." (1 Pet. 1:3). Today, when I worship the Lord, something rises within me that lets me know I'm doing what He desires. Bach said, "All music should have no other end and aim than to the glory of God and the soul's refreshment." When I sing the praises of the King eternal, I want those listening to see only the crucified Christ. Jesus is the answer for a desperate world enslaved by sin. And the beauty of life is that, with all surrendered, God will use us for His glory.

When Julius Caesar returned to Rome after many years of fighting its battles abroad, he planned grand festivities and victory processions to celebrate his triumphs over Gaul, Egypt, Pontos, and Africa. His goal was to hold the people spellbound by his greatness. The parades wound through the streets and ended at the temple of Jupiter, displaying treasures, large paintings of battles, and maps. Then came the prisoners with their barbarian kings, the Roman officials, then the commander, riding on a chariot drawn by three white horses. He wore a laurel wreath and purple toga, carried the eagle scepter, and colored his face red to represent Jupiter, whose power was thought to have made the armies victorious. Standing over Ceasar was a slave holding a golden wreath. Yet the same enslaved person also counseled this great ruler by repeating in his ear, "Remember, you are human; remember you are human." Richard J. Foster tells a story about working among the Inuit people of Alaska as a teenager. He said these people "had a deep sense of the wholeness of life" with no distinction between prayer and work. One day, he was making a trench through the frozen soil. An Inuit man watched him for a while and then said, "You are digging a ditch for the glory of God." Foster never forgot it. Nobody would remember that he dug that ditch — or perhaps even that a ditch had been dug in the first place. But he said, "I dug with all my might because every shovelful of dirt was a prayer to God."

There is an exciting conversation Moses has with God in Exodus 33. Moses asks God to show him His glory. As fascinating as the request was, even more impressive is that God honored his request, but only to a degree. Charles Spurgeon said, "Now, what attribute is God about to show Moses? His petition is, "Show me thy glory." Will God show him his justice? His holiness? His wrath? His power? No. Hear the still, small voice – "I will make all my goodness pass before you." Ah! The goodness of God is God's glory. God's greatest glory is that he is good… "I will make all my goodness pass before you." As believers, we say that we exist for God's glory. We talk about doing everything for the glory of God. We sing songs about His glory. We pray that Christ will be glorified in our lives, homes, and churches. But what does all this mean? What exactly is the glory of God? Often, it refers to the display of His creative power. The heavens declare His glory (Ps. 19:1). Therefore, God's glory is an outward expression of His excellence. It could also mean praise and honor to His great name (Acts 4:31). Wayne Grudem says, "God's glory is the created brightness that surrounds God's revelation of himself." Glory is the light that speaks of the revelation of God's true nature. Our knowledge and understanding of God's glory are manifest through the grace of Jesus Christ, which far outshines the glory of the Old Testament law (2 Cor. 3:13). We read in John 1:14, "The Word was made flesh and dwelt among us, and we beheld his glory, the glory as of the only begotten of the Father, full of grace and truth." The apostle John wanted us to know that Jesus is the absolute revelation of God, heralded to the shepherds on the hillside in Luke 2:9. In Revelation, we are told that the heavenly city of God has no need of the sun, neither of the moon, to shine in it, "for the glory of the Lord did lighten it, and the Lamb is the light thereof" (Rev. 21:23).

The theme of God's glory and majesty is declared throughout the Bible. In Isaiah 43:1-7 we read, "But now saith the Lord that created thee... I am the Lord thy God... fear not: for I am with thee... even everyone that is called by my name; for I have created him for my glory..." God's glory is revealed through creation (Ps. 19:1-2). It is identified with God's people (Isa. 40:5) and linked to the exodus (Ex. 13:31). The glory of God is identified as Christ in His incarnation (John 1:1-18), His birth (Luke 2:9), miracles (John 2:11), transfiguration (Matt. 17:1-13), crucifixion (John 7:39), resurrection (Acts 3:13-15), ascension (1 Tim. 3:16), supreme reign (Mark 10:37), and His coming victory (Titus 2:13).

William Carey, the great missionary to India who translated God's Word into forty different languages, was first a shoemaker. Some call him "the cobbler who gave the world a Bible." The most excellent Christian vocation is to be what you are to the glory of God. As the moon reflects the sun's light, we can reflect God's power, grace, and truth. (Isa. 60:1-6, 1 Cor. 10:31). We are created for God's glory (Isa. 43:7). So how can we give glory to "the King of glory" (Ps. 24:8)? First, we embrace the Cross of Christ as the only way to salvation (John 14:6, Gal. 2:20). Then we willingly submit to that which is revealed in Scripture as the will of God for our lives (Rom. 12:1-2). In other words, we take what comes to us providentially by the good hand of

God. We recognize and acknowledge the nature of God's goodness and praise Him with our lips (Ps. 63:3). We obey His words (Acts 5:29). We produce spiritual fruit (John 15:8). We give generously (2 Cor. 9:13), live honorably among men (1 Pet. 2:12, Rom. 12:18), remain faithful in suffering (1 Pet. 4:16), and rejoice in the promise of Heaven (John 14:3). Through the years, I have beheld the light of God's glory in many of His faithful believers.

After an evening of talk at Sagamore Hill, William Beebe, and Teddy Roosevelt would go out on the lawn and search the skies for a particular spot of light near the lower left-hand corner of the Great Square of Pegasus. Then Roosevelt would say, "That is the Spiral Galaxy. It is as large as our Milky Way. It is one of a hundred million galaxies. It has one hundred billion suns, each larger than our sun." Then Roosevelt would say, "Now I think we are small enough! Let's go to bed." When Solomon's temple was dedicated, everyone assembled for the occasion. The people surrendered, and the Lord received His rightful praise. In this place, the weight of God's splendor was displayed. The Bible says the glory of the Lord was so heavy that "the priests could not stand to minister by reason of the cloud; for the glory of the Lord had filled the house of God" (2 Chron. 5:1-14). Oh, my friend, God's glory was then, is now, and forever will be! Soli Deo Gloria! To God alone, the glory!

God and Sinners Reconciled

PROCLAIMING THE GLORIOUS COMING OF THE WORLD'S SAVIOR, CHARLES Wesley's song is loved by many: "Hark, the herald angels sing; glory to the newborn King! Peace on earth and mercy mild; God and sinners reconciled." When we talk about putting Christ back in Christmas, we generally think of a Christmas that is already pretty good, and we're making it a bit better. But the connection is much more than just applying a religious component to a season of celebration. Christ came from Heaven to defiant people to rescue them from their rebellious ways (Ezek. 12:2). He came to unclean people to purify them and make them holy (1 John 1:7). He came to his enemies to make them his friends (Rom. 5:10). He came to those who had rejected him to open their hearts in worship (Acts 7:51). He came to sinful people so that he might die for them and pronounce them forgiven (1 Pet. 2:24). He came to people who were dead in their sins so they could live again (Eph. 2:1-6). He visited condemned people to grant them a full pardon (Neh. 9:17). He did not come to earth to do something nice for friendly people. He came to do something extreme for wicked people. Christ came to earth so that God and sinners would be reconciled.

What is this reconciliation between God and sinners? The definition of reconciliation is to make good again, to bring into harmony, and to restore. In Romans 5:8, the Bible says God demonstrated his love for us on the Cross while we were sinners. Regardless of our perceived moral system, we must admit we have sinned and come short of the glory of God (Rom. 3:23). The Bible is a story about reconciliation where we discover a God so intent on being reunited with His creation that He's willing to pay the penalty for their disobedience (Eph. 1:7). To understand this, we must first understand what happened to the relationship between God and humankind. We were created in the image of God, walking in perfect harmony with Him and each other (Genesis 2). But because of disobedience to the words of God, the relationship was severed (Genesis 3). This is what prompted the apostle Paul to declare, "For all have sinned, and come short of the glory of God" (Rom. 3:23), and because we are born into an inherent sinful nature, we have fallen short of the very thing for which we were created: revealing God's glory (Col. 1:16).

When we look at the relationship between God and humanity in the Old Testament, we see a difference between forgiveness and reconciliation. Texts like Isaiah 43:25 speak to a future hope in which God longed to reconcile with His people despite their repeated failings. This is a prophecy of Christ's atoning work on the cross, where forgiveness was fully realized. Jesus the Redeemer would become sin (2 Cor. 5:21) and pay the price for reconciliation, presenting forgiveness beyond the temporary sacrifices of the old covenant. We see this in our relationships. We may forgive what someone has done to us, but that doesn't necessarily restore the relationship. God wanted to make peace with us when we were neither interested in nor capable of being His friend. This is where Jesus comes in. If we believe in His death, burial, and resurrection as the only way to a relationship with God, we are made holy, without blemish, and free from condemnation. Speaking of those who accept this gospel of Christ (1 Cor. 15:1-4), Paul said, "Therefore if any man be in Christ, he is a new creature: old things are past away; behold all things are become new" (2 Cor. 5:17).

Two young boys attended the same school: George Washington and Peter Miller. Time changed the course of their lives. Washington became the United States' first president, and Peter Miller grew up to become a preacher of the gospel. Following a 16-month stay in New York City, George Washington occupied the President's House in Philadelphia from November 1790 to March 1797, and the humble Miller lived at Ephrata, a village seventy miles away. In Ephrata, a corrupt man named Michael Wittman also lived and did all in his power to torment the man of God. He inflicted personal violence, damaged the preacher's building, and publicly denounced his testimony. In time, Wittman was arrested for treason and sentenced to death. Upon hearing this, the old preacher walked the seventy miles to Philadelphia to plead for the life of his enemy. He presented himself before President Washington and said, "For our old acquaintance's sake, George, I have come to beg the life of the traitor Wittman." "No, Peter; this case is too black: I cannot give you your friend's life." "My friend! He is the most bitter enemy any man ever had." Miller told the President what he had suffered from this man for over twenty years. "Ah, then, Peter; this puts another aspect upon the matter. I could not give you your friend's life, but I will freely pardon your enemy." On the third day, the preacher and his old-time antagonist walked back the seventy miles to Ephrata. The pardon and Miller's forgiving spirit melted the man's heart. There, he was brought into the joy of God's salvation. Jesus Christ came before our executioner with more than the pardon papers. He came to take the place of the Wittmans of the world, who were sentenced to death. He willingly sacrificed His life so our lives might be saved and fit for eternal glory. This is the message of the Cross: justice and mercy. God deals in both (Rom. 3:26). He pronounced the severity of His justice on Christ, the sinner's substitute, and set the offender free. This is reconciliation through the cross of Christ!

In 1862, Confederate General Simon Buckner proposed a cease-fire to negotiate a settlement with Union General Ulysses S. Grant. General Grant told Buckner: "No terms except an immediate and unconditional surrender can be accepted." His words became a Union battle cry. We do not come to God and negotiate peace; we do not dictate the terms. He comes to us and declares the war over, requiring nothing less than unconditional surrender. All we brought to the table was our enmity; God brought full forgiveness. This is the grace of which no one can boast and say, "I made peace with God." We can only boast about the God who made peace with us. "Let us now go even unto Bethlehem, and see this thing, which is come to pass, which the Lord hath made known unto us," the shepherds said after the angels had left them and gone into heaven. May we never limit the coming of Christ to just a historical event. It is bigger than that. It is where we meet God. It is where our lives are sustained for all situations. It is where our souls are saved from eternal punishment. The "good tidings of great joy" (Luke 2:10) is that Jesus loved us enough to leave heaven and come to earth and suffer. The heavenly Father values us more than we can comprehend: "For God so loved the world, that he gave his only begotten Son, that whosoever believeth in him should not perish, but have everlasting life" (John 3:16).

An apology had been made, but Ricky could not reunite with a friend who had committed an indiscretion against him. He went to his pastor and said, "It's a huge wall between us, and I can't get through it." His pastor replied, "Ricky, imagine that you had just confessed a serious sin to God, and for the first time in your life, he spoke to you audibly: 'I forgive you, but I can't ever be close to you again.' How would you feel?" There was no answer. Pastor continued, "Now, imagine instead that God said, 'My son, I forgive you. I promise I will never think about your sin again. I promise never to bring it up and use it against you. I promise not to talk to others about it. And I promise not to let this sin stand between us or hinder our relationship.' After a long silence, tears began to fill Ricky's eyes. "Then I would know true reconciliation."

In the book of Isaiah, God refers to Abraham as "my friend" (Isa. 41:8). In Exodus we learn that "the Lord spake unto Moses face to face, as a man speaketh unto his friend" (Ex. 33:11). In the Gospel of John, Jesus calls his disciples "friends" (John 15:15). What could possibly be greater than having God as one's friend? How is such a relationship possible? It begins with reconciliation. While friendship with God shares similarities with human friendships, there are important differences as well. To begin, we must remember that this is not a relationship between equals. Friendship with God must be accepted and pursued on His terms—not ours. God is the Creator, King, and Lord of the universe; we are mere creatures—and fallen ones at that. Friendship with God thus finds its origin in reconciliation with Him. We must humbly recognize that our sin has separated us from God (Isa. 59:2), and the relationship must be restored. Mercifully, God has taken the initiative of providing for us to be reconciled with Him through "the death of his Son" (Rom. 5:10). Reconciliation brings peace with God, restoring the relationship that our sin had broken. God sent His Son to forgive us for our sins, and His precious atoning blood will cover all who put their faith in Him. He took the penalty of death for your sin upon Himself. Believe that God's love and justice were satisfied because

God raised Jesus from the dead. When you believe in the crucified and risen Lord Jesus Christ, God takes the righteousness of Christ and credits it to your account.

In Jesus, God has taken the initiative to bring those who will believe the gospel message into fellowship with Him (2 Cor. 5:14-19). He who knew no sin, laid down His life for us so that we might become the righteousness of God (2 Cor. 5:2). Romans 10:9-10 tells us, "That is thou shalt confess with thy mouth the Lord Jesus, and shalt believe in thine heart that God hath raised him from the dead, thou shalt be saved. For with the heart, man believeth unto righteousness, and with the mouth, confession is made unto salvation." The old, sinful nature is gone, and the new has come (2 Cor. 5:17). This is the "good tidings of great joy, which shall be to all people" (Luke 2:10). Being born from above is more than an outward reformation. A born-again believer is given a new heart. He acts upon new principles with new ends. He is the workmanship of God, created in Christ Jesus unto good works (Eph. 2:10). For, when we share this gospel, lives are changed, sinners are reconciled, and God is glorified!

Addictions and the
Struggle Within

I OFTEN SHARE MY HEART WITH THOSE RECOVERING FROM SUBSTANCE abuse and other addictions. Recognizing their struggle and wanting to support them in their recovery, I seek to encourage them with the Word of God. Recently, I challenged a group of men with the following message of truth in love (Eph. 4:15):

The Bible speaks of a war that rages. Satan would have us believe we are no longer lovable or valuable when we fall short of pleasing God. And because of this, we can become consumed with negative, self-condemning thoughts that leave us guilt-ridden and spiritually paralyzed. The central declaration of the gospel is that Christ has come, he has died, and he has risen again so that we who believe in Him might be free. Christ has come to give us freedom from bondage to evil habits. He has come to release us "that we may be blameless (single-eyed and sincere)" (Phil. 2:15). Jesus Christ offers new life (Rom. 6:23). We "have redemption through his blood, the forgiveness of sins, according to the riches of his grace" (Eph. 1:7). And all who trust Him for salvation have been released from the condemnation of sin and death (Rom. 8:1-17). Believers will not practice sin as a way of life. Still, we will never know the complete absence of sin until we are with the Lord in Heaven (1 John 3:2).

In Romans 7, the apostle Paul speaks of an intense, unrelenting battle of the mind. He said, "For I delight in the direction of God after the inward man: But I see another law in my members, warring against the law of my mind, and bringing me into captivity to the law of sin which is in my members. O wretched man that I am! Who shall deliver me from the body of this death?" A guilty Christian is not a happy Christian, so let's examine this passage of Scripture. When Paul penned these words, he had walked with Christ for several years. In Romans 7:5-13, he is describing his pre-conversion experience. But in verses 14-25, Paul speaks in the present tense as one free from captivity but not from warfare. The apostle also describes this experience in Galatians 5:17, where he writes to believers. To paraphrase, he says, "Even though I am determined not to do what is wrong, I suddenly find myself in such circumstances that my determination melts away, my resolve is gone, and I end up doing what I had said I would not do." The apostle finds - as we do - that our fleshly bodies quickly and eagerly respond to the impulses and desires aroused by sin. There is a division here. Paul says that the redeemed spirit wants to do what God desires. And yet there is an alien power, a force that he calls sin, that springs to life. Satan's strategy is to afflict and oppress. If the enemy of our soul cannot seduce us with our sin, he will let us sink in our guilt. The devil wants to instill doubt, fear, and uncertainty in the lives of God's children.

In 2 Corinthians 10, we are told to cast down imaginations, "bringing into captivity every thought to the obedience of Christ" (v5). John Stott said, "The battle for the Christian life is the battle for the Christian mind." As your mind goes, so goes your life (Prov. 23:7). Your mind is the steering wheel of your heart (Eph. 4:23); it is the initial battlefield where the battle is won or lost (Rom. 12:2). Purify your mind and you will purify your life (Col. 3:2). Too often, we attempt to handle this sin problem by trying to do our best through the exercise of willpower. Then, we come away angry with ourselves. "What's the matter with me? Why can't I do what is right? Why am I so weak?" This is right where we live. The heart's cry at that moment is Romans 7:24: "O wretched man that I am!" Right here, you arrive at where the Lord Jesus began the Sermon on the Mount: "Blessed are the poor in spirit, for theirs is the kingdom of heaven" (Matt. 5:3). Blessed is the man who comes to the end of himself. Blessed is the man who has arrived at spiritual bankruptcy. If we believe we can control evil in our lives by simply determining to do so, then we have not yet come to the end of ourselves. We are bound to fail miserably until we cry,

"Who shall deliver me from the body of this death?" And the answer comes immediately in verse 25, "I thank God through Jesus Christ our Lord." In Christ, we are a new creation (2 Cor. 5:17), a child of God (1 John 3:1), and our minds are being transformed (Rom. 12:2). We are not poor, struggling, bewildered disciples left alone to wrestle against these powerful urges. With the Holy Spirit's power, we can say, "No!" and walk away to be free in Jesus Christ.

It is impossible to live victoriously without daily prayer and Bible reading. These are lifelines that must become a lifestyle. Furthermore, we cannot ignore the commands of God by deflecting them with our opinions or philosophy. The commands of Jesus are not to be argued. They are to be believed. They are not to be symbolized. They are to be obeyed. Move away from your cleverness. Such has been the ruin of intelligent men and women for generations. We usually know exactly what to do but refuse to do it. Be honest. There are choices to be made. Are you searching for a humanistic approach to recovery? Are you seeking a secular program to help you with self-confidence and personal growth? Stop. The only solution to the struggle within is to kneel at the Cross and surrender everything to God. What time and place have you set aside for daily prayer? When and where do you read the Bible? Do you read verses of Scripture that relate to your battle, trusting that God is speaking to you? Do you meditate on passages that establish a greater determination to live for the Lord? Stop relying on what you think. Stop listening to what your friends think. Dig in and find the timeless, life-changing truths of God's Word! We are helpless to battle sin alone.

Counsel with a trusted friend and share your heart. We need godly friends to help us make the right decisions when we've made the wrong ones. We need social and spiritual support to keep us accountable. Pride will keep us from seeing the truth (Heb. 10:24). Humble yourself. Decide that you will take every opportunity to be in the house of the Lord. Make an effort to be with the family of God in singing, worship, prayer, and fellowship. Free yourself from people who do not have your spiritual interests at heart. This may include former friends who are not saved because you are now walking a different path. You cannot associate with unregenerated people and survive. Yes, we witness and pray for everyone, but we must use wisdom in choosing our new neighborhood (physically and spiritually). Very often, the fatal mistake made by those coming out of bad company is that they return to bad company. Do what you must to guard yourself. Find a place far from your old life and continue with people of faith who live according to the guidance of the Holy Spirit. As you search God's Word for answers, you learn that Christ Jesus has set you free from the law of sin and death (Rom. 8:2). Learn to walk, not according to the flesh, but according to the Holy Spirit (Rom. 8:4), and He will become more precious to you.

The good news is that through Jesus Christ, we can overcome our sinful nature. Every battle is won or lost in the mind, so bring your thoughts under control. The Bible tells us to be sober, obedient children, not fashioning ourselves according to former lusts. The apostle Peter says, "So be ye holy in all manner of conversation" (1 Peter 1:13-16). Replace thoughts that lead to immoral acts. Make Philippians 4:8 your daily focus: "Whatsoever things are true, honest, just, pure, lovely, and of a good report; if there be any virtue; and if there be any praise, think on these things." Pay attention to triggers that have caused you trouble in the past. I'm acquainted with a former alcoholic who will not so much as taste rum-flavored candy. The enemy of the soul is in the bondage business, and he wants to keep you entangled in sinful attitudes and lifestyles. Meditate on the Word of God every single day. Create a time to pray and be committed to it. Do not skip a day! Remember, the battle against the flesh is not physical but spiritual (Eph. 6:12), so you must use the right weapons. What are the weapons we fight with? The Word of God, prayer, and obedience to the Holy Spirit. We defend ourselves against the enemy with the truth that we are saved by grace and not by works (Eph. 2:8-9), that if we resist Satan, he will flee (James 4:7), and that if we confess our sins, God will cleanse our hearts (1 John 1:9). God's Word is our weapon. Jesus repeatedly fought the enemy, saying, "It is written" (Luke 4:1-4). Call on the Lord of hosts, the commander of the heavenly armies, to win the war (Dan. 10:11-14). When the error of our way is revealed in Scripture, we must immediately correct it. God will not bless us until we deal with the issue at hand. In chapters 7 and 8 of the Book of Joshua, the people of God suffered defeat in battle. Their leader, Joshua, fell on his face before God in repentance. But notice what happened next. The Lord told Joshua,

"Get thee up." Why? There was something he needed to do. Sin had to be dealt with before the people would be victorious. Sometimes, prayer involves initiative, and by our actions, we surrender in obedience to the voice of God.

Let Jesus Christ be the master of every area of your life. Be mindful of what you see, the places you visit, the people you hang out with, or anything that will bring temptation your way (Ps. 1:1-2). Jesus said, "He that follows me shall not walk in darkness" (John 8:12). Ask the Lord to keep you on the righteous pathway. Be accountable to someone—partner with a person of strong faith. Creating accountability for yourself makes you more careful not to sin and keeps you alert. Do not become complacent. The world is not a playground. It is a battleground. But God has not left us defenseless. In Ephesians 6:10-17, we are told to put on the whole armor of God: truth, righteousness, the gospel of peace, the shield of faith, the helmet of salvation, and the sword of the Spirit, which is the word of God. Acquire biblical knowledge, then pray for wisdom and conviction. Overcoming a sinful addiction requires complete dependence upon God for direction, purpose, and strength. Accepting the forgiveness of God and forgiving yourself means leaving the past and experiencing the power of God's transforming love. Peter failed the Lord miserably (Luke 22), yet we consider him a repented church leader (Acts 2). Accepting the forgiveness of Jesus allowed Peter to live a new life. The same can be said of you. Having an addiction does not define who you are. Believe what Jesus accomplished at the Cross (2 Cor. 5:17). Leave your sins with God, then move on to be the person you were meant to be. No matter the struggle, we all can faithfully run this race to the end!

Things Too High For Me

A SCIENCE TEACHER WITH LITTLE REGARD FOR GOD'S WORD RECENTLY posted on social media, "If God wrote the Bible, I would expect it to be clear, concise, accurate, and full of useful teachings. I would expect details on the early beginnings of the universe. I would expect chapters about sociology to guide us in creating great, loving societies where everyone can live in harmony. I would expect it to be full of knowledge we cannot yet imagine or understand." After reading his post several times, I thought about how I might respond: The truth is that God's Word is all of this – and more. How much more? As the heavens are higher than the earth! God is the Creator of all things (John 1:3), forever working to reveal His glory and redeem His people. The instant we are awestruck by the grandeur of God's creation, we are inspired to seek the Creator. And praise God; we can know Him in the person of Jesus Christ (John 1:18; 14:9)! Yet, there are matters in Scripture and the spiritual realm that cannot be understood this side of heaven (Ps. 139:6). The Psalmist said, "Lord, my heart is not haughty, nor mine eyes lofty: neither do I exercise myself in great matters, or things too high for me" (Ps. 131:1). In another passage, he said, "Great is our Lord, and of great power: his understanding is infinite" (Ps. 147:5). The Bible says there are things known only to God (Deut. 29:29, Rom. 11:33). David had no conceited opinion of himself or his own merits, nor did he have all the answers. He was satisfied with everything the Lord ordained or allowed. He left what he could not understand with the One who could.

As we study the Scriptures, our understanding of God will grow, our love for our Lord will deepen, and our faith will be strengthened. Even so, we tend to try to explain things beyond our reach. But, admitting we don't know everything is okay. At the end of his trial,

Job appropriately confessed that he had spoken of things he did not understand as though he did (Job 42). In Psalm 139, David admitted that some things are so high that he could not "attain unto it." Isaiah 55:8-9 tells us that, as the heavens are higher than the earth, so are God's thoughts above ours. Job said the measure of God is "longer than the earth and broader than the sea." He said the number of God's years is unsearchable (Job 11:9, 36:26). Moses said, "The secret things belong unto the Lord our God" (Deut. 29:29). To the Romans, the apostle Paul declared, "O the depth of the riches both of the wisdom and knowledge of God! How unsearchable are his judgments and his ways past finding out! For who hath known the mind of the Lord? Or who hath been his counselor?" (Rom. 11:33-34). Scripture teaches that we can have a genuine knowledge of God (1 Cor. 2:1-16), but this does not mean we will ever fully understand Him. His greatness, power, thoughts, ways, wisdom, and judgments are beyond our ability to fathom (Job 26:14). But our knowledge of God in the person of Jesus Christ should be our greatest delight (Jer. 9:23-24, Gal. 6:14), for this is the basis of inheriting eternal life (John 17:3). Jesus Christ is God making Himself known. In Christ, God has provided personal, relational, and sufficient knowledge of Himself for fruitful, faithful, godly living. Peter said, "According to his divine power have given unto us all things that pertain unto life and godliness, through the knowledge of him (Jesus) that hath called us to glory and virtue" (2 Pet. 1:3). We cannot understand everything God does or why He does it. Still, we trust Him to reveal what is necessary. And in all this, we can rest in peace, for He is good and faithful (Lam. 3:21-26).

We read Isaiah 66:1-2: "Thus saith the Lord, The heaven is my throne, and the earth is my footstool: where is the house that ye build unto me? And where is the place of my rest? For all those things hath mine hand made, and all those things have been, saith the Lord." In Job's great distress, he had a dialogue with his friends about the meaning of his suffering. Eventually, they had nothing more to discuss (Job 3-27), and Job took up his final position before God (Job 29-31). He laments the days of his health when his life was filled with family and friends. Then, in verses 35-40 of chapter 31, he demands an explanation from God. And so, after enduring the long-winded words of Elihu (Job

32-37), God speaks up and responds to Job in a series of speeches (Job 38-41). God asks Job impossible questions like, "Where were you when I laid the earth's foundations? Please tell me if you know. Have you ever commanded the morning light? Where does light live, or where does darkness reside? Can you lead out a constellation in its season?" And, of course, the correct response to all these questions is for Job to say, "No, I do not command the universe, and I don't know the answer to any of these questions." This good man of God finally understood that God is aware of perspectives and details he never imagined. We see this in his answer, "Behold, I am vile; what shall I answer thee? I will lay my hand upon my mouth" (40:4). God has made His point. Whatever God's reasons for allowing Job's suffering, neglect is not a viable option. Job never finds out why he suffered, nor does the reader. The book's goal was never to offer us that information but to clarify that God's perspective on the universe has a broader range than any human will ever have. Job evaluated God's knowledge and ability based on the limited horizons of his life experience. We are finite. Our brains and sensory skills are not designed to take in the information necessary to evaluate God's choices. Job questioned God's design, and God responded that he had insufficient knowledge.

There are divine mysteries that have not been identified and will be kept sealed until the end of time (Rev. 10:4). John Walvoord said, "This illustrates the principle that while God has revealed much, there are secrets which God has not seen fit to reveal to man at this time." Science is a powerful tool for explaining the dynamics of the physical universe. But science cannot examine or explain the universe's purpose (Ps. 19:1-4). These things are known only to God. Louis Pasteur said, "Too little science leads away from God, while too much science leads back to Him." Scientific law stems from God's creative activity, who speaks his Word and brings forth the creation! None can fully describe the attributes of God, the manner of His existence or manifestation. His power to create, to produce something out of nothing, is beyond human understanding. In Him, there is height and depth that human intellect cannot measure. God is infinite. There is no limit to His being; therefore, He cannot be compressed into any particular definition. David closes 2 Samuel 7 with a blessing for his family and friends.

In humility, he becomes content with God's actions in his life and theirs. Rather than debate what we cannot comprehend, let's rejoice in knowing that God is love, truth, and life (Ps. 33) while celebrating the transforming power of Christ, the Savior!

Sometimes, there are clear answers, and we are satisfied. But something deep within us often feels unsettled when the question goes unanswered. An unsolved question often leads to a restless spirit, but there is a better way to live. Unanswered questions are part of the Christian faith. It seems that most of our serious questions revolve around the issue of God's sovereignty. We don't get the full answer sheet to the quiz on life. But that's okay. As one author prayed, "I cannot grasp your mind, but with my whole heart, I trust your love." We may use intelligence to make sound decisions and connect more effectively with other people. In doing so, we feel a sense of control and ownership over the spaces in which we learn or work. However, when the limitation of human intellect is reached, all that is left is to accept and adore. It is good for us to know what we believe and to be able to defend it. But admitting we don't have all the answers takes the arrogant edge off of our testimony. We don't always have the answers we wish we had. But we can rest in God's character when we don't understand His activity.

An excellent chess player sees all sixty-four squares and all the pieces on the board. He won't move his bishop and think: "I moved my bishop there because it puts my opponent's king in check." Instead, an excellent chess player will be thinking: "I moved my bishop there because it puts his king in check, blocks him from moving his knight where he wants to, protects my queen, opens up space to move my rook, and sets me up to take his bishop two moves down the road." The Bible says God's ways are perfect in judgment and truth, without iniquity (Deut. 32:4). God is sovereign and works all things after the counsel of His own will (Eph. 1:11). When we feel anxious about the future, it's easy to race ahead and try to explain what is happening. And if we're not careful, we will regard knowledge and learning as our prime objectives. But the great end is to fellowship with God. There is no higher way of living than to be a servant of the One who created, loved, and redeemed us in Christ, for He is worthy of all praise!

The Psalmist said, "Exalt ye the Lord our God, and worship at his footstool; for he is holy" (Ps. 99:5). Do you want a God you can explain or extol? The God of infinite majesty cannot be measured. The One who unleashes miracles will not be controlled. He whose love is eternal will never be explained. The Book of Wisdom reminds us: "As thou knowest not what is the way of the spirit, nor how the bones do grow in the womb of her that is with child, even so, thou knowest not the works of God who maketh all" (Eccl. 11:5). God operates in ways beyond our comprehension (Isa. 55:8-11), and if we agree to follow Him only when we understand what He's doing, we'll always stop short of His wonder. Sometimes, we beat on heaven's door for answers, but we know that all things will be woven into the fabric of His plan and purpose (Rom. 8:28). In Romans 11:33-36, Paul climbs as high as he can to the summit of truth. Yet, he is still a long way from the peak. Unable to climb any higher, Paul bows low to worship the Lord. His mind is now empty, but his heart is full. And with a sense of adoration, Paul celebrates the God who is too deep and too high to be figured out. The cross of Jesus is the wisdom of God at work (1 Cor. 1:17-31). The truth of God is shallow enough for a child to drink from it without the fear of drowning (2 Tim. 3:15). But it is so deep that scholars can dive in and never reach the bottom (Ps. 147:4-5). I want to see life as the constant movement of God's wise and sovereign purposes. Yes, there are things too high for me. Still, I will serve God. I will love Him. I will embrace the truth of His excellence and celebrate the wonder of His majesty!

God's Refining Fire

THE BIBLE OFTEN USES THE DESCRIPTION OF GOLD BEING REFINED TO illustrate God's work in the life of a Christian (Zech. 13:9, 1 Pet. 1:7). Gold is not always recognizable when extracted from the earth due to the impurities that spoil its appearance. Yet, for the refiner, the potential for beauty is evident. The Academy of Art in Florence, Italy, houses a beautiful statue of King David from the Bible. When asked how he carved such a magnificent statue from a block of marble, the sculptor, Michelangelo, said, "I just removed everything that wasn't David." Just as fire removes everything that is not gold – and just as Michelangelo removed everything that was not David – the Holy Spirit uses trials and testing to remove everything from us that is not Christlike (1 Pet. 1:15-16). The disciplines of God are the refining fire by which we become dead to sin and useful for His Kingdom (Acts 28:31). Job, a man who was "perfect and upright" (Job 1:1), did not understand everything God had allowed to come upon him. Yet he said, "He knows the way that I take: when he has tried me, I shall come forth as gold" (Job 23:9-10). In Romans 5:4, Apostle Paul speaks of a refinement process for those justified by God's grace through faith. He says, "We glory in tribulations also; knowing that tribulation worketh patience; and patience, experience; and experience, hope: and hope maketh not ashamed; because the love of God is shed abroad in our hearts by the Holy Ghost which is given unto us." If we want to please God, we will behold every divinely orchestrated circumstance as an opportunity to be more like Jesus.

The prophet Isaiah labels adversity as the "furnace of affliction" (Isa. 48:10). God is not just interested in what we do but in what we are becoming. Adversity builds passion, perseverance, and character.

The single most validating reality of your faith is trials. What can your faith survive? Does your trust in God stay intact? When we understand the Refiner's work in us, consolation replaces pain, peace replaces turmoil, and hope replaces sorrow. In Isaiah's words, God gives us "beauty for ashes, the oil of joy for mourning, the garment of praise for the spirit of heaviness." Why? "That he might be glorified" (Isa. 61:3). The apostle James says, "My brethren, count it all joy when ye fall into divers temptations; knowing this, that the trying of your faith worketh patience. But let patience have her perfect work, that ye may be perfect and entire, wanting nothing" (James 1:2-4). The Romans were persecuting many believers for their faith in Christ, and Peter knew what that was like firsthand. He explains, "That the trial of your faith, being much more precious than of gold that perishes, though it be tried with fire, might be found unto praise and honor and glory at the appearing of Jesus Christ" (1 Pet. 1:7). The psalmist said, "It is good for me that I have been afflicted; that I might learn thy statutes" (Ps. 119:71). In the same context, David said, "Before I was afflicted, I went astray: but now have I kept thy word" (v67). The pain was his professor. The trial was his teacher. Through the darkness, he experienced God's faithfulness. He was saying affliction should refine rather than defeat us.

There is always a purpose beyond the pain of God's refinement (Gal. 6:9, James 1:12). It is a purification meant to conform us to the character of Christ. In Isaiah 43:2-3, God told His people, "When you pass through the waters, I will be with you; and through the rivers, they shall not overflow you; when you walk through the fire, you shall not be burned, neither shall the flame kindle upon you, for I am the Lord your God, the Holy One of Israel, your Savior." Sometimes, we fail to endure victoriously in trials because we think they are random happenstances and, therefore, have no purpose. There have been times when I have prayed, "Lord, as I go through troubling times, please help me to see the benefit. You are teaching me, so help me learn the lesson." I say this because I know there is nothing random, unplanned, or unforeseen with God. Citing coincidence is how we humans explain unexpected events and surprise meetings. But just because we are taken by surprise doesn't mean God is. What appears to us as coincidence is overseen by a sovereign God who knows the number of hairs on every head (Luke 12:7). Jesus said that not even a sparrow falls to the ground without our Father's notice (Matt. 10:29). In Isaiah 46:9-11, God states explicitly that He is in charge of everything: "I am God, and there is none else; I am God, and there is none like me, declaring the end from the beginning… my counsel shall stand." And because "all things were created by him and for him" (Col. 1:16), I believe all sorrow can have redemptive purposes. The Lord's wise purposes stand, and they endure forever. Trials come from God's heart, not His fist (Heb. 12:9-10). And, no matter how difficult things get, we are taught to do everything without murmuring. Through challenging circumstances and clear priorities, we become children of God without rebuke, shining bright in a dark world (Phil. 2:14-15).

When faith survives the refining heat, the beauty of the gold is lovelier than the cost is painful. Trials increase our fellowship with God (2 Chron. 20:12). They grow our knowledge of Scripture, build character, and equip us to comfort others. With a correct response, hardship will cause us to believe the promises of God more firmly than we did before. Suffering prepares an eternal weight of glory and reminds us that Earth is not our home. How? Because in times of loneliness, we yearn for God's presence. We long for a place where there will be "no more death, neither sorrow, nor crying, neither shall there be any more pain" (Rev. 21:4). Just as God tested Gideon, so too, God uses our trials to show that he alone deserves the glory (Judges 7). Trials make it clear to the world that we do not have the ability or strength to overcome. Therefore, our Christlike behavior will show others that God is faithful to His children. Changing from a human perspective to God's point of view is where we see life's struggles as opportunities for God to do something transformational in our lives. The dark events in our lives aren't hurdles that God puts before us to see how high we can jump or how hard we stumble. No, our God is more loving than that. He wants our infinite trust in the journey He has planned for us (Prov. 3:5-6).

Have you ever looked up at a plane flying by and wondered where it's coming from and where it's going? Thanks to technology, it's relatively easy to find out. These days, flight trackers provide real-time updates about an airplane's location, altitude, speed, departure, and arrival times. This knowledge can be used to monitor nearly all commercial flights. Recently, a friend was scheduled to fly out of a Texas airport to return home through Sacramento Airport. Several small storms were in the atmosphere, so she knew her flight would be delayed. This inconvenienced the passengers and their loved ones waiting for them at the gate. But that night, I was looking at a computer screen that showed everything happening from a satellite view far above the actual event. I noticed a thin blue line between the airports offering the standard flight route. But, more importantly, the active flight path was displayed in real-time. I watched as the plane circled back around the airport on departure to miss storm activity. I saw a "bird-eye view" of how this was taking place. And, while some turbulence was likely felt on the plane, things could have been much worse: the pilot could have been left to an educated guess of the aircraft's position. Life is a journey, and most of the time, we see only the immediate circumstances. What we consider to be interruptions can cause us to feel anxious - or even angry. Jesus said, "If any man serve me, let him follow me; and where I am, there shall also my servant be: if any man serve me, him will my Father honor" (John 12:26). He said, "Rejoice, and be exceedingly glad: for great is your reward in heaven: for so persecuted they the prophets which were before you" (Matt. 5:12). Then comes the promise, "Let not your heart be troubled: ye believe in God, believe also in me. In my Father's house are many mansions: if it were not so, I would have told you. I go to prepare a place for you" (John 14:1-2). We often focus on a delayed flight when our Lord is more interested in a safe arrival. Christian friend, this world is not our home, and God is leading us to our destination in Heaven!

Scott O'Grady, a U. S. pilot operating over Bosnia, was shot down and forced to evade capture for six days before being rescued by American forces. O'Grady says. "The inspiration that carried me through this difficulty came through the things I cherish the most in life. I look at my entire combat experience through my faith." When Scotty Smiley lost his eyesight while serving in Iraq, he became the U.S. Army's first blind active-duty officer. He wrote about it in his book, 'Hope Unseen.' He says, "Life isn't just nice softball pitches you can crank over the fence daily. You have struggles, you have trials, you have tribulations no matter what."

Even more remarkable than these, the Bible contains the accounts of many who persevered through struggles, deepened their faith in God, and inspired generations of believers. We desire to be like them because they lived for God despite the most trying times. Joseph was imprisoned for a false accusation, yet he showed us that God will bless us in places and ways we least expect as long as we remain faithful to Him (Gen. 45:7-8). Moses had many struggles that would have made any other leader give up. But his perseverance reminds us to always call upon God for deliverance (Ex. 14:13-15). The story of Ruth starts with tragedy and misfortune. As a poor widow and an outsider in her community, Ruth could have quickly abandoned her family and continued her life elsewhere. But Ruth's faithfulness to God and her loyalty were her foundation for navigating life's challenges (Ruth 1:16). Facing Goliath was not David's most significant test. Despite his remarkable leadership, David's reign was stained when he committed adultery. The consequences were severe. But beyond the wrongdoings, we see a man who truly repented. David was a man whose words about God are etched in history forever because of his faith (2 Sam. 22:7). Having persevered to overcome many personal struggles; Apostle Peter preached the Gospel in the face of heavy persecution. The story of Job is one that many people quote to try and answer the question, "Why do bad things happen to good people?" Yet, while his dialogue with God was void of answers, Job still managed to exclaim praises and worship (Job 1:21). We are also called to live by faith – purified in God's refining fire.

Spiritual Growth

SPIRITUAL GROWTH. WHAT IS IT, AND HOW IS IT ACCOMPLISHED? FIRST, if you have been born again (John 3:1-21), "by the washing of regeneration, and renewing of the Holy Ghost" (Titus 3:5), the Bible says your salvation is immediate and secure (John 10:28-29). Jesus said, "Verily, verily, I say unto you, he that heareth my word, and believeth on him that sent me hath everlasting life, and shall not come into condemnation, but is passed from death unto life" (John 5:24). The words Jesus uses place this eternal life at this moment—in the present. Those who trust in Christ have a never-ending life that will be fully realized in His heavenly presence (2 Cor. 5:1-8, Phil. 3:20-21). A believer's passing from death to life has already happened (John 6:47). Salvation is an act of God through which He declares a sinner to be His child, positionally secure through adoption (John 1:12). Salvation is not a lifetime achievement award. It is God's grace received through faith (Eph. 2:8), immediate and complete (Rom. 5:18). This is justification by faith (Rom. 5:1) wherein we are declared righteous by God (Rom. 4:5)

When the transformation of salvation takes place, spiritual growth begins. This is grace applied to life, often called sanctification (Rom. 6:19, Phil. 3:13-14). Spiritual growth is the process of becoming more and more like Jesus Christ. When we place our faith in Jesus, thankfulness for His amazing grace will motivate us to pursue Christlike behavior (Titus 2:11-14). The Holy Spirit begins the process of conforming us into the image of Christ (2 Pet. 1:3-8) through the knowledge of Scripture. As we develop this way, fewer acts of the flesh (Gal. 5:19-21) will be evident in our lives. Spiritual growth manifests when love, joy, peace, longsuffering, gentleness, goodness, faith, meekness, and temperance (Gal. 5:22-23) become increasingly evident. To "grow in grace and in the knowledge of our Lord and Savior, Jesus Christ" (2 Pet. 3:18) is a lifelong process that depends on applying Biblical principles and obedience to the Holy Spirit's leading. Spiritual maturity is increased faith that develops over time. Therefore, the question becomes, "How do we respond when God calls us into a more meaningful relationship?" We have a choice. We can continue in what is familiar or move toward greater understanding by searching the Scriptures and relying on the Spirit for direction. And, while we cannot do anything to grow God's unmerited favor, we can develop a deeper appreciation of it. Just as a young child hardly grasps the full extent of his parents' actions, his awareness of their love and care deepens as he matures. As a result, the relationship becomes more precious.

In Matthew 13:3-8, our Lord describes the scene of a farmer planting seeds. He explains that just as a seed grows, followers of Christ grow in spiritual maturity when they accept His teachings with a receptive and obedient heart. Simply put, an individual who hears and applies the principles of the Bible will grow in their relationship with God. The apostle Paul describes this process in Colossians 1:9-10: "That ye might be filled with the knowledge of his will in all wisdom and spiritual understanding; that ye might walk worth of the Lord unto all pleasing, being fruitful in every good work, and increasing in the knowledge of God." No relationship will thrive without intentional communication. Listen to the Holy Spirit and be willing to trust Him with your heart. As you draw closer to God, He will reveal more of Himself to you (James 4:8).

Pablo Casals was considered the most outstanding cellist ever to live. When he was 95 years old, he was asked why he continued to practice 6 hours a day. He answered, "Because I think I'm making progress." God wants to be involved in every area of our lives. He wants to communicate with us daily. The truths of the Bible are vital to Christian living. But without a relationship with God, there will be no life in them. The words of God must be operational to be effective. Jesus said, "Behold, I stand at the door, and knock: if any man hear my voice, and open the door, I will come in to him, and will sup with him, and he with me" (Rev. 3:20). The word sup in that verse carries the idea of fellowship with Jesus. The better we know God, the easier it is for us to trust Him. God's work will continue in the life of a believer. In Philippians 1:6, we read, "Being confident of this very thing, that he which hath begun a good work in you will perform it until the day of Jesus Christ." Jesus said, "Blessed are they which do hunger and thirst after righteousness: for they shall be filled" (Matt. 5:6). Life's trials are opportunities to grow (James 1:2-4). John Bunyan said, "It is said that in some countries trees will grow, but will bear no fruit because there is no winter there." Truth, grace, and time are essential for spiritual growth. The truth of God's Word is profitable for doctrine, reproof, correction, and instruction in righteousness (2 Tim. 3:16). Grace is experiencing God's patient forgiveness, and time is essential for any relationship.

A godly lifestyle will develop as we learn and obey the Bible. In 2 Corinthians 4, Apostle Paul describes the difficulties of his life. What kept him going? In verse 13, he quotes Psalm 116:10, saying, "I believed, and therefore have I spoken." This is the conviction that shaped Paul's life and ministry. There was no alternative for him but to live for God. Andrew Murray (1928-2017) said, "Let the divine presence be felt, and no lot is hard. Let me but see His hand, and no event is unwelcome." John Bunyan, the great Puritan preacher and author of The Pilgrim's Progress, remained in jail for twelve years, but it wasn't the prison bars that held him there. He only had to agree not to preach publicly to go free. Faced with that option, Bunyan replied: "If I were out of prison today, I would preach the gospel again tomorrow with the help of God." When the Word of God shapes our convictions, we are growing spiritually. The Psalmist David said, "As the hart panteth after the water brooks, so panteth my soul after thee, O God" (Ps. 42:1). David is not talking about merely reading the words of God for intellectual stimulation or gathering ammunition to win an argument. He was hungry for the nourishment he so desperately needed. If we approach the Word with hunger, we will always be satisfied.

There is wisdom in spiritual maturity. One day, Ray, a barber, was excited about sharing his newfound faith with his customers. He told the Lord, "Today, I'm going to witness to the first customer who walks through my door." A man came in as he opened the shop and said, "I need a shave." Ray said, "Yes sir… just have a seat." As Ray approached the man's neck with his razor, he remembered his promise to God about witnessing, so he asked, "Sir, are you ready to meet your maker?" The man was last seen running down the street with a towel around his neck, his face covered with shaving cream! Zeal for God? Abundant! Wisdom? Not so much. Discernment is a sign of spiritual growth. The Bible says, giving all diligence, we add to our faith virtue, and to virtue knowledge, and to knowledge temperance, and to temperance patience, and to patience godliness, and to godliness brotherly kindness, and to brotherly kindness charity (2 Pet. 1:5-8). Spiritual maturity involves glorifying God (1 Cor. 1:31), sharing the gospel with lost souls (Acts 1:8), serving in our local church (Eph. 4:16), caring for other believers (Col. 3:16), helping the poor and needy (James 1:27), and comforting the brokenhearted (2 Cor. 1:4). As we grow in grace, we become more useful and effective in God's earthly kingdom. Jesus said, "Herein is my Father glorified, that ye bear much fruit; so shall ye be my disciples" (John 15:8). By the time we reach the age of 75, we will have completed nearly two million decisions. Our life will be the sum of them. A fruitful Christian is a productive Christian who makes the most of their time on earth for the glory of God. As we expand our knowledge of God, we will make better choices (2 Peter 1:9).

When we are growing spiritually, it will not be a secret. Several things make it evident: A desire to spend time with God (2 Pet. 3:18), digging deeper into the truths of the Bible (2 Tim. 3:16-17, 1 Pet. 2:2), learning and teaching others, growing in grace with forgiveness (Titus 2:11-14), and desiring to obey God (John 14:15, James 1:19-25). Spiritual maturity looks different for every person. Therefore, compare yourselves to what the Bible says and not how others do. Are you living more for God and less for yourself? Have your thoughts and actions toward God and others improved, or have they remained the same since your life with Christ began (Heb. 5:12-14)? In Paul's letter to the Ephesian believers, he said, "That we henceforth be no more children, tossed to and fro, and carried about with every wind of doctrine... but speaking the truth in love may grow up into him in all things, which is the head, even Christ" (Eph. 4:14-15).

Are you growing in the knowledge of God? Can you discern false teaching when you hear it (1 John 4:1)? Do you examine scriptures against what you hear (Acts 17:11)? Are you learning when to engage in - or refrain from − carnal behavior (1 Cor. 10:23)? Spiritual growth will manifest in how we live (James 1:26). An unknown writer said, "The Bible is the mind of God, the state of man, the way of salvation, the doom of sinners, and the happiness of believers. Its doctrines are holy, its precepts are binding, its histories are true, and its decisions are immutable. Read it to be wise, believe it to be safe, practice it to be holy. It contains light to direct you, food to support you, and comfort to cheer you. It is the traveler's map, the pilgrim's staff, the pilot's compass, the soldier's sword, and the Christian's character." We yearn for shortcuts. But shortcuts usually lead away from spiritual maturity, not toward it. It's been said that hunger makes a good meal, and we should desire to gain knowledge from the Holy Scripture. Amy Carmichael once penned these thoughts: "Sometimes, when we read the words of those who have been more than conquerors, we feel almost despondent. I feel that I shall never be like that. But they won step by step by little bits of will, little denials of self, little inward victories by faithfulness in tiny things." She said, "No one sees these little hidden steps. They only see the accomplishment, but even so, those small steps were taken. There is no sudden triumph, no spiritual maturity. That is the work of the moment." We become what we are. As the Holy Spirit changes us in the areas we know about, we become aware of new areas needing the work of God. So, what is spiritual growth? It is the beautiful and continuous journey of a lifetime with Jesus!

Thy Will Be Done

In Matthew 6:9-10, Jesus taught His disciples, "After this manner therefore pray ye: Our Father which art in heaven, Hallowed be thy name. Thy kingdom come. Thy will be done in earth, as it is in heaven." What is this kingdom? God reigns supreme; therefore, His kingdom can be universally defined as the entirety of creation (Ps. 103:19, Isa. 66:1). The Psalmist said, "The Lord hath prepared his throne in the heavens, and his kingdom ruleth over all" (Ps. 103:19). In John 18:36, when Jesus answered Pilate, "My kingdom is not of this world," He spoke of a spiritual kingdom that would be revealed in the hearts of men and women. This kingdom is not merely an empire of social change subject to the earthly principles and broken practices upon which kingdoms of the earth are founded. To be a child of God is to be in the "kingdom not of this world" (John 1:12), free from all sin and guilt, with the promise of eternal life and peace with God through the sacrificial atonement of Jesus' precious blood (1 John 1:7, 1 Peter 1:18-23). The glory of God is in Jesus Christ (2 Cor. 4:6), and we who regard His name as holy will make the invisible kingdom of Heaven visible on the earth. How? By living the reality of His lordship. As believers (Rom. 10), we are citizens of heaven, and we owe our highest allegiance to our ultimate authority, King Jesus.

Jesus also taught us to pray that His will would "be done in earth as it is in heaven." In heaven, the will of God is performed entirely and without hesitation. There is no mission on which the angelic hosts will not go, nor is there reluctance in their service (Matt. 26:53, Heb. 12:22). In Psalm 115:1, we read, "Not unto us, O Lord, not unto us, but unto thy name give glory." We are praying that something will happen that has not yet happened. We are making ourselves available to fulfill His purpose. This was the prayer of Mary after the angel

Gabriel had revealed to her the will of God in bearing his son Jesus. She said, "Behold the handmaid of the Lord; be it unto me according to thy word" (Luke 1:38). Praying for the will of God to be done in our lives means that we are willing to, by the power of the Holy Spirit, overcome whatever might prevent that purpose from being accomplished. William Barclay said, "When we pray, 'Thy will be done,' we are not praying for resignation but for triumph." Prayer is not an invitation to passively accept what will happen. It is to pray for the spirit of victory, not defeat. It is to pray for perseverance until the victory is won rather than surrender by retreating from the conflict. Everything that happens is woven into the purpose of God. Jesus said, "I am Alpha and Omega, the beginning and the ending" (Rev. 1:8). Nothing is beyond God's purpose and control (Isa. 46:9-11). What God does in time, he planned from eternity. Precisely how the events of our lives are woven into the Father's plan, we may not know (Deut. 29:29). But the Christian journey is a walk of faith, and that which is good, acceptable, and perfect can be realized through prayer and applying the principles of Scripture (Rom. 12:2).

The story is about a sailor who repeatedly gets lost at sea, so his friends give him a compass and urge him to use it. But as usual, he became hopelessly confused and could not find his way. Finally, he was rescued by his friends. Disgusted and impatient with him, they asked, "Why didn't you use that compass we gave you?" The sailor responded, "I did. But I wanted to go north, and as hard as I tried to make the needle aim in that direction, it just pointed southeast." It's difficult to hear God's voice when we have already decided what we want Him to say. We dare not live this way. God reveals His plan to those committed to it (Ps. 25:14). In 1902, Adelaide Pollard hoped to go to Africa as a missionary, but she could not raise the funds necessary to make the journey. Greatly discouraged, she attended a prayer service one evening, and as she sat there, she overheard a woman say, "It really doesn't matter what you do with us, Lord, just have your way with our lives." This inspired Pollard. She contemplated the potter's story from Jeremiah 18:3, and upon returning home that evening, she wrote all four stanzas of the song "Have Thine Own Way, Lord" before retiring for the night:

Have Thine own way, Lord; have Thine own way
Thou art the potter, I am the clay.
Mold me and make me after Thy will,
While I am waiting, yielded and still.

The prophet Jeremiah did as the Lord commanded; he obeyed the divine will. He went down to the potter's house to hear what the Lord had to say and to observe such things from which he might learn instruction. He watched a potter there, having prepared his clay, fashioning a beautiful vessel of honor (2 Tim. 2:21). Praying for God's will is laying down our pride and selfishness, trusting that God knows better than we do. Just as the clay finds its highest purpose when it remains pliable in the hands of the potter, our lives fulfill their highest purpose when we let our Potter have His way with us. The sovereignty of God is the most comforting doctrine in Scripture, for the Lord will "shew himself strong in the behalf of them whose heart is perfect towards him" (2 Chron. 16:9). You may ask, "What is God's will for my life?" First, it is God's will that every individual be saved from the penalty of sin and death (1 Tim. 2:3-4, 2 Peter. 3:9). Therefore, if you commit to sharing your faith with others, you will be at the center of God's will (Matt. 28:18-20). The will of God is that we obey His Word, bow to His providence, and respond to His grace with wholehearted surrender (Matt. 6:25-34). It is God's will that we love the Lord with all our hearts and our neighbors as ourselves (Mark 12:29-31). It is God's will that He be glorified through us (Matt. 5:16). It is His will that we rejoice evermore, pray without ceasing, give thanks in all things, and embrace that which is good (1 Thess. 5:15-21). We are called to live by every word that proceeds from the mouth of God (Matt. 4:4). The Creator of the world, the Ruler of the universe, does not adjust His pitching to where we're swinging the bat. We're the ones who must make the adjustments.

Sometimes, the stories of the Bible seem far away, and we cannot see how the two worlds link up. But understand, the connection is God himself. Godliness and spiritual maturity are developed through doing those things we know will bring us closer to God (Col. 1:9-14, Heb. 10:22), disciplines that include Bible reading, study, prayer, fellowship, service, and stewardship. After Jesus raised himself from the grave, He appeared to His closest followers. They were afraid of what lay ahead of them. But rather than leave them with detailed instructions about everything they needed to do from then on, He gave them the ultimate Gift and source of guidance. He promised that His Spirit, the Holy Spirit, would come and guide them (John 20:19-23). The same Gift has been given to all who have believed in Him (Acts 2, Eph. 1:13). When our desire to follow God outweighs our desire for a particular outcome, we are ready to hear from heaven. Meditate on God's Word and spend focused time in prayer. Find dedicated Christians and seek biblical advice (Prov. 15:22). Ask them to pray about your decision. God can open and close the doors of opportunity, using events to point you in a specific direction. Life is a journey that is filled with possibilities. Trust that God will reveal your next steps at the best time and in the best ways. Be open to God's leading and seek to learn from your circumstances (Phil. 4:6-7, Isa. 26:3). If you are God's child, your Father will equip and empower you to fulfill the purposes He intends for your life. Trust Him to lead you into a future filled with hope!

God's desire is not to get us to a destination in the quickest, easiest, most straightforward route possible. Instead, he wants us to know him deeply. His will is not a feeling or a formula but a relationship. There is very little in the Bible about procedures for understanding God's plan, but many verses speak about developing a loving relationship with Jesus. W. A. Criswell noted something interesting about the Mississippi River. Even though everyone knows it flows from north to south, if you fly the length of the river, you will find it flows north at times and west at other times. But ultimately, the river flows south. It starts near Canada and empties into the Gulf of Mexico. What really matters is not the river's temporary direction but its ultimate destination. If your life flows "west" instead of "south" right now, remember that God is in charge. Life's twists and turns are less important than where it ends (2 Cor. 4:16-18). 1 Corinthians 1:9 tells us, "God is faithful, by whom ye were called unto the fellowship of his Son Jesus Christ our Lord." Remember the commandments in Mark 12:30-31 to love the Lord with our whole heart, soul, mind, and strength and to love our neighbor as ourselves? When Jesus said, "There is none other commandment greater" (v31), He shows us that the highest earthly ministry involves a personal relationship with God through which we can better care for those around us. What an incredible privilege God gives us when he calls us to demonstrate what mercy looks like to a confused world (Micah 6:8). In Romans 15:13, we read, "Now the God of hope fill you with all joy and peace in believing, that ye may abound in hope, through the power of the Holy Ghost."

Heavenly Father, fill us with wisdom and power so that we may present the riches of your grace to a perishing world. The imagery of the potter and the clay represents your dealing with us. You alone hold the sovereign right to shape our lives through your wise and loving hands. May we remember that the power of the Holy Ghost is alive and active in our lives. Your plans extend far beyond our understanding, your faithfulness knows no bounds, and your promises are fulfilled with perfect timing. May your Spirit empower us, comfort us in times of trouble, and lead us into a deeper understanding of truth. May our lives be a reflection of your transforming work within us. We pray for your will to be done in us as it is in heaven. Dear Lord, Thy will be done.

The Measure of a Man

WHAT IS THE MEASURE OF A MAN? IS HE GOOD WITH HIS FISTS? OR MAYBE with his wits? Perhaps the measure of a man is his work ethic, his character, or the capacity to provide for himself and his family. What do a man's tears or lack of tears say about his manhood? If a man is a nurturer, is that part of his masculinity? Is his manhood diminished if he is open to sharing his feelings or talking with other men about something besides cars and sports? The roles of men have been undermined and confused to the extent that many are left wondering what it means to be a good man. The great news is that the Bible contains instructions on how to be a godly man. Every facet of a man's life – his family, his work, his friendships – is strengthened as he grows in the most important relationship, which is his relationship with Jesus Christ. Let's check a higher authority instead of listening to society's definitions of manhood. I invite you to open your Bible to Psalm 15. Let's see what God has to say about manhood.

When God measures a man, He observes how he lives. Does he do things God's way or his way? Does he lead his own life or allow the Holy Spirit to lead? The man who does things God's way tries to do what is right. He tells the truth. He treats people fairly. He doesn't assassinate the character of others. And the man knows how to pick out good role models for his life. He doesn't make heroes out of the ungodly, try to fashion his life after them, or win their approval. Instead, he honors those who love the Lord with the mark of Christ on their lives. His words are his bond, even if it costs him. He is generous. He shares his resources with others and would never exploit anyone for profit. When God measures a man, he looks for humility and integrity (Micah 6:8), not perfection. A godly man is not two-faced. He's not a pretender. His life is hidden with Christ in God, and he's the same man always – no matter what kind of crowd he's with. He takes responsibility for himself. He doesn't blame others for his faults and failures. He genuinely tries to do the right thing, "providing for honest things, not only in the sight of the Lord but also in the sight of men" (2 Cor. 8:21). Men who meet God's measure live with integrity before the Lord and their fellow human beings. And they do it no matter the cost.

Are you in a leadership position? Godly leaders begin with love. They set the example. They do the right things. They create the right mindset. They do their best and allow for mistakes. In a time when winning is everything, integrity is a Georgia high school basketball coach named Cleveland Stroud. His team won the state championship but willingly relinquished it after discovering that a scholastically ineligible kid had played 45 seconds in the first of the school's five post-season games. Said Stroud, "We didn't know he was ineligible at the time; we didn't know until a few weeks ago. Some people have said that we should have kept quiet about it, that it was just 45 seconds, and the player wasn't an impact player. But you've got to do what's honest and right. I told my team that people forget the scores of basketball games; they never forget what you're made of." Titus 2:7-8 tells us, "In all things shewing thyself a pattern of good works: in doctrine shewing uncorruptness, gravity, sincerity, sound speech that cannot be condemned: that he that is of the contrary part may be ashamed, having no evil thing to say of you." Integrity. Men, how much integrity would you measure if you were to measure your own lives? What grade would you give yourself on your Psalm 15 report card? And what grade would the people who know you best assign you on your integrity report card? I can tell you this: Nobody's grading a hundred. Nobody's getting a perfect score. For me, Psalm 15 is less a pat on the back than a swift kick. It doesn't so much tell me what I'm doing right as what I'm doing wrong… wrong with the way I use speech, bad with the way I treat my neighbor, wrong with the way I choose my role models and the way I use the resources God has given me. I'm not a total Psalm 15 failure, but it describes more where I need to grow than where I am right now. Psalm 15 shows me that I don't meet God's standards. It shows me that I am a sinner. I'm hit-and-miss at best. I got a few singles, but I'm no

Psalm 15 home run hitter. It would be easy to be discouraged. And I would be, except for one thing: Jesus Christ. Jesus is a Psalm 15 home run hitter. Jesus got it all right. Jesus lived a sinless, perfect life. And then He chose to go to the cross and sacrifice His life to cover my sins and make me righteous before God.

In 1 Timothy 6, Apostle Paul tells us to flee envy, strife, pride, and the love of money. Then, he gives six virtues that men of God should pursue: righteousness, godliness, faith, love, patience, and humility. He tells us to "Fight the good fight of faith, lay hold on eternal life, whereunto thou art also called, and has professed a good profession before many witnesses." Look at this passage of Scripture in 2 Corinthians 5:21: "For he (God) hath made him (Jesus) to be sin for us, who knew no sin; that we might be made the righteousness of God in him." This is the good news: I can't measure up to God's standards, but Jesus can, and Jesus did, and Jesus does. Only when we put our trust in what Jesus did for us on the cross and in his resurrection can we be assured that we can sojourn in God's tent and dwell on His holy hill now and forever. Jesus is the way! Jesus takes up the slack for us, saves us from our sins, and makes us holy in God's sight. When our lives are hidden with Christ in God, God forgives our sins, sees us as righteous, and continues to help us become more like Jesus through the guidance of the Holy Spirit. This is God's work in us. We cannot do it on our own. And maybe that's the best way we could say it: When God measures a man, He wants to see Jesus in that man. Not every man will like the same things, enjoy the same hobbies, express the same emotions, and share the same passions. But all will bear the mark of Christ Jesus. There it is, God's measure of a man—a God-chasing, integrity-living man in whom both God and the rest of us can see Jesus in his face. Men, be that man. The life we live before others will show the love of Jesus.

How can we live a life that is pleasing to God? Psalm 1 tells us, "Blessed is the man that walketh not in the counsel of the ungodly, nor standeth in the way of sinners, nor sitteth in the seat of the scornful. But his delight is in the law of the Lord; and in his law doth he meditate day and night." Consider David, the second king of Israel, the man after God's heart (1 Sam. 13:14). When we study David's life, we discover that a heart for God is not a supernatural gift, nor is it merely an emotional one. It is a surrendered lifestyle made up of God-honoring choices. A person with a heart for God will hold Him in the highest esteem (Ps. 42:1, 145:3), made possible only through prayer and the study of Scripture. Someone asked their pastor, "Which is more important... praying or reading the Bible?" The pastor replied with a question of his own, "Which is more important... breathing in or breathing out?" Both are essential. So, what does it mean that David was a man after God's heart? Indeed, it doesn't mean he was blameless. In 2 Samuel 11, we are told of the terrible sins he committed for which he suffered great sorrow. But the Bible also says, "David did that which was right in the eyes of the Lord and turned not aside from anything that he commanded him all the days of his life, save only in the matter of Urijah the Hittite" (1 Kings 15:5).

I believe the reason God spoke so highly of David is found in Acts 13:22, where we read, "I have found David, the son of Jesse, a man after mine own heart, which shall fulfill all my will." David devoted his life to fulfilling God's purposes. He loved what God loved. In Psalm 119:47, he said, "I will delight myself in thy commandments, which I have loved." He was compelled to act upon whatever God desired. Yes, he was flawed. Who among us is perfect? Not one! We are all sinners needing a Savior (Rom. 3:10-23). But in humble submission, David asked God to bend his heart toward righteousness (Ps. 119:33-40). And with a continuing spirit of repentance, he received new mercies and forgiveness (Ps. 51). He loved the ways of God (Deut. 5:33). He loved the law of God (Ps. 119:97). When God spoke, he paid close attention. He wanted to live according to all that God intended for him. Psalm 119:2 says, "Blessed are they that keep his testimonies, and that seek him with the whole heart." David wanted to follow the Lord with a clean heart and a right spirit (Ps. 32:5). This is a great testimony of what God desires in us. I believe the fundamental disciplines of prayer, Scripture, brotherhood, accountability, and personal ministry will be found in godly men. The great and mighty success in Noah's life was building an ark. What an incredible act of obedience! Yet the time spent for this high calling was equal to just twelve years in the life of an eighty-year-old man. What does this mean to me? It means that life's highest calling is to walk with God. Not before Him, nor after Him; but beside Him. Noah decided to obey God for a lifetime. He chose to be upright in a twisted world and preach God's gospel. The Bible says, "Noah found grace in the eyes of the Lord... and (he) walked with God" (Gen. 6:8-9). He walked with God. This is the measure of a man!

What Grief Taught Me

IF YOU GRIEVE THE PASSING OF SOMEONE YOU LOVED DEARLY, I WANT TO share my story with the hope that something I say will help you. God has been my strength in very dark days, and He will do the same for you if you let Him. The Psalmist said, "The Lord is my light and my salvation; whom shall I fear? The Lord is the strength of my life; of whom shall I be afraid?" (Ps. 27:1). My remarks are based on the Word of God because I choose to experience my journey of life with an eternal perspective.

By July 2020, millions of people had tested positive for the dread Coronavirus, and hundreds of thousands had died. It was Tuesday morning, July 28, 2020, and Marjorie had not slept well the night before. She was up early. By about 9:00 a.m., it seemed the best thing to do was to take my wife to a hospital that was about ten miles from our home. When I got home, I knelt beside our bed and prayed that God would bring strength and healing to her. This was the beginning of what I would do for several days after that. It felt as if I was suffocating. I could not catch a deep breath. I was being crushed by something beyond my control, so frightened at the possibility of losing her that my heart would palpitate rapidly. I would read my Bible and pray. I would think about what had transpired in my nearly 52 years with Marjorie. I met her at age sixteen, and we were married almost four years later, in 1972. I asked God to give her physical strength and peace of mind as she lay in her room. And God granted my request. I had written several devotionals about being confident in God's provision, but it was more challenging to live the promise. It was such a dark and painful time for me. But considering her difficulty and that of so many others with the disease, I asked God to forgive my self-centered attitude.

On August 3rd, I received an alarming phone call from Marjorie's doctor. He said he would do what he could to arrange a visit for me. I rushed to the hospital and met my children there. I grabbed my Bible and phone and walked into the lobby. I was directed to the third floor, where I met the most wonderful and accommodating nurses. They helped me put on the protective gear and allowed me into Marjorie's room. My sweet wife was lying on her right side, an IV in each arm and wearing a full-face oxygen mask. I knelt at her side and rubbed her hand. I stroked her hair and told her how much she meant to me and that I loved her more than anything. She nodded slightly. I reached over to pat her leg, and she patted her leg simultaneously. I was unsure if she thought she was patting my hand, but I did not care. I was so glad to see her! At one point, I could hear her faintly trying to say something. I told her I would talk for both of us; after all these years together, I knew how she would answer anyway. She nodded, and I could see a light in her eyes. I told her our kids and grandkids were all gathered outside the hospital, that they loved her and were praying. She nodded again with a little twinkle in her eyes. I spoke of the many who were praying for her. Each time, she would nod. She understood. When I began to pray, she closed her eyes and prayed silently with me. I thanked God for the opportunity to see her, His wonderful gift of salvation, and his many blessings. I prayed for physical strength and peace of mind. When I finished, she opened her eyes and seemed very relaxed. I told her repeatedly how much I loved her. I reached to take her left hand and rubbed the back side of her arm. When I started to let go, she grasped my hand the best she could and then patted it. It was time for me to go. I said, "I love you so much, but I have to say goodbye for now." I told her I would see her soon. With that, I left the room.

Sitting in my car in the hospital parking lot, I talked with God. My part of the conversation went like this: "Dear Lord, she was yours before she was mine. You love her more than I ever could. You can care for her in ways I cannot." I told Him, "As a child, I gave my life to you. She is now part of my life and, therefore, part of that giving." On August 19th, at nearly 5:00 a.m.. I received a call from the hospital. Marjorie had passed from this life a few minutes earlier, peacefully and with music playing in her room. Lying there

63

in the darkness, I thought of all she meant to me. Precious memories turned into treasures more valuable than anything I would ever own. Through all this, I am more determined to live as Marjorie did - with lots of love, joy, and a heart of giving. I know we will be together in heaven (1 Thess. 4:13-18), and I believe it will not be long before I see her again. Oh, how I look forward to that day! On September 3, 2020, after nearly 48 years of marriage, I rested my sweet wife at Cherokee Memorial Park in Lodi, California. The graveside service was beautiful, and everything was as she would have wanted it to be.

So, what has grief taught me?

None of us is alone in our grief, though it feels like we are. Grief is a road well traveled, and getting to know those who journey with us gives perspective. The question becomes, "Do we move on, or do we learn to live with it?" I choose every day to see the positive and be grateful for what Marjorie and I had together, for the love we shared. And my days are bright. I have met a wonderful woman who shares a similar story of love and loss. With very thankful hearts, Yolanda and I talk about all the wondrous things God has done for us. God is so good!

I have learned that life is fragile and to be grateful for those who are near and dear. I have fantastic choices and possibilities all around me. I love to write, and I've taken this joy to a higher level.

Grief has taught me that not everyone grieves the same. There is no timeline and certainly no right or wrong way to grieve. We all have different responses and reactions to losing a loved one. Your loss is personal, and the grieving process is personal. The real challenge is simply doing something positive with your new life. Each day, you can carve out renewed joy and purpose. This starts by taking the focus off of yourself and beginning to do more things for others. Serving people is not only the right thing to do. It is vital to recovery and leads to more profound healing. One of the best ways to help yourself is through selfless acts of kindness. This is so important! Grief has taught me that little moments count. Forgiveness and love should always be on your lips.

We live in a very broken world, and it is up to each of us to bring some comfort (2 Cor. 1:3-5). To some, grief is seen as embarrassing and weak, and they don't understand that time and kindness are the most important things that should be offered to the bereaved. I have learned that it isn't my job always to be strong, and sometimes, I must rely on those who love me to do the heavy lifting.

Grief teaches compassion. If you respond God's way, losing someone you love will soften your heart and cause you to see the loss and grief of others more clearly. Encountering loss and dealing with grief has taught me to empathize with others better. I have something to share out of my own experience. I can relate to them; therefore, I can assist them. Grief is a gift that will teach you the importance of caring, loving, and sympathizing. Serving *others* can allow you to discover gifts and talents you didn't realize you had, and this will help you regain control.

Sudden bursts of grief will happen when least expected, and you will have emotional breakdowns. Sadness can disappear for days - and then overwhelm you when you least expect it. The triggers can be anywhere, at any time. For me, it has happened when shopping for groceries, hearing a favorite song, using one of Marjorie's kitchen utensils, and any number of other things. Death and grief make people uncomfortable, so don't judge them too harshly for their silence. Do not judge them for saying too much. Most people try to be helpful, but sometimes, it comes across differently than expected. The good news is that they are paying attention.

Grief has prompted me to live life more fully. Be kind to yourself. Don't play the 'what if?" game. God knows the future precisely because He wills the future. There is no "what if?" in a God whose providence reigns supreme. Because God is invisible to us, we often fail to recognize His active presence in human affairs. I have not seen all of God's purposes, but I have seen enough. The battle is ours; the outcome is His. How do we stand the pressures of a changing world? Apostle Paul answers, "I know whom I have believed" (2 Tim. 1:12).

Living another day is both a privilege and a joy; I will make the most of it. I am so grateful for the joy, love, and laughter moments! I promise you, things will get better. We must come to a place of experiencing a faith grounded in the belief that God is love and that His motive is always for our good. The Psalmist says He has hedged me in behind and before and that He has laid His hand upon me (Ps. 139:5). When I see God for all He is, I see myself for all I am not (Isa. 6:5). When I stumble in the darkness of emotional pain, the Lord gently nudges me back to an eternal perspective. One day, Jesus Christ will make all things right for those who believe in Him (2 Pet. 3:13). He will come again in power and glory, and all this world's sin, suffering, and death will be destroyed (1 Cor. 15:24-29). In His dying, He destroyed death; in His rising, He restored life (John 19 and 20). Friend, you are not alone. God hears your pleas, and He understands the pain of every kind. Cast your burden on the Lord, and He will sustain you (Ps. 55:22). Rest in Him. God is continually aware of every detail of your life. Not only is He aware, but He is with you to heal every emotion when you trust Him for all outcomes. I pray that you will receive the sweet comfort of God in your life today!

A God-Honoring Legacy

OUR CHILDREN AND GRANDCHILDREN DECIDE HOW IMPORTANT THEIR faith will be to them by watching how important our faith is to us. As we cherish the old, rugged Cross, so will they. Any worthwhile legacy is really about just being faithful to Jesus Christ. And much of that is about how we treat people. What are we doing to make a positive difference for the glory of God? In my writings, I have tried to weave in my thoughts about life's lessons, my own spiritual journey, and choices that must be made. I want to model faithfulness, integrity, love, and generosity. I want to celebrate my family and friends by encouraging them to live for God. I want to say things that will leave an impression on people. I will have been helpful if I give a smile, hope, pleasure, and encouragement. I want my grandchildren to know that their grandpa was a man who loved Jesus and studied God's Word.

Is your mission worth inheriting? Nowadays, we tend to consume too much energy on the wrong questions: What do I want? Who do I want to become? What do I want my life to look like in five years? How can I achieve more? These are all excellent questions, but they are self-centered. They neglect to factor in how deeply our actions touch the lives of others. We must begin each day with a timeless overarching question that we can revert to repeatedly, reflecting our core values and guiding our actions. I believe that question is, "How do I want to be remembered?" For a Christian, the question has three benefits. It tells what we stand for, how we want to live for Christ, and how deeply we are rooted in Him. We are all writing a story of how we want to be remembered for our time on earth. Our faith, followed by actions, will more clearly shape who we become. The apostle James said, "For what is your life? It is even a vapor that appears for a little time, and then vanishes away" (James 4:14). The wisest man in history told us our days are numbered (Eccl. 7:2). The Psalmist David prayed, "Lord, make me to know mine end, and the measure of my days, what it is; that I may know how frail I am" (Ps. 39:4). C.T. Studd (1860-1929) spent his life in dedicated service to the Lord, serving in China, India, and Africa. He said, "Only one life, twill soon be past; only what's done for Christ will last." Our legacy is not about celebrating our life or achievements but maximizing our influence for Christ (1 Cor. 15:58).

What can we learn from Bible heroes about how to leave a God-honoring legacy? Moses prepared Joshua to lead the Jews into their new homeland (Joshua 1:1-5). When Moses ascended Mount Sinai to talk with God, young Joshua was at his side (Ex. 24:13-14). Joshua witnessed firsthand the power and glory of God. Elijah successfully equipped Elisha to be his prophetic successor. Soon after Elijah called fire down from heaven and single-handedly slaughtered the prophets of Baal, God asked him to anoint the young farmer Elisha as his successor (1 Kings 19:19-21). Then, without leaving his mentor's side, Elisha witnesses his spiritual father's ascent to heaven in a chariot of fire. The young prophet would not rest until he walked in the same power and anointing as Elijah (2 Kings 2:13-15). Christ's entire ministry was spent "passing the torch." Jesus called a roughshod fisherman to drop his fishing nets and fish for men (Matt. 4:18), then tested Peter's faith several times. He pushed Peter out of the nest. Sometimes he would fly, and sometimes he would fall. But when the Holy Spirit descended at Pentecost, Peter was ignited with divine passion and power (Acts 2:1-41). Look behind you. Who is following in your footsteps, and where are you leading them? It's never too late to leave a God-honoring legacy.

A legacy is not a resumé or a list of accomplishments but the imprint you leave on the future, either by default or design. Leaving a Godly legacy means telling the stories of God's goodness and faithfulness in your life (Deut. 6:6-7). Too often, older people tell the next generation everything they are doing wrong instead of positioning them for success. Be honest with them, and do not downplay the challenges of the coming adult days. But reassure them by pointing them to Jesus. Christ spoke of the things of the higher life hereafter. So, it should be with us. We should talk and teach of the mercy and lovingkindness of God. Our words should be words of praise and thanksgiving. By revealing His character, we can influence others for the Kingdom of God. One fundamental principle taken from Proverbs 13:22 is the value of transferring values and wisdom for the benefit of future generations. This way, we equip them to navigate life with purpose. To impact lives eternally, share the message of hope, forgiveness, and salvation with those you love. Let's determine to build a legacy that echoes through time, enriching lives. And may we be a testament to a love that endures!

People who positively impact others dedicate themselves to what gives their life meaning and purpose. They use what they've learned as a means of serving. They spread what they know. They're not afraid to connect with others, share their knowledge and talents, and offer their viewpoints and opinions. They have learned that mutually supportive relationships can catapult both parties to a higher level. They want to affect change because they believe change will bring a better way to live. People of influence are happy to help. They use their power and influence to uplift others because their motives are not self-serving. Make an impact for Christ. Influence others to live with an eternal perspective. How? Ask the Lord to help you see the world as He sees it and do what He did. Are you moved with compassion? Jesus was saddened when He saw how much people were suffering, but He wasn't discouraged. Instead, He ministered to them. We are never too young, old, poor, or rich to serve God. He only requires a willing heart.

In 1867, a Swedish chemist, Alfred Nobel, invented a new high explosive named "dynamite." He believed his invention would make war so horrible that it would never happen again. Surprisingly, he was wrong. Instead of ending wars, dynamite made them more devastating and wide-ranging than ever before. He was horrified. And then something interesting happened. One morning, around the turn of the century, he awoke to read his obituary. It read: "Alfred Nobel, the inventor of dynamite, who died yesterday, devised a way for more people to be killed in a war than ever before. He died a wealthy man." The newspaper had made a mistake. Alfred's older brother was the one who died. But the obituary had a profound effect on him. So, what did Alfred Nobel do? He founded the Nobel Prize - an award for scientists and writers who foster peace. Nobel said, "Every man ought to have the chance to correct his epitaph in midstream and write a new one." Alfred Nobel was given a chance to make a change. And ultimately, when he did pass away, he would be known for creating dynamite and the most well-known peace prize in the world.

John Livingstone had set his mind on making money and becoming wealthy, and he did. His brother David had knelt and prayed, surrendering himself to Christ. He resolved, "I will place no value on anything I have or possess unless it is in relationship to the Kingdom of God." The inscription over the Scottish missionary's burial place in Westminster Abbey reads, "For thirty years, his life was spent in an unwearied effort to evangelize." But under his name in an old edition of the Encyclopedia Britannica, John Livingstone is listed simply as "the brother of David Livingstone." Sometimes, God takes our most significant failures into our greatest successes. Charles "Chuck" Colson had risen the ladder of national political success at breakneck speed. After a tour in the Marines, Colson served in the office of the Assistant Secretary of the Navy, ran a political campaign, and joined a law firm before becoming special counsel to the President (Richard Nixon) in 1969, at the ripe old age of 38. And then it all came crashing down when Colson was sent to prison for his involvement in the Watergate scandal. As one pastor put it, Colson's career was over, but his calling was beginning. While in prison, Colson converted to Christianity and fought for the rights of the incarcerated. Today, Prison Fellowship serves in all 50 states in the U.S., impacting more than 1,000 prisons and over 365,000 incarcerated men and women each year. In his 1983 book Loving God, Colson shares the realization that his legacy came not from his successes but from his failures. He said, "God chose the one experience in which I could not glory for His glory."

Have you ever imagined what your friends and family might say at your funeral? If you see yourself in that place, be encouraged! You are still here, and your life has not been entirely written yet. You and I still have that precious gift of time on our side. A God-honoring legacy begins with a relationship with God, a relationship that is built, not inherited. When my acquaintances hear my name, I want them to think about the evidence of salvation (Gal. 5:22-23). I want to be remembered as a person of kindness, a good listener, a father, grandfather, and friend with a good sense of humor, and perhaps someone who seems to know song lyrics for almost anything. I hope to be remembered as helpful and funny, someone who sought to help alleviate someone's suffering. Perhaps you're like me, thinking of all the times you could have done better in raising a family. But at least from this day forward, we can know that we are fervent in our pursuit of God. Let no one call us moderate ever again. There will come a time when we'll be center stage. It will be the last days of a lifetime performance—no do-overs, no take-two. The audience will be our family, friends, and neighbors. And if our faith is genuine, there will be no difference between who we are and the character we played in life. Our masks and our faces are the same. We are the person we wanted others to think we were. We are the same as when we lived in the most pressure-packed moments of life. When Jesus reached that moment, He said, "Father, into thy hands I commend my spirit" (Luke 23:46). That's how I want to leave the stage of life: full of faith, peace, anticipation, and hope!

That I May Know Him

WE MAY KNOW LITTLE ABOUT THE LORD JESUS HIMSELF WHEN WE BEGIN our Christian journey. But the lessons we are to learn will come in time, for we all will walk the road to Emmaus with Him (Luke 24:1-35). When hope hangs by a thread, our broken hearts will be restored. Jesus will reveal Himself more clearly, and our perspective will change. In John 3, we read about a man who wanted to know God better. His name was Nicodemus, and he was a Pharisee, a ruler of the Jews. Jesus patiently explained to Nicodemus that he must be born again. Therefore, we understand that the Christian journey begins with faith. The first step to knowing God is to accept his son, Jesus, as your Savior. Admit you are a sinner and receive the precious blood that He shed on the cross of Calvary as payment for your sin debt (Rom. 10:9-10). When we are born again by the power of the Holy Ghost, we can truly begin to learn about God, His character, and His will (1 Cor. 2:10). Prayer, preaching, fellowship, and Scripture reading are all essential to living victoriously in Christ. But I want to talk about how we can draw closer to the Lord through life's difficult experiences. I want to experience a strength that begins when mine ends.

Life is defined by the choices we make. In Philippians 3:10, Apostle Paul expressed his desire: "That I may know him and the power of his resurrection, and the fellowship of his sufferings, being conformed to his death." Paul had been a Christian for 25 years, sitting in a Roman prison. He had known Jesus for a quarter of a century, yet he wanted to know Him better. He could aim no higher. In verse 8, Paul referred to "the excellency of the knowledge of Christ Jesus my Lord." Paul's singular ambition was to connect with Jesus on the closest possible relational level, and nothing else mattered. He was willing to lose every earthly possession and pursuit for intimately knowing Christ. For Paul, to experience a relationship with Jesus in this way meant sharing in the fellowship of His sufferings, even if that meant death. To know Jesus is not the same as knowing His historical life. We can say that we know someone because we recognize him: we can distinguish what is different about him from others. We can say that we know someone because we are acquainted with what he does; we see the baker because we get our bread from him. We can say that we know someone because we are on speaking terms with that person. We can say that we know someone because we spend time in his house and with his family. But we can honestly know someone because we have committed our life to him. We live with him daily, sharing every circumstance. And when we draw near God, His promises will become real. Peace, strength, hope, joy, and love will begin to characterize our lives. Yes, there is a way of knowing Jesus Christ in the power of His resurrection!

No one wants to suffer. No one invites life-altering pain. No one wants to lie awake agonizing over where a disastrous situation is headed. No one wants to experience a loss so profound that we wonder how to go on. We understand that rain falls into everyone's life, but no one wants a deluge. We don't pray for it. We don't seek it. And all we can think about is relief. But in the Book of Job, we discover a surprising truth: sometimes deliverance comes by affliction (Job 36:15). You may ask, "How does this make sense? If I want relief *from* affliction, how can I possibly find it *by* affliction?" The answer is that we can be delivered from things worse than the affliction itself. Now, you may think, "What is more precious than immediate relief from pain?" Deliverance from indifference. We learn to recognize God's voice as Samuel did because we actively listen for it (1 Sam. 3:4-14). The prophet Isaiah said, "And though the Lord give you the bread of adversity, and the water of affliction… thine ears shall hear a word behind thee, saying, This is the way, walk ye in it…." (Isa. 30:20-21). Trials can awaken us to more of God, and our faith will increase if we respond to the circumstances as we should. The Roman Centurion never heard Jesus preach a sermon. He never saw Him heal or calm the wind. He only witnessed the way He died. But that was all it took to make a hardened soldier take a giant step of faith (Luke 23:47). The reality of one's belief is revealed in pain.

Truth and character are unveiled in hardship. Time spent in the fog of pain may be God's greatest gift. It could be that the hand that extends itself to lead you out of the mist is a pierced one. The manufacturing process of a brass trumpet involves extreme heat, rigorous stretching, a bending block, a frozen solution, repeated hammering, abrasion, and polishing, all of which are necessary to hear the instrument's beautiful sound! Faith is at its best, not in pews on Sunday mornings but at hospital bedsides, cancer wards, and cemeteries. The principle is simple: tears are most apt when words are most empty. A tear falling on a casket says what a spoken farewell never could. Heeding the voice of the Holy Spirit through Scripture and prayer will radically transform us and ultimately reshape who we are. There is a changing power in pressure. The more I pray, the more I realize He hears me. The more I read my Bible, the more I realize how true and unchanging He is. The more I trust Him, the more I have witnessed His faithfulness.

The psalmist said, "It is good for me that I have been afflicted; that I might learn thy statutes" (Ps. 119:71). Affliction will draw us to the things of God when we realize that the things of earth are broken. Pain causes us to search for meaning and hope beyond our present circumstances. It opens our eyes to the power and beauty of God's Word. When life falls apart, we cling to God, forgetting our foolish pride. We taste and see for ourselves God's goodness and grace. Speaking of the God of all comfort, Apostle Paul said, "But we had the sentence of death in ourselves, that we should not trust in ourselves, but in God which raises the dead" (2 Cor. 1:11). God will teach us to depend on Him through times of hardship. He will give us patience, endurance, and hope, all because the love of God is shed abroad in our hearts (Rom. 5:1-5). Affliction prevents us from loving the world because we become increasingly aware that this world is not our home (1 John 2:15). The greatest joy of heaven will be seeing the glory of God in the face of Jesus (2 Cor. 4:6). Everything in this life will pale in comparison!

Sometimes, we find ourselves walking an untrodden path where we are brought to a standstill. The way may be new to us, but not to our God. All things are equally present to His eye, and nothing surprises Him (Ps. 139:16). We have His Word to guide us and are given the privilege of prayer (Matt. 6:9–13). Nobody knows grief better than

Jesus Christ, and He can be trusted with mine. I want Him to prove His power in my weakness (2 Cor. 12:9–10). When a crisis occurs in our lives, we seek God for relief and answers of every kind. Yes, we experience pain and confusion. But in times of trouble, we need more than logic. We need hope. Jesus Christ is that hope! Having never received an answer from God as to his suffering, Job said, "I have heard of thee by the hearing of the ear: but now mine eye seeth thee" (Job 42:5). There is a difference between hearing God's goodness and experiencing it. I know He is always at work in my life, but sometimes, I cannot see Him do much of anything. I have even prayed, "Lord, I just need to know you have not deserted me and that you hear me" (Psalm 13). My time in the valley will depend on my obedience to God in the valley. I do not praise Him for the circumstance but for being my Deliverer. In Christ, we become satisfied by acknowledging His wisdom, justice, and goodness.

What does it mean to trust God? To trust is to believe in the reliability, truth, ability, or strength of something. Trusting in Him means believing that what He says about Himself, the world, and you is true. Having faith in what He says is a choice, even when your emotions and circumstances would have you believe something different. We can learn more about God when life is uneasy because we lean into Him more. We realize we cannot make it without Him, so we pray more. And through all, we experience His faithfulness like never before. God is present and is making Himself known. You need only to look. Trust grows as you look for God's presence in what feels dark and heavy. He never leaves. We are not obliged to say, "I like these circumstances," to be content with them. Contentment is found in His promise, "I will never leave thee, nor forsake thee" (Heb. 13:5). A satisfied spirit is a silent, cheerful, and thankful spirit! No matter the difficulty, I live in the promise of my salvation. Heaven gets sweeter with each passing day. Friend, you are not alone. God hears your pleas, and He understands the pain of every kind. Cast your burden on the Lord, and He will sustain you (Psalm 55:22). Rest in Him. He is with you to heal every emotion when you wholly trust Him for all outcomes (Matt. 6). Someone said, "The only way to meet affliction is to pass through it solemnly, slowly, with humility and faith, as the Israelites passed through the sea. Then the waves of misery will divide and become a wall to us, on the right side and left, until the gulf narrows before our eyes, and we land safely on the opposite shore."

When we face pressures that are too great for us to resolve ourselves, adversity gets our attention. It reminds us of our weaknesses (2 Cor. 12:7-10). In February 1862, President Abraham Lincoln grieved over the death of his favorite son, eleven-year-old Willie. The sorrow intensified his tendency to suffer from depression, making it more difficult for him to deal with his mentally unbalanced wife while coping with the greatest domestic crisis in American history. It also caused the president to reflect more profoundly on the ways of God. Affliction drives us to communicate with God (Ps. 107:6). Desperate times lead to desperate prayer. Suffering humbles us. Paul said, "There was given to me a thorn in the flesh… lest I should be exalted above measure" (2 Cor. 12:7). Pain makes us rely on divine power. It positions us to receive grace (2 Cor. 12:9). When we realize how powerless we are, the Lord can display His glory in our lives. When we are afflicted, we can experience the comfort of God in a wonderful way (2 Cor. 1:3-4). Through our adversity, we can gain greater compassion for others. And lastly, affliction reminds us that this world is not our home. We are told in Hebrews 13:14-15, "For here have we no continuing city, but we seek one to come. By him, therefore, let us offer the sacrifice of praise to God continually, that is, the fruit of our lips giving thanks to his name." When I join the Psalmist in saying, "Bless the Lord, O my soul, and forget not all his benefits," I will include those He gives me through difficult times. Oh, that I may know Him!

A New Day Dawning

THERE IS SOMETHING VERY SPECIAL ABOUT DAWN. THE SUN CLIMBS OVER the horizon, inviting us to share the marvelous opportunities of a new day. The Bible uses this imagery to communicate the reality of new beginnings. The psalmist teaches that each new day should be a source of rejoicing (Ps. 118:24). Jeremiah tells us that the mercies of the Lord are new every morning (Lam. 3:23). We see this description of dawning throughout the Bible. The first recorded words spoken by God are "Let there be light" (Gen. 1:3). The Bible also tells of a day coming when the "sun of righteousness shall rise with healing in its wings" (Mal. 4:2), bringing a wonderful newness into this fallen world. This newness will make everything perfect.

During the Passover, the message of Jesus to the disciples was clear. He spoke of a new promise for all who would believe. Jesus said love would be the new standard (John 13:34-35), and the next day, our Lord proved His love at Calvary. Then, three days later, He raised Himself to life. This was the dawning of a new day! God opened to us a new life in Jesus (2 Cor. 5:17), and the early morning of the empty tomb was the beginning of all things made new. We testify of the resurrection, not only because of the historical evidence but because the power of the risen Lord has transformed our lives (Rom. 6:5-14). The resurrection of Jesus Christ is at the heart of the Christian message (1 Cor. 15:1-4), and Resurrection Day is the celebration of the accomplished Gospel. Absent the resurrection, Christianity becomes a mere human philosophy on balance with all other religious teachings. When Sir Michael Faraday, a great scientist of the 1800s, was dying, someone questioned him about the speculations of life after death. "Speculations!" he said, "I know nothing about speculations. I'm resting on certainties. I know that my Redeemer lives, and because He lives, I shall live also."

What does the resurrection of Christ mean to you? It meant freedom from spiritual bondage to Mary Magdalene, for she had been delivered from the hand of Satan. To fearful and guilt-ridden people, Jesus comes with peace, bringing the gift of a fully restored relationship with Him. For Peter, the resurrection meant forgiveness and a second chance. With sins forgiven, the apostle expressed his love for the Master (John 21:15-19), and, once again, Jesus presented the challenge, "Follow me!" Just as dawn broke once more for Peter, Jesus will see us through to a new day if we accept God's renewal of grace. The Spirit that raised Jesus from the dead empowers us to walk in victorious faith and obedience (1 Pet. 1:3-5). This is not behavior modification. It is the life-changing power of the Holy Ghost. It is not wishful thinking. It is the sure and confident expectation that our future is in His hands. The good news of the empty tomb is that our eternity is sealed in Jesus Christ (1 Pet. 1:3-9).

For the twentieth anniversary of *Larry King Live*, Barbara Walters interviewed the man who became famous for interviewing others. She asked him direct and revealing questions. Two of the most telling responses came when she probed fear and faith. Walters asked King, "What is your greatest fear?" He immediately replied, "Death." This interview occurred in 2005 when Mr. King was at the top of his career and had much to lose. But none of that mattered compared to his fear of death. Barbara's follow-up question was, "Do you believe in God?" King replied, "Not sure. I'm agnostic." To be uncertain about God is to be fearful of death. But Resurrection Sunday reminds us that the fear of death dissolves when we walk with the One who walked out of the tomb.

Have you ever supposed that the angel came and moved away the stone so Jesus could come out? It didn't happen that way; that verse is not in the Bible. The angel moved the rock so Mary and those with her could see. They were not walking up the hill rehearsing what they would say or do. But when they got there in the darkness, God rewarded their faithfulness with light and let them look in. Jesus Christ raised Himself that day! Death will not have the last word, for Jesus conquered the grave. And, because He arose, all who believe shall also rise. In Romans 6:5, Paul writes, "For if we have been planted together in the likeness of his death, we shall also be in the likeness of his resurrection." Jesus said, "I am the way, the truth, and the life: no man cometh unto the Father but by me." He was delivered for our offenses and raised again for our justification (Rom. 4:25). The life of our Lord is marked by a virgin's womb and an empty tomb. Christmas was the promise. Easter is the proof. And the ultimate victory has come, for Jesus has risen. Indeed, the Lord has risen!

In a cemetery in Hanover, Germany, there is a grave on which enormous slabs of granite and marble were cemented together and fastened with heavy steel buckles. It belongs to a woman who did not believe in the resurrection of the dead. Yet, just in case she was wrong, she asked that her grave be made so secure that it could not reach her if there were a resurrection. On the marker were inscribed these words: "This burial place must never be opened." A seed, covered over by the stones, grew in time. Slowly, it pushed its way through the soil and out from beneath them. The great slabs gradually shifted as the tree trunk enlarged, and the steel buckles were wrenched from their sockets. A tiny seed that had become a tree is a faint reflection of God's power to call to life all who are in the grave. When Jesus rose from the dead, he conquered death. He defeated the spiritual forces of evil and took them captive. He ascended to the throne of God and sent the Holy Spirit to teach and guide us in the life he has called us to.

Years ago, Sir Winston Churchill planned his funeral, and he did so with the belief in resurrection and eternal life. He instructed that after the benediction, a bugler stationed high in the dome of St. Paul's Cathedral would play Taps, the universal signal that says, "The day is over." But then came a theatrical moment. Another bugler was placed on the other side of the massive dome, and he played Reveille, the universal signal that says, "A new day has dawned, and it's time to arise." Churchill believed that, beyond the grave, Jesus Christ would open the door to his eternity. The Resurrection is the perfect act of God's love for us. This is not Lazarus rising from the dead only to die again eventually. Nor is it the daughter of Jairus or the son of the widow of Naim, who both rose from the dead and died again. These people were restored to the life they had before. They were no different after their restoration than before their death. Christ was not restored to the life He had before. He did not experience death again at some later time, and neither shall we! After death, resurrection will come into the new life God has prepared for us (1 Cor. 15:42-58). The resurrection of Jesus opened a door between the fallen, groaning world into which He was born and the renewal of all things (Eph. 1:18-23). He lived the life of perfect righteousness we have failed to live. He died as a lamb led to the slaughter, offering Himself as the perfect sacrifice to atone for the sins of the world, once and for all (Isa. 53:7). If Jesus has not risen, we who trust in Him are to be pitied because our hope extends no further than wishful thinking. If Jesus has not risen, our faith is meaningless, and we remain in our sins (1 Cor. 15:17-19). But because He arose, we are raised to a new hope. Christ prevailed over the power of the curse of sin that we also may be overcomers.

If you are a born-again believer – if you have received that gift of eternal life, your new life has already begun. Jesus said, "Verily, verily, I say unto you, He that heareth my word, and believeth on him that sent me, hath everlasting life, and shall not come into condemnation, but is passed from death unto life" (John 5:24). Through faith in Jesus, we have passed out of death into life, and by the power of the Holy Spirit, our new life has already begun. Our citizenship is now in heaven, and we are living the resurrection life right now! Just as Christ rose to a new and different life, so will we, who have been transformed by the infilling of the Holy Spirit, rise to a new and different life. Our greatest need is not only to see or hear about the resurrection but to have the power of the resurrection dwell in our hearts. Nothing is more important than becoming fully persuaded that God leads His children on a journey from earth to heaven. Every good and perfect gift comes from our heavenly Father (James 1:17). The Psalmist said, "The Lord will command his lovingkindness in the daytime and the night his song shall be with me" (Ps. 42:8). Study the Scriptures to discover its meaning for your life. Live as God intended. Do not take on tomorrow's anxieties today (Matt. 6:31-34). There is so much ahead for us, and God is in every moment. In Christ, you are never alone. Cast your cares on Him (1 Pet. 5:7), for we serve a God of new beginnings. He truly does make all things new! I love the words of the 1708 hymn written by

Isaac Watts. He paraphrased the 90th Psalm: "O God, our help in ages past, our hope for years to come, our shelter from the stormy blast, and our eternal home. O God, our help in ages past, our hope for years to come, be thou our guide while life shall last, and our eternal home."

Christian friend, we have an anchor of the soul, sure and steadfast (Heb. 6:19). The resurrection of Jesus Christ is that morning of history that gives us the courage to endure the hours of darkness, even the night of death. No longer do I fear death, for Christ has triumphed over it (Rev. 1:18). This is what led the apostle Paul to write: "O death, where is thy sting? O grave, where is thy victory?" (1 Cor. 15:55). And just as the first day of creation began with darkness and ended in the light, so shall our days be. Open your Bible to the beautiful promise in John 14:19, "Because I live, ye shall live also." I find comfort in knowing I will live forever with the One who would rather die for me than live without me! The resurrection of Jesus is the most significant and meaningful event in the history of the world. God's power is beyond measure, His strength is without end, and His mercy never fails. The promises of God are great and precious; they are bright and true; they are "yes and amen" (2 Cor. 1:20). And because Jesus lives in our hearts, we stand forgiven in the presence of God. Oh, how we long for the day when all things will be made new (2 Peter 3:13). For when Jesus returns, we will see the fullness of God's glory revealed (Rev. 21:23) at the most beautiful dawning of a new day!

The Expression of Gratitude

IF WE LIVE WITH GRATITUDE, OUR GENEROSITY WILL SHOW IT. AND those who appreciate the grace of God understand the importance of advancing His purpose in the world through cheerful giving (2 Cor. 9:7). The apostle Paul speaks of a grace received and a heart of thankfulness from which flows a commitment to give (2 Cor. 8). And in his pointing to the churches in Macedonia as an example of charity - even as they were themselves struggling under the affliction of extreme poverty - we should recognize that giving to others will be the conclusion of Christlike love for them. The temple offering provided by the widow in Luke 21 illustrates generosity - not in terms of quantity - but of sacrifice. Giving of ourselves is a work of God's grace in us. What, where, when, why, and how we give says something about our commitment to the Lord. Unwillingness to freely give our time, talent, and treasure speaks volumes about our profession of love for the One who first loved us.

Generosity begins in the heart. It begins when we stop complaining over what we are giving up and start rejoicing in all we have gained in Jesus Christ (Matt. 19:29). A thankful person knows that God is the source of all things, and His blessings are to be shared (1 Chron. 29:14-17). From a practical standpoint, a quick review of our financial records will speak volumes. If we give grudgingly, our approach will be "I must do it." If we give dutifully, our approach will be "I need to do it." But if we give thankfully, our approach will be "I want to do it." The Bible says, "For God so loved the world that He gave..." (John 3:16). In simple terms, our relationship with God is made known by our willingness to live as Jesus did (Phil. 2:4-5). If you think about it, isn't thankfulness and generosity a choice? Paul tells us that the Macedonian Christians "first gave themselves to the Lord" (1 Cor. 8:5).

Years ago, a gentleman was baptized in northern England. He was a prominent man in the community, a man who was known for his great wealth. This man was also known for having no interest in Jesus or the church. But someone had invited him to a Bible study, and as a result of his research, he had come to understand who Jesus was and why He came to die on the cross. In time, the man offered his life to Christ in response to God's grace. He appeared in dramatic contrast to the others waiting to be immersed on the evening he was baptized. Most wore jeans, a T-shirt, or other simple clothing. The wealthy man came dressed in an impeccable three-piece suit and a fabulous silk tie. He looked ready to present a business opportunity in London, which he had always been prepared for. And in his testimony, he explained why he had dressed this way. He said he recognized that his suit, his tie, and the quality of his shoes represented all he once held dear and built his life upon: everything that gave status and significance to him when he walked into a meeting. And now he says, "I've decided to be baptized in all of this attire so that I might remind myself always from this day that Jesus Christ has all of me." William Booth was asked to explain the extraordinary usefulness that God had made of him in the founding and framing of the Salvation Army. Mr. Booth replied without any pride, "Jesus Christ has all of me." We will not get beyond the starting block of godly living until we are convinced that God's grace is cause for giving.

God's favor is not granted to us because of anything we have done (Rom. 11:6). But this does not mean that good works are unrelated to a new life in Christ. Good deeds will not save us, yet we should be committed to acts of kindness that glorify God (Eph. 2:8-10). Living according to the teachings of Jesus is an expression of our thankfulness for God's wondrous grace (Phil. 2:13). When we live with an awareness of God's grace and forgiveness, we will use what we have in praise and worship. To the extent we appreciate the love of God, there will be joy in helping others. Developing a heart of gratitude often comes from our struggles, for we are more prone to recognize the troubles of those around us. Much of our character development happens during the storms of life and in the refining fire of difficult circumstances (1 Pet. 1:7).

A dear woman writes, "My name is Wendy, and this is the backstory about One Exceptional Life and how it all began. Have you ever had a time when your life was turned upside down? That was me back in 2011 when what started as flu symptoms progressed to a life-threatening illness within three days. The doctors told my husband and kids that I had less than a one percent chance of survival and to plan for my passing. My husband replied, "You don't know my God and what He can do!" My family never lost faith. Word spread, and hundreds of people prayed. God saved my life, but I lost my limbs. After three weeks in a medically induced coma and three months in the hospital, I came home to a new way of living. My family loved, supported, and cared for me. But the life I previously had was over. I questioned for a long time, "What do I do now?" I knew God had a plan for me. But what was it? Why did this happen to me? I dug into God's Word, and I continually counted my blessings. But there was still doubt, hopelessness, depression, and frustration. One day, I realized I could do more than I was giving myself credit for. That was the day my pity party ended, and my quest to help other women move past their challenges began. That was the day One Exceptional Life was born." If we open our hearts, the grace, gratitude, and generosity cycle will start and finish with God.

Paul said the Macedonian saints gave even beyond their ability (v3). They were willing to forego a legitimate want to supply a legitimate need; that is, they squeezed themselves so others wouldn't feel the pinch. And they did it without external prodding. Who among us is not a product of God's grace demonstrated through the contribution and influence of others? When Christ is our treasure, we will pledge our resources - our money, our time, our talents - to His purposes in the world (Col. 3:23-24). The eternal reward that awaits a child of God will far outweigh any inconvenience of this life (Rom. 8:18). When we consider the love of God and His grace toward us, the only appropriate response is to offer ourselves a living sacrifice to Him (Rom. 12:1). This is the only logical response to such a generous, merciful, and forgiving God!

Generally speaking, we start living small and live larger and larger. As we get more prosperous, we're a little less careful with what we have. We are a little more relaxed about our spending and how we use our time. We take up golf, fishing, or photography. Our standards are getting higher and higher. We trade fast food restaurants for better dining. What we have in abundance, we're less careful with. But we must recognize that we are stewards, not owners, and that our audience is God Himself. And when we understand our accountability is to Him, we will lead a life that loves people. Only two things in this life are eternal: people and the Word of God. Therefore, I want to invest heavily in both. Money and possessions are fleeting, and they must be subservient to reaching souls with the gospel of Christ (Matt. 28:16-20). The closest we can come to things of eternal value on earth is our influence in the world; that is, the people we reach for Christ (2 Cor. 3:2-3) and a sincere faith that inspires our brothers and sisters in the Lord (2 Tim. 1:5). Our godly witness is a legacy that will long endure beyond our passing.

J.L. Kraft, head of Kraft Cheese Corporation, said, "The only investment I ever made which has paid consistently increasing dividends is the money I have given to the Lord." Missionary Jim Elliott said, "He is no fool who gives what he cannot keep to gain what he cannot lose." Theologian Murray J. Harris says, "The steward needs an open hand to receive from God and then an active hand to give to God and others." Crusader F.B. Meyer said, "He is the richest man in the esteem of the world who has gotten the most. He is the richest man in the esteem of Heaven who has given the most."

One of the greatest misconceptions about giving is that what we part with to help the needy or spread the gospel disappears and is gone forever. We even buy into the devil's lie that giving will rob us of the good life. We could not be more wrong (Matt. 6:19-21). Martin Luther is credited with saying, "I have held many things in my hands, and I have lost them all. But whatever I have placed in God's hands, that I still possess." Rooted in our fallen human nature is a conflict between two value systems: the earthly and the eternal. Our natural inclination is to look to and be shaped by temporal things as if they were lasting. But that value system only delivers what it promises. It leads to futility and delusion. Jesus taught us not to store treasures that can be destroyed or stolen (Matt. 6:19-20). We will only find true fulfillment, reality, and wisdom when we embrace the eternal value system. This does not mean we ignore temporal things; it only means we leverage them in light of eternity. Psalm 90 is a prayer that God would teach us to number our days, that His glory would appear to our children, and that His beauty would be upon us to establish the work of our hands. When we consider the brevity of this life and the eternity of the life to come, we will not lose heart when temporal things fail us (2 Cor. 4:16). When we recognize that our days on earth are finite, we will have an appreciation for God's grace that leads to thankfulness and generosity (Ps. 90:12).

Saved By Grace

WHERE THERE IS A VICTORY, WE TEND TO BECOME PRIDEFUL. WHEN WE receive any gift from God, we are tempted to use it for self-glorification. In Deuteronomy 9, God promised victory to his people. They would take and possess the enemy's territory for their own. However, calculating the prideful tendency of their hearts, God first wanted them to understand that the victory would be His alone. He made clear that defeating the enemy would have nothing to do with their integrity or righteousness. God does not choose people to further His purposes based on merit - but only by His mercy. He seldom uses people who appear to be the most likely to succeed. In the Old Testament, God worked through dysfunctional kings and prophets. Moses was an escaped fugitive who made excuses. Adam, the first man, was a blame shifter who couldn't resist peer pressure (Gen. 3:12). Lot, who lost his father early in life, had a severe problem choosing the wrong company (Gen. 18-20). Rebekah, the first "mail-order bride," turned out to be a somewhat manipulative wife (Gen. 27). Jacob, who wrestled God, was pretty much a pathological deceiver (Gen. 25, 27, 30). David, the friend of God, concealed his adultery with a murder (2 Samuel 11). God used "foot in mouth" Peter to proclaim His gospel. He chose a man who once persecuted Christians to establish churches and record much of Scripture. Paul summed up God's amazing way of using the most unlikely people when he wrote, "God hath chosen the foolish things of the world to confound the wise... that no flesh should glory in his presence" (1 Cor. 1:17-31).

We often fall victim to the mistaken idea that we must be better than the rest to be used by God. But, in all of Scripture, God used flawed people. Grace is an all-inclusive, no-strings-attached gift. Some will say, "Lord, join my righteousness with Christ's righteousness," as if the two together could accomplish something. Not so. There is no righteousness but God (Jer. 9:23-24, Rom. 3:10). Here are three practical and productive takeaways: Dysfunction cannot be equated with our standing before God (1 John 3:20, 1 Cor. 4:3), sin does indeed have consequences (Gal. 6:7), and there is most certainly grace to be had (Heb. 4:16).

Grace is the love of God shown to the unlovely, the peace of God given to the restless, and the unmerited favor of God offered to the sinner. It is His kindness toward the undeserving (Rom. 3:23, 5:1-2). Earthly descriptions of grace, such as elegance of form, a charming characteristic, or a short prayer at a meal, do not begin to define the grace of God. B.B. Warfield said, "Grace is free sovereign favor to the ill-deserving." John Stott said, "Grace is love that cares, stoops, and rescues." Jerry Bridges said, "Grace is God reaching downward to people who are in rebellion against Him." Shorthand for grace is mercy, not merit. Grace focuses on the giver's goodness, with little focus on the recipient. Divine favor is about a relationship with God made possible by the sacrifice of Calvary. Speaking of Jesus, Charles Spurgeon said, "His agony and bloody sweat have forever taken away the consequences of sin from believers." Society tells us we are defined by what we do and that doing something will make us feel good. Work is what we do, but the relationship is who we are. Activity is easy, but relationships require more. Action can be done by a hypocrite, but a relationship is always genuine. Religious enterprise doesn't always mean we know Jesus. It could just mean that we know a lot about Him. On the day Jesus cleansed the temple, there was much activity - but there was no healing, worship, or communion with God (Matt. 21: 12-17). Activity involves wearing the right clothes to God's house... grace is loving God's people.

We can only begin to understand the grace of God when we know the holiness of God. His grace is mind-boggling, not just because He is gracious, but because He is merciful even though He is holy. God must judge sin to be true to His nature, but His amazing grace is given to those who come under righteous judgment. He chooses to be merciful toward us! Our smallest offense deserves the full wrath of a God set apart in His perfection, glory, majesty, and holiness. So, what are we to do with this question of our sinfulness and God's holiness that clings so close to us? Repent and receive God's amazing grace. We who first believed in the gospel of Jesus have received forgiveness according to the riches of God's grace (Eph. 2:7). But there's more. Grace is not only for the moment we realize we have nothing to bring to God and everything to receive. Grace is also for the long cultivated growth season following our rebirth. By grace, we set out. By grace, we are also sustained. Grace has as much to say about endings as it says about beginnings. The apostle Paul tells us, "For the grace of God that bringeth salvation hath appeared to all men, teaching us that denying ungodliness and worldly lusts we should live soberly, righteously, and godly, in this present world" (Titus 2:11). Grace transforms, and holiness follows. Grace encourages godly living. It changes our desires, motivations, and behavior. As we "grow in grace, and in the knowledge of our Lord and Savior Jesus Christ" (2 Pet. 3:18), grace becomes the basis of our identity (1 Cor. 1:10), the foundation of our position with God (Rom. 5:2), and the cause of our behavior (2 Cor. 2:12). It is our strength for living (2 Tim. 2:1), the root of our speech (Col. 4:6), and our sufficiency of life (2 Cor. 2:9). Grace is our response to suffering (Heb. 4:16), and our hope beyond death (Rom. 5:21).

We want to think that we can take care of ourselves. We can punch our ticket, clean up our mess, and make our way. Many of us are taught from a young age to be self-sufficient and not ask for help if we don't have to. But all of this contradicts the teaching of Ephesians 2:8-9: "For by grace are ye saved through faith, and that not of yourselves; it is the gift of God: not of works, lest any man should boast." Let's define the keywords in these two verses. Grace: undeserved assistance for our sanctification. Saved: deliverance from sin and eternal damnation. Faith: complete trust and confidence in something or someone. Gift: something voluntarily transferred to another without compensation. Boast: excessive pride or self-satisfaction about one's achievements. To be saved, we must first acknowledge our need for a Savior (Rom. 3:23, 6:23). I have done nothing to deserve mercy, but God delivered me from death and eternal separation from Him when I placed my confidence in Jesus Christ. During the Second World War, some soldiers serving in

France wanted to bury a friend and fellow soldier who had been killed. They found a well-kept cemetery with a low stone fence around it, a picturesque little Catholic church, and a peaceful outlook. But when they approached the priest, they were told that unless their friend was a baptized Catholic, he could not be buried there. He wasn't. Reluctantly, the soldiers buried their friend outside the wall of the cemetery. They returned to pay their final respects the next day but could not find the grave. Confused, they approached the priest. "Last night, I couldn't sleep," said the priest. "I was troubled that your friend had to be buried outside the cemetery walls, so I got up and moved the fence."

Some suggest various religious practices be observed to be saved, but the Bible formula is always faith in God's grace plus nothing. Grace refers to God's blessings on the undeserving, and the very idea of unmerited favor negates all attempts to earn salvation. The apostle Paul said, "And if by grace, then is it no more of works: otherwise, grace is no more grace" (Rom. 11:6). Some will turn to James 2:24 to argue the idea of adding works. But what James is saying is that works are an outward manifestation of genuine faith in the grace of Christ. In Titus 2:14, Paul says those who believe in His death and resurrection will be eager to do what is good. A song written by David Hamilton and Phil McHugh says, "Were it not for grace, I can tell you where I'd be, wandering down some pointless road to nowhere with my salvation up to me... so here is all my praise, expressed with all my heart, offered to the Friend who took my place and ran a course I could not start." The believer's salvation is outside himself, in the action of God alone – and all of grace (Rom. 5:6-11). Indeed, there is no peace until we turn from our insufficiency to an all-sufficient God.

From Genesis to Revelation, God is portrayed as gracious, loving, and merciful. Grace is first mentioned in Genesis 6:8, where we read, "Noah found grace in the eyes of the Lord." To Moses, God describes himself as "merciful and gracious, longsuffering, and abundant in goodness and truth" (Ex. 34:6). In Psalm 145:8-9, David wrote, "The Lord is gracious and full of compassion; slow to anger, and of great mercy." King Hezekiah proclaimed, "For the Lord your God is gracious and merciful, and will not turn away his face from you, if ye return unto him" (2 Chron. 30:9). The apostle Peter said, "The God of all grace" has called us into his eternal glory by Jesus Christ (1 Pet. 5:10). Our Lord offers pardon from sin and eternal life to those who, by faith (Rom. 5:1-2) will humbly confess their sins (1 John 1:9). It is essential that we form our view of God and ourselves from Scripture, not from the prevailing opinions of our times. When we examine Scripture, we find that God is far more holy than we ever imagined, and we are far more sinful than we ever fathomed. Grace is power, not just pardon. By definition, grace rejects the slightest hint that human merit contributes to a righteous standing before a holy and perfect Creator. We bring nothing with us to our redemption (Eph. 2:1-7). "For God so loved the world that he gave his only begotten Son, that whosoever believeth in him should not perish, but have everlasting life" (John 3:16). The indescribable glory of our salvation is that Christ bore our sins. We receive His righteousness (2 Cor. 5:21). God's grace removes sin's guilt, and it empowers us to live holy from the inside out. The "gratitude response" to God's love is obedience to His Word. Thank God we are saved by His amazing grace!

Such As I Have

WHEN WE SHARE THE BLESSINGS OF THE LORD WITH OTHER PEOPLE, THE kingdom of Heaven is increased, and God is glorified. The account in Acts 3:1-10 is a powerful example of such an event. It's especially remarkable because it takes place in the shadow of the cross, the ascension of Christ, and the infilling of the Holy Ghost. Something drastic happened to the disciples. With the coming of the Holy Spirit to the upper room at the festival of Pentecost (Acts 2:1-13), God's anointing transformed them. There, the three-thousand-year-old language barrier of Babel (Gen. 11) was supernaturally overcome when about 120 believing Jews began to speak in foreign languages. In one story, language separates the people. And in the other, it connects them. The "other tongues" spoken in verse four were no less than fifteen unlearned languages described in verses five through eleven, symbolizing the gospel being preached to all nations.

The anxiety that had caused the disciples to cower in the shadows (John 20:19) was gone. The fearful had become bold. The timid were now brave. And on this day, Peter and John went to the temple at the hour of prayer with a promise they had never experienced before. The anticipated Comforter that Jesus spoke about in John 14 had come to abide within. When the apostles arrived at the temple gate, Peter directed his attention to a lame man who sat there expecting to receive money and declared, "Silver and gold have I none; but such as I have, give I thee: in the name of Jesus Christ of Nazareth rise up and walk" (Acts 3:6). Consider what was given to a person in need that afternoon. Indeed, the apostles shared their presence, time, and a hand to lift. But more importantly, they shared the miraculous healing of the Holy Spirit. Speaking to the onlookers who had gathered, Peter turned the spotlight on the crucified Christ, Jesus, "the author and finisher of our faith" (Heb. 12:2). And to the glory of God, the kingdom of Heaven was increased by three thousand people who had heard the good news in their respective languages!

How did these men of God receive such an authoritative ministry? It would be easy to assume that God's special love for his people comes from something special about his people, something they've got that no one else does. But listen to how Deuteronomy explains why God made Israel his treasured possession out of all the peoples on earth: It was not because you were more in number than any other people that the Lord set his love on you and chose you, for you were the fewest of all peoples, but it is because the Lord loves you and is keeping the oath that he swore to your fathers (Deut. 7:7-8). It would perhaps be even more natural to assume that God chooses his people based on whether or not they follow the rules. Performing for approval is familiar to many religions, but not with a true believer's Christianity. In ourselves, we fall victim to an expectation of others that will only produce conditional love. But God relates to His people in forgiveness and acceptance, not perfection. There are no strings, no expectations, and no hidden agendas. He loves us despite our persistent lack of righteousness (Rom. 5:8). The message of God's love is to be shared in this very broken society. It can unlock healing and restoration like the world has never seen. The message of love is simple, yet to live daily in it is something few people truly know. When our Savior appeared, He saved us from sin and eternal punishment according to His lovingkindness and mercy. In Mark 10:45, we read, "For even the Son of man came not to be ministered unto, but to minister, and to give his life a ransom for many." Jesus Christ is our example for giving, and we are to live a life set apart for Him (Rom. 12:1). The apostle Paul said he was obligated to preach the Gospel to all people. When we have a revelation of the grace of God, we realize that we are a debtor to Jesus for all that we are and have. It is not a debt to pay for grace, for then it would cease to be grace. Instead, it is an attitude of gratefulness for undeserved mercy.

A pastor writes, "It was a frigid day for May. There, walking into town, was a man who appeared to be carrying all his worldly goods on his back. He was carrying a well-worn sign that read, "I will work for food." My heart sank. As he sat on a bench near the church, I approached him. "Looking for the pastor?" I asked. "Not really," he replied, "just resting." "Have you eaten today?" "Oh, I ate something early this morning." "Would you like to have lunch with me?" "Do you have some work I could do for you?" "No work," I replied. "I commute here to work from the city, but I would like to take you to lunch." "Sure," he replied with a smile. As he began to gather his things, I asked some surface questions. His eyes were dark yet clear, and he spoke with startling eloquence and articulation. He removed his jacket to reveal a bright red T-shirt that said, "Jesus is The Never Ending Story." Then Daniel's story began to unfold. He had seen rough times early in life. He'd made some wrong choices and reaped the consequences. Fourteen years earlier, he had stopped on the beach in Daytona while backpacking across the country. He tried to hire on with some men putting up a large tent and equipment. A concert, he thought. He was hired, but the tent would not house a concert but revival services, and in those services, he saw life more clearly. He gave his life over to God. "Nothing's been the same since," he said, "I felt the Lord telling me to keep walking, and so I did, some 14 years now." "Ever think of stopping?" I asked. "Oh, once in a while, when it seems to get the best of me. But God has given me this calling. I give out Bibles. That's what's in my sack. I work to buy food and Bibles and give them out when His Spirit leads."

I sat amazed. My homeless friend was not homeless. He was on a mission and lived this way by choice. The question burned inside for a moment, and then I asked: "What's it like?" "What?" "To walk into a town carrying all your things on your back and to show your sign?" "Oh, it was humiliating at first. People would stare and make comments. Once, someone tossed a piece of half-eaten bread and made a gesture that didn't make me feel welcome. But then it became humbling to realize that God was using me to touch lives and change people's concepts of other folks like me." We finished our dessert. Just outside the door, he paused. He turned to me and said, "Come, ye blessed of my Father, inherit the kingdom prepared for you from the foundation of the world: For I was hungry, and ye gave me meat: I was thirsty, and ye gave me drink: I was a stranger, and ye took me in" (Matt. 25:34–35).

I felt as if we were on holy ground. "Could you use another Bible?" I asked. He said he preferred a particular translation. It traveled well and was not too heavy. It was also his personal favorite. "I've read through it 14 times," he said. "I'm not sure we've got one of those, but let's stop by our church and see." I found my new friend a Bible that would do well, and he seemed very grateful. "Where are you headed from here?" "Well, I found this little map on the back of this amusement park coupon." "Are you hoping to hire on there for a while?" "No, I figure I should go there. I figure someone under that star right there needs a Bible, so that's where I'm going next." He smiled, and the warmth of his spirit radiated the sincerity of his mission. "The Lord is good." "Yes, He is. How long has it been since someone hugged you?" I asked. "A long time," he replied. And so, on the busy street corner in the drizzling rain, my new friend and I embraced, and I felt deep inside that I had been changed. He put his things on his back, smiled his winning smile, and said, "See you in New Jerusalem." "I'll be there!" was my reply.

The biblical truth that to whom much is given, much is required (Luke 12:48) was spoken by Jesus in the context of faithful and wise stewardship. We are held responsible for what we have, with the expectation that we will use it to glorify God and benefit others. It's easy to assume that only wealthy people have been "given much." But in truth, born-again believers have all been given a gift more precious than gold! As Peter and John had received, we have been granted God's abundant grace (Eph. 1:3-10). We have been given His holy Word, and the principles and practice of biblical generosity will bless both the giver and the recipient. Making our time and possessions available for God's ministry is the essence of giving such as we have. J.H. Jowett said, "Giving is the language of loving; indeed, it has no other speech." According to God's Word, giving ought to be done purposefully, cheerfully (2 Cor. 9:7), proportionately (1 Cor. 16:2), unselfishly (Matt. 6:1-4), sacrificially (Luke 21:1-3), freely (Matt. 10:8), generously (2 Cor. 9:6-7), and willingly (Ex. 35). Jesus Christ is our pattern and our power for living out His love. How? In practical deeds of helpfulness for the gospel's sake. In John 13:34, we read His words, "A new commandment I give unto you, That ye love one another; as I have loved you...." Our Lord put aside His sense of entitlement and served. And so must we.

How often do we miss opportunities to share our faith with others because we don't speak up? I am guilty. Perhaps we don't know what to say, so we say nothing. Or maybe we fear rejection for not having all the answers. First, spending time in prayer, Bible reading, and a fresh look at Calvary will cause us to spread the "good tidings of great joy" intended for all people (Luke 2:10). Secondly, people can debate religion all they want. Still, they cannot argue with our testimony of salvation. As believers, we are called to identify hurting people, interact with those who need to learn more about Jesus and help those who need our love. The Bible says the love of God compels us to live, not unto ourselves but unto Him who died for us and rose again. We are new creatures in Christ, reconciled to God. And because we have been reconciled, we are chosen for a ministry of reconciliation (2 Cor. 5:14-18). Therefore, without pretending to know all the answers, we look for common ground, build relationships, and wait for God to open doors. The Holy Spirit will always be our guide when, with compassion and grace, we are willing to offer such as we have!

Don't Lose Heart

In James 4:8, we read, "Draw nigh to God, and he will draw nigh to you." Cleland McAfee (1866-1944) suffered the loss of two infant nieces to diphtheria in 1903. His daughter described the account in her book, *Near to the Heart of God.* "The family and town were stricken with grief. My father often told us how he sat long and late thinking of what could be said in words and songs on the coming Sunday. So, he wrote the song:

1. There is a place of quiet rest,
    Near to the heart of God;
    A place where sin cannot molest,
    Near to the heart of God.

    o   *Refrain:*
        O Jesus, blest Redeemer,
        Sent from the heart of God;
        Hold us, who wait before Thee,
        Near to the heart of God.

2. There is a place of comfort sweet,
    Near to the heart of God;
    A place where we our Savior meet,
    Near to the heart of God.

3. There is a place of full release,
    Near to the heart of God;
    A place where all is joy and peace,
    Near to the heart of God.

The choir learned it at the regular Saturday night rehearsal, and afterward, they went to Howard McAfee's home and sang it as they stood under the sky outside the darkened, quarantined house. It was sung again on Sunday morning at the communion service." The stanzas affirm that near to God's heart is a meeting place with the Savior, a place of 'quiet rest,' 'comfort,' 'full release,' and 'joy and peace.' This song expresses the relationship between the believer and God. Let's be encouraged today by the promise that God will draw nigh to us if we draw nigh to Him. Indeed, a place of quiet rest is near God's heart.

Life is a battle. Therefore, the Christian life is a battle. The Bible speaks of believers as soldiers who are obedient and committed to God's will (Eph. 6:12-13). Serving God means acknowledging His Lordship in our lives, demonstrated by a commitment to help others as Jesus did (John 13:34). There He was, offering His Kingdom in exchange for their pain. Serving God means reaching lost souls with the gospel of Christ (Matt. 28:19-20). It means facing adversity with hope (Ps. 46:10). It means making our Lord visible in everything we think, say, and do by our obedience to the Bible (2 John 1:6). There will be times that, as you hold to the morality of Scripture, you will feel the assault of the world (Eph. 6:12). You will grow weary of the Christian journey. You will wonder if anyone cares (2 Cor. 4). But quitting is not an option. God never said our traveling would be easy, only that our destination would be glorious (Rom. 8:18). As an ocean buoy rings only during storms, the beating of the waves and wind will bring out the music within us. Trials reveal character. Do not quit. John Wittier wrote, "When things go wrong, as they sometimes will; when the road you're trudging seems all uphill; when funds are low, and the debts are high, and you want to smile, but you have to sigh; when care is pressing you down a bit, rest if you must, but don't you quit."

The temptation to give up is usually experienced during a difficult season. But if there is one thing the apostle Paul seemed to repeat repeatedly, it was don't quit! To the Galatians (6:9), he said, "And let us not be weary in well doing: for in due season we shall reap, if we faint not." This verse has a straightforward command and an incredible promise. We will be rewarded if we do not become complacent in the work of the Lord. Paul uses the terms "persevere," "press on," or "strive" many times in his writings to the New Testament churches. He linked perseverance to integrity and hope. When we lose heart, our days seem empty, and we lose hope. When we lose hope, we lose the ability to dream for the future. Therefore, quitting is not an option. Our "labor is not in vain in the Lord," and we have victory in Jesus Christ (1 Cor. 15:57-58).

The key to endurance is remembering that we no longer exist to serve our agenda. We are the Lord's (1 Cor. 6:19-20), and the "well doing" part of Galatians 6:9 is returning God's love for us through worship and cheerful obedience! We all live for something. It could be our family, career, friendships, athletic or academic achievements – and many other things. To say we are "living for" something is just another way of saying, "This is the motivation behind what I do." On June 5, 1998, Timothy Stackpole was injured in a five-alarm fire in Brooklyn. He spent over two months in the Burn Center with severe burns over forty percent of his body. He endured many surgeries and months of painful rehabilitation. He had two goals: to recover and spend as much time as possible with his family, and turn to full duty at a job he loved. He was a great firefighter. He was enthusiastic about his work and was soon promoted to captain. Three years later, at forty-two, Timothy was one of the firefighters who ran into the second tower of the World Trade Center to try to save people on September 11, 2001. When he did, it collapsed and took his life. His wife Tara says, "Timmy had a huge heart. He shared his faith, compassion, and love with everyone he met. He was a loving husband and friend, an adored father, and a loving,, devoted son and brother. He was a hero not only because of how he died but, more importantly, , because of how he lived." Timothy knew his calling; it was to save people. We must know our calling. God has called us to a life of service and ministry with eternal value. Don't forget your purpose. Do not give up on sinners. Whether they fully understand or not, they are dying without God (Rom. 6:23), desperate for someone to share the good news of Jesus Christ. This is God's agenda, and our privilege is to partner with Him in the power of the Holy Spirit.

The apostle Paul said, "I therefore, the prisoner of the Lord, beseech you that ye walk worthy of the vocation wherewith ye are called, with all lowliness and meekness, with longsuffering, forbearing one another in love" (Eph. 4:1-2). Why do some people abandon their calling to Kingdom work? Maybe the guilt and shame of the past weighed heavily on their mind. It could result from bad relationships with fellow believers or disagreements with church leadership. Then, some people left the local church assembly, saying it was imperfect. I have news: There are no churches but imperfect ones. And the fact that Jesus started His church with bad people should make us marvel at God's incredible grace!

A faithful church attendee stopped going to church. The pastor found the man at home, alone, sitting by the blazing fire. Guessing the reason for the pastor's visit, the man welcomed him, led him to a comfortable chair near the fireplace, and waited. The pastor made himself at home but said nothing. In silence, the pastor took the fire tongs, carefully picked up a brightly burning ember, and placed it alone on one side of the hearth. Then he sat back in his chair, still silent. The host watched all this in quiet contemplation. As the one lone ember's flame flickered and diminished, there was a momentary glow, and then its fire was no more. Soon, it was cold and dead. The last time the man had spoken was before the initial greeting. The pastor glanced at his watch and realized it was time to leave. He slowly stood up, picked up the cold, dead ember, and placed it back in the middle of the fire. Immediately, it began to glow again with the warmth of the burning coals around it. As the pastor reached the door to leave, his host said, with a tear running down his cheek, "Thank you so much for your visit, especially the sermon. I'll be back in church next time the doors are open."

We can become discouraged for many reasons. But I believe one's departure from following Christ is most often tied to the experience of pain or death. The typical "Why?" questions surrounding these events have caused good people to reject the sacrificial road that Jesus walked. "Why this? You are not who You say you are. I can tell by what's happening to me." Yes, our Lord wants to bear our burdens (Ps. 18:6). But questioning the sovereignty of God with a rebellious, untrusting heart will take us to ruin. Many will say they cannot accomplish what the Bible says. We are to honor the Lord with fruit (John 15:8), not insult

Him with excuses. Indeed, life is hard, and there will be reasons for disappointment. But not one is reason enough to walk out on the Savior! We must understand that we have a bright and everlasting eternity no matter what we face. D.L. Moody said, "If I had ten thousand lives, Jesus Christ should have every one of them."

In Hebrews 12:3, we are told to "consider him that endured such contradiction of sinners against himself, lest ye be wearied and faint in your minds." Satan is our enemy, and there is nothing more damaging to his evil influence than Spirit-filled people who love God. Living for Jesus is a choice. We made the decision when we knelt at the Cross. We are saved by grace through faith (Rom. 6), striving to live as Jesus did (1 Cor. 11:1). Pleasing the Lord is our highest aim (Col. 1:10), and growing weary should not change any of this. In Luke 9:23, Jesus said, "If any man will come after me, let him deny himself, and take up his cross daily, and follow me." It's important to acknowledge the unfortunate fact that the enthusiasm of Christianity can wear off, mainly if we are not "abiding in Christ" (John 15:5). In Revelation 2:1-7 Jesus commended the believers in Ephesus for their labor, patience, and endurance. But he faulted them for having lost their "first love." Love is the difference between religious people and relational people. It is our testimony in the world (John 13:35).

Discouragement and weariness can rob us of our joy. The danger of not taking our burden to the Lord is that we will eventually become disillusioned with the Christian journey altogether. We have a powerful promise that "we will reap" if we do not faint. Think about the fruit of the harvest: dear people rescued from slavery to sin and set free in Christ, and then believers are strengthened in their faith! Did not God call you to do work for Him? Go to Him in prayer. Read His Word. Seek the wise counsel of a trusted friend if you must, but do not quit! We are all called to follow Christ with equal depth and commitment, serving the people God has put in our lives. When you feel like quitting, consider why you began walking with the Lord. Think about God's love. Take another look at the Cross on which your Savior died. It will be worth it all when we see Jesus!

Finding God Instead
of Learning Why

As all parents know, every child's favorite question is, "Why?" The truth is, our "why" questions, though now of a more severe kind, continue into adulthood. When a relative dies in a tragic accident, a parent is afflicted with a disease, or our children are plagued with problems, we will ask the same question. Our favorite question at the beginning of great trouble is, "Why?" But in all forty-two chapters of the Book of Job, God never answers the question. Instead, He shows us that if we get to know Him in times of difficulty, any 'why' will be okay (42:1-6). Like a parent who has come to the end of a child's string of questions with, "Because I said so," God says to us, "I am your heavenly Father. Trust me; not only when you do not understand, but because you do not understand. Live by faith; not just with the first step of your Christian journey, but with every step" (Ps. 46:10). We may be bewildered at things that happen to us, but what God is after is the handling of our affairs. In time, Job said of God, "Though he slay me, yet will I trust in him... He also shall become my salvation..." (13:15-16). Job questioned God's actions, but he never stopped trusting.

When trouble comes our way, it is our nature to ask God why it happened. Moses asked, "Lord, wherefore have I not found favor in thy sight?" (Num. 11:11). David asked, "O Lord, why hidest thou thyself in times of trouble?" (Ps. 10:1). Habakkuk asked, "Why dost thou shew me iniquity?" (Hab. 1:3). Job asked, "Why has thou set me as a mark against thee?" (Job 7:20). The disciples asked, "Master, who did sin, this man, or his parents, that he was born blind?" (John 9:2). We tell God how we feel, for He wants to bear our burdens. Jesus said, "Come unto me, all ye that labor and are heavy laden, and I will give you rest" (Matt. 11:28). We know that God welcomes a sincere question from a sincere heart. The Psalmist said, "The eyes of the Lord are upon the righteous, and his ears are open to their cry" (Ps. 34:15). When in distress, David cried, "Hear my prayer, O Lord, give ear to my supplications: in thy faithfulness answer me" (Ps. 143:1). The apostle Paul says, "Be careful for nothing, but in everything by prayer and supplication with thankfulness let your requests be made known unto God" (Phil. 4:6). In Matthew 7:7 Jesus tells us to ask, seek and knock. And I am so thankful for the privilege of coming before the throne of God to "obtain mercy and find grace to help in time of need" (Heb. 4:16)! At issue is not whether we should ask God why, but in what manner and for what reason. Some have a relentless need for answers, even to the point of demanding explanations. They want to live the abundant life spoken in John 10:10, forgetting that Jesus also said we would face tribulation (John 16:33). In light of the Cross, anything we experience ceases to be a liability. Instead, it becomes an asset to be used for God's glory. What is your chief joy? Is it to be healthy, happy, and prosperous? Indeed, these are blessings from God. But our chief joy should be to do God's will and finish the work He has designed for us. This was the passion of our Lord (John 4:34), for Jesus said, "As my Father hath sent me, even so send I you" (John 20:21). No matter the circumstance, we exist to glorify God.

The Christian experience is a journey of faith. What is this way of faith? It is that we find the world of the unseen more convincing than this one. In the uncertainties of life, there is certainty in what God has promised: "Which hope we have as an anchor of the soul, both sure and steadfast... even Jesus" (Heb. 6:13–20). Let us hold fast the profession of our hope without wavering, for He is faithful that promised (Heb. 10:23). He is with me to accomplish His perfect will in my imperfect life. Indeed, I have found a faithful friend and Savior! When trouble comes, our faith changes. It either diminishes or deepens. Why? Because it has been challenged. We will either step toward or away from the Cross but cannot walk out in neutral. A choice is demanded. We want to figure things out and understand the reasoning behind everything happening. But there are so many things we cannot understand. And for those who are suffering, any intellectual response seems inadequate. Yes, we experience pain and confusion. But in times of trouble, we need more than logic. We need hope. Jesus Christ is our hope! Do not stumble at the mysteries of life where there is no explanation. Instead, find comfort in the knowledge that you are a child of God, living by faith with heaven in view (Rom. 1:17). Jesus taught us to live one day at a time (Matt. 6:11).

Remember the man with an infirmity lying beside the pool called Bethesda for thirty-eight years? He was waiting to be healed. And when Jesus saw him there, He had compassion (John 5:1-15). But notice the Lord did not ask the man, "Do you need to get well?" The need was evident, and the situation seemed hopeless. The question was, "Do you want to get well?" God knows our hearts and understands that deep sorrow can rob us of the willingness to do anything about it. He wants to see if we desire the healing strength to help us pick up and walk by faith. The question that was asked that day speaks volumes. I have met those whose continual questioning has become an excuse for not accepting the sovereignty of God. Why? Because asking questions is easier than submitting to His authority and yielding to His lordship. The first thing Adam and Eve did after they sinned was to hide from God (Gen. 3:8). To be free from the God who calls sinners into accountability has been a constant goal of humanity from the beginning. A life spent requiring answers will not bring glory to God. He is glorified through our obedience and praise (John 15:14, Ps. 150:6). We read in Psalm 100:3: "Know ye that the Lord he is God; it is he that hath made us, and not we ourselves… be thankful unto him, and bless his name." Sometimes, asking "Why?" suggests a hostility toward God's character or that He cannot be trusted. Simply put, He is God, and we are not (Ps. 100:3). There is a difference between questioning God and asking Him a question. The difference is found as we humbly acknowledge that His thoughts are not our thoughts; neither are His ways our ways (Isa. 55:8).

The human mind will never fully understand the grandeur and authority of God. But enough is written in Scripture that we do well to know all we can about His nature, His power, and His majesty, for we gain both the strength and the freedom to trust. God has no rival.

He is subject to no other power, and He reigns supreme. Heaven is His throne, and the earth is His footstool (Acts 7:49). The vast universe is evidence of the glory of God. He is clothed with majesty, and His throne is established forever (Ps. 92:8). He is Almighty on the throne. All will bow before Him whose grandeur no one can surpass. His majesty is displayed with lightning and thunderous voices going out from the throne proclaiming His holiness (Rev. 4:5). He is God Almighty. He always has been, is now, and forever will be (Psalm 90:1–2). Power and glory are His. His dominion is everlasting, a kingdom that will never pass away nor be destroyed (Dan. 7:14). All authority in heaven and earth belongs to Him (Rev. 4). None can fully describe the attributes of God, the manner of His existence or manifestation. His power to create, to produce something out of nothing, is beyond human understanding. The foundation of the earth and the heavens are the works of His hands (Heb. 1:10). He is the Creator and sustainer of the universe (Gen. 1). He owes His existence to no one. God is not subject to, altered, or aged by time. He is eternal (Ps. 90:2). In Him, there is height and depth that human intellect cannot measure. God is infinite. There is no limit to His being; therefore, He cannot be compressed into any particular definition. In His hand is the soul of every living thing and the breath of all humankind (Job 12:10). God's work is majestic in creation. He has all the authority to free people from the curse of sin. God's power will affect how we live and save us for eternity. He is love. He is the truth. He is life. His transforming Spirit is released into our lives, and the power of the gospel is regeneration. His grace changes how we live here and assures us eternal salvation in heaven (Acts 11:16–18). God is not subject to human limitations. The angels of heaven cry, "Holy, holy, holy, is the Lord of hosts: the whole earth is full of his glory."

The Old Testament patriarch Job understood that he could not demand anything from the Lord (Job 23:13). Many heroes of the Bible experienced trouble for decades before they saw God's plan. And for some, the reasons were never made known. Do not continue with a lifetime of questions without spiritual growth. Somewhere deep inside, the repeated questioning and lack of answers feed a sense of entitlement. And when that sense of entitlement grows, it usually leads to bitterness. I have seen the effects of anger in the hearts of good people, and so have you. Do not live with an angry, quarrelsome attitude (Eph. 4:31). There is a better way to live. Focus on the goodness and majesty of God! Make an intentional decision to believe that He is teaching you something for your ultimate good (Phil. 3:8). Knowing there is something to learn in a trial makes it easier to bear (James 1:2-12). The answers we think we must have may never be known in this lifetime. The Bible does not promise it, and we are not entitled. We read in Romans 9:20, "Shall the thing formed say to him that formed it, Why hast thou made me thus?" He is the potter; we are the clay. We are "the work of His hand" (Isa. 64:8). Jehovah says, "I am God, and there is none else... my counsel shall stand, and I will do all my pleasure" (Isa. 46:9-10).

God does not suggest that our stories will make sense in and of themselves. But He does promise we will one day find our greater purpose in light of His eternal plan of redemption (Eph. 3:9-13, 2 Cor. 1:3-6). Oh, friend, our faith in God must be greater than our need to know. If we want peace, we must give up the need to understand. Knowing that God's glory can be displayed even in the brokenness of our lives will bring hope, and those around us will be encouraged. We will find more purpose and joy if we set aside the question "Why?" and begin to worship Him with our lives. How might God use your circumstance to display His glory? Can He use your heartache to show His power? What can He reveal about Himself in your trial? Will you allow Him to turn your mess into a message and make you a person who walks by faith and not by sight (2 Cor. 5:7)? For every child of God, there has been – or there will be – an experience that will change Romans 8:28 from a memorization quote to a belief system. Will you allow your prayer to move from "God heal me" to "God, use me for your glory, and help me cope?" Only then will you find that joy can co-exist with uncertainty, pain, and confusion. Thank God because He is worthy of praise (Ps. 18:3). Glorifying God is expressed by a lifestyle. He is perfect in truth, holiness, love, power, and wisdom. Praise Him for what He has done. Worship Him for who He is! Indeed, God can use your situation to show you the peace that is found only in Jesus Christ (John 14:27). He can use the death of your loved one to stir the hearts of others and show them the importance of surrendering their lives to Him (John 11:45). We cannot see the big picture. We cannot see around the corners. But we know that God will never leave or forsake us (Deut. 31:6). We also know He loves us. He hears our cries, and He cares (1 John 5:14-15). So, take a moment and ask for divine wisdom in moving forward with your life (Prov. 4:7). Trust God. Commit your cause to Him, and He will work things out according to His plan. When we visualize Him in majesty and power, we will find that God is in complete control without understanding why things happen. He is with you!

The Blessing of Godly Friends

WHAT'S THE BEST THING A FRIEND HAS EVER DONE FOR YOU? PERHAPS someone supported you emotionally and financially, giving you a fresh start. Maybe they dropped their plans and drove several hours to be with you. Many of us remember a friend who helped us achieve a major goal. Some have become self-proclaimed family members, showing up when we need help the most. Things like a surprise birthday party, unexpected assistance with a house project, and volunteering to watch our kids are simple, but we all know how much these things mean when we're on the receiving end. We have all heard stories about friends surprising someone with a fabulous vacation after a challenging event like a job loss or a divorce. These are acts of kindness not soon forgotten. Friends make us feel good. We don't always have everything in common, but trustworthy friends support us anyway. Indeed, good friends are among the greatest gifts in life!

How would we define such a relationship in the context of God's Word? A godly friendship is a supportive relationship filled with mutual service and affection based upon a shared devotion to the gospel of Jesus Christ (Phil. 2:3–5). In the second chapter of Mark's Gospel, we read where faith was expressed by four men determined to get their paralyzed friend to Jesus for healing. The scene is set with Jesus teaching inside a private home, overflowing with people who came to hear him. The only way the paralyzed man's friends could get him close to Jesus was to tear up the roof and lower him down through the hole. The Bible says Jesus acknowledged their efforts as a sign of their faith and healed the man. And, just as the paralyzed man's friends had exercised faith in bringing him to Jesus, he exercised faith when at the words "Arise, and take up thy bed," he immediately stood up and walked. While the story's setting in Capernaum is known, neither the person with paralysis nor his friends are named. Thus, the emphasis remains on Jesus, whose mission was to make known His divine power to forgive sins through the visible act of healing (v10). So, too, it takes faith for us to come to Jesus (Heb. 11:6), to allow him to heal our souls and forgive our sins (Gal. 2:16). Recovery of the body is wonderful, but may we always glorify God for the more remarkable thing!

God has placed in our hearts the desire to share a close bond with others. The paralytic man depended on the grace and compassion of those around him for daily survival. For his friends, there was no separation between being and doing. Moreover, their collective faith was enough to capture the attention of the Lord, and everyone was rewarded. How essential are friendships in the body of Christ? Of 353 people interviewed about the first time they attended a new church, 311 mentioned the church's friendliness. Out of those 353 people, 117 specifically mentioned greeters or welcome centers. Fifty-seven percent of formerly unchurched people said that relationships played a part in choosing their church. Thirty-six percent of those who transferred their membership said the same thing. A British publication once offered a prize for the best definition of a friend. Among the thousands of answers received were: 'One who multiplies joy and divides grief.' 'One who understands our silence.' The winning definition read: 'A friend is the one who comes in when the whole world has gone out.' Friends are those rare people who ask how we are - and then wait for the answer. Surround yourself with people who will influence you in a godly way. Much of our lives is determined by the input we get when making decisions and whether we heed wise counsel when we receive it (Prov. 27:9). Many came to Jesus that day, but these men did something that set them apart. For the sake of a friend, they put aside their schedule and accomplished a task that could not have been done otherwise (1 Cor. 10:24). Immobile, confined to a stretcher, unable to enter, with great effort, the man's friends showed great compassion. It has been said that the measure of a man's character is what it takes to stop him, and some will stop at nothing to help us grow in our relationship with the Lord.

What are the characteristics of godly friends? They ask God for bigger things than you pray for yourself (Phil. 1:9). They believe in you when your faith is weak (Rom. 15:1). They make space for you when life falls apart (Rom. 12:10). They rejoice with you when all is well, and weep with you in your sorrow (Rom. 12:15). They heighten your joy in God (Psalm 20). They encourage you to obey God (Eccl. 12:13). They bring you to God in your weakness (Gal 6:2). Christian friends are a treasure because they help us cling to our greatest Treasure. Above all will be their love for you (1 Pet. 4:8). The Mark 2 story has left me wondering: How would things change if I took my friendship queues from these four men? What if I was as dedicated to my friendships as they were? How would God use me if I had more faith? The example of the lame man's friends speaks powerfully about our need to love other people. Jesus said, "By this shall all men know that ye are my disciples if ye have love one to another" (John 13:35). These unnamed men loved a friend so deeply that they took extreme measures to get him into the presence of the Savior. Friendship takes intentionality and effort. Jesus models true friendship for us in His ministry. He was present. He took time to know His friends. He cared for them (John 3:22). He prayed earnestly and often for them (John 17:1-26).

Dying to self is the key to living for Christ. A man healed, people amazed, Christ's power made known, but most of all, God is glorified! Is it more important that one man is temporarily healed of paralysis or that many people understand the forgiveness of God? The eternal salvation of souls is the goal of godly friends. Supporting soup kitchens is terrific. Hospitals, clean water, and homeless shelters are all worthy causes, but only as we share the Gospel as part of the effort. We're amazed by the thought of Jesus making a lame man walk, but the real miracle is that he had peace with God through faith in Christ (Rom. 5:1). Jesus provides the most profound healing: forgiving sins. He is the One who helps us with our greatest need! A godly friend will be committed to helping you grow physically, emotionally - and spiritually (Prov. 27:17).

We must not underestimate the wonderful friends in this story. Nor should we overlook the one whose roof was damaged. Can you see the homeowner thinking to himself, "Oh great... I just fixed that roof and need to do it again!" Have you ever been inconvenienced in some way as part of your ministry? Today, a site stands in Capernaum that archaeologists suggest may have been Peter's house. I love thinking about the power of the Savior, the faith of the friends who brought the paralyzed man to Jesus, and just maybe it was Peter who was willing to let go of the broken roof to focus on a bigger miracle. Do we appreciate friends with faith? Can a brother or sister rely on our faith if they are in need? The Lord has given us much; let us give much in return! There are times when we stand frozen by fear, and our heart nearly breaks; times when we can barely muster a prayer, and when it comes out, it's a plea for a friend. Saul must have been physically spent nearing Damascus (Acts 9). He had traveled 120 dusty miles to stop the church from thriving there, and with one deafening statement and a blinding light from heaven, Saul discovered that everything he believed to be true was false. Jesus wasn't the enemy. Jesus was Lord! And in the depth of Saul's darkness and loneliness, God was about to reveal the power of faithful friends. Saul was about to meet two of the best friends he would ever have: Ananias and Barnabas. They helped him change the world. As Paul and these men eagerly defended and confirmed the gospel, their bond of fellowship strengthened. It is impossible to overstate the value of a faithful friend, and it's so important that we be that friend to others.

Together is better on the journey of life (Eccl. 4:9-10)! Think about the way Ananias and Barnabas helped change the world. Saul, who became known as Paul, eventually would become the most influential missionary in Christian history, a leader equal to Peter and John in the early church, and the most prolific writer in the New Testament. How many millions, becoming Christians, have been freed by the Ephesians 2:8-9 truth of salvation by grace and not by works? How many marriages have been saved by 1 Corinthians 13? How many anxious hearts have been calmed by the Philippians 4:7 peace that passes all understanding or the Romans 8:23 knowledge that God works all things for our good in every situation? Paul's letters, written under the inspiration of the Holy Spirit (2 Pet. 1:20-21), have changed the lives of millions of believers! Flashback now to the day when this man lay crumpled in the dirt on the outskirts of Damascus. A bright light and an overwhelming Savior had just taken his eyesight, spiritual foundation, and emotional health. Saul didn't want food or water as he stumbled into the city. But he needed a friend. So, God reached down and asked Ananias and Barnabas to be friends with a man in desperate need. Perhaps today, a person near you needs the blessing of a godly friend. Are you willing to be their blessing? Our daily prayer should be, "Dear Lord, give me the courage to step out in faith and take the initiative to build godly friendships. Help me to be a godly friend to those you put in my life."

Answering God's Call

THE PASTOR WAS WALKING TO THE PULPIT WHEN HIS PHONE RANG. Somewhat embarrassed, he pulled the device from his pocket and, in an audible whisper, said, "Lord, it's nice to hear from you, but right now, I'm really busy!" It seems the preacher was too busy for what matters. Inconvenient calls to serve happen to every believer. And, when the call comes, we quickly justify why we cannot answer. Some will even turn up the volume of life to avoid hearing God's call. But if we are fully surrendered to the service of the Lord, our phone is always on and fully charged as we anticipate that heavenly ringtone.

There are eight billion people on Earth, and every Christian has received the call to share the gospel of Christ's death and resurrection (Mark 16:13). The gospel message is for everyone (Rom. 1:6). When Jesus died on the cross, He died for all (2 Cor. 5:15). The Bible compares the gospel to a seed that first must be planted – and then the harvest. The 'Macedonian Call' in Acts 16:9 was given to the apostle Paul, and he was continually awed by the privilege of being used by God. Our Lord always seeks people who respond to His call with a willing heart. He asks us to love when loving is difficult, to serve when serving is inconvenient, and to forgive when forgiving is awkward. Nothing else will go with us to eternity but the souls we have led to Jesus. I'm sure Paul would have loved a comfortable life with safe streets at night, but his desire was beyond the temporal. He lived with an eternal perspective. God's call upon his life was often inconvenient. In John 12:26, Jesus said, "If any man serve me, let him follow me; and where I am, there shall also my servant be: if any man serve me, him will my Father honour."

Robert Morse talked about his resentment for a particular period of his ministry. He and his family were missionaries to Burma.

During this time, they were kicked out of that country and could not return to America for various reasons. Instead, they had to hike over the Himalayan Mountains and live in the jungle. This 'temporary inconvenience' lasted six long years. Looking back, however, it was a significant and productive time during which Morse completed a translation of the New Testament in the native language. A surrendered individual says, "Not my will but thine be done" (Luke 22:42). God will give us many opportunities to respond to the 'voice of billions' if we intentionally make Christ known to those we meet. We can become overwhelmed by the thought of reaching the world for Him, but Jesus connected with individuals one at a time. There was the woman at the well, the rich young ruler, Zacchaeus, Matthew, and many others. Indeed, He taught the multitudes. We also preach to congregations. We teach in the classroom with collective prayer, singing, and worship. This is all part of the work of God's kingdom. But no other ministry is so richly rewarding as establishing a friendship and leading that person to Jesus Christ!

Think about something you could do, some role in helping others cherish the old, rugged Cross. What comes to mind first? Perhaps you're thinking, "This is inconvenient, and I don't have the time." But maybe the actual interpretation is, "I don't care enough to be inconvenienced." Oh, how often I have been guilty! I ask myself, "Does my reluctance to serve come from a lack of calling or convenience?" Will you at least ask this convenience question before saying no to what God may call you to do? Stop for a moment and think of Jesus' commission's privilege and responsibility for us to continue His ministry on earth. This is most humbling to me. We are sinners, yet in Christ, we are His ambassadors, led by Scripture, to do as He did while on the earth. When Jesus spoke, things changed. Lives were made whole again by the power of the Holy Spirit. He made the kingdom of God known. He made the gospel precious. Jesus was tender toward people condemned under the law (John 8:1-11), and He was tough on those who appeared to keep the law piously (John 8:44). He delivered a Gentile girl from demons (Matt. 15:21-28). He kindly blessed bothersome children (Luke 18:15-17). He also called scribes and Pharisees hell-bound serpents (Matt. 23:33). Those who heard Him said, "Never man spake like this man"

(John 7:46). Consider the message and the authority of the commission we are given: "Go ye therefore and teach all nations, baptizing them in the name of the Father, and of the Son, and of the Holy Ghost, teaching them to observe all things whatsoever I have commanded you…" (Matt. 28:19-20). Each person has a job to do. We have been commissioned to a specific task.

Hudson Taylor, one of the fathers of the modern missionary movement, greatly emphasized the *'go'* aspect of the Great Commission. He understood that, through our witness, Jesus Christ, the God of glory, the Creator of all things, and the Redeemer of souls, will speak change into the lives of all who listen. In John 5:24, Jesus said, "He that heareth my word, and believeth on him that sent me, hath everlasting life." The voice of the Holy Spirit is consistent with His revealed Word (Rev. 22:18-19), and hearing God's voice is synonymous with obeying His commands (James 1:21). This "hearing" is not just a function of the ears but a willing response of the heart. Remember the story of the disciples on the road from Jerusalem to the village of Emmaus? Their beloved teacher had been put to death. Jesus had been crucified, and these men were devastated. The One they thought would rescue them from their enemies had been crucified. For them, the story of the resurrection had become an idle tale. Everything was confusing and very inconvenient for them! But life had new meaning, and their spirits were lifted by the understanding that the Savior had overcome the grave. This is the message of hope we bring to the world, that the Messiah came to save the souls of all who will believe (Acts 16:31)!

How did Jesus interact with people, and what happened in the conversation? In John 4:7-42, he talked with a Samaritan woman, and she was set free from the guilt of the past. In John 5:1-15, he spoke with a crippled beggar who was made whole. Jesus talked with people in ways most familiar to them. He didn't need a particular religious environment to discuss things of eternal value. Our Lord included questions in His conversations. He connected with people's thoughts and feelings. He was interested in establishing common ground with them. Likewise, we cooperate with the Holy Spirit in our conversations. Then, we leave the results to God. By all external measures, there was nothing exceptional about the mother of Jesus. As a young teenage girl in a backwater town in Galilee, Mary lacked social status. She was an unwed peasant engaged to an ordinary carpenter. Despite her humble circumstances, Mary's shock at the angel's visitation did not give way to doubt. Mary neither scoffs nor asks for proof when told she will conceive the long-awaited Messiah. Without question, the announcement was an inconvenience to her! Nevertheless, Mary submitted to the angel's message with, "Be it unto me according to thy word" (Luke 1:38). But what about us? How do we react when God calls us to something beyond our abilities and understanding? Do we snicker like Sarah (Gen. 18:12)? Do we ask for certainty like Zechariah (Luke 1:20)? Do we demand proof of success like Gideon (Judges 6:17)? Do we make excuses like Moses (Ex. 3:11-13, 4:1-13)? Do we run and hide like Jonah (Jonah 1:3)? Or do we rush to share the joy of the encounter with a close relative as Mary did (Luke 3:39-56)? I have responded in most of those ways. There was a nudging, and my response was, "Is this a call, or just my imagining?" I couldn't say. All I knew was that it was inconvenient. Two thousand years ago, a sincere girl in Nazareth believed in God in the face of unbelievable circumstances. And she was blessed with the greatest gift ever bestowed upon a human being. There may come a time when it feels like you have outlived your usefulness and purpose. You start to believe that although you may have had a call on your life, it's over now. But the truth is, God is never through with you. What may be true about what you are experiencing is that life, as you know it, is changing. God may call you to rework the details of your present walk or set you on a new path. Trying to keep things from changing only makes the process miserable. It's far less upsetting to let the old go and walk step by step with God into the new life He has for us. Follow the leading of the Lord as you put your hand in His, and trust that the light in you can never be put out.

Following Jesus can be inconvenient. There is a cost. True discipleship calls us out of our comfort zone, the rhythm and routine of daily life, and the ease of the familiar. In an age of consumer Christianity, many want the blessing and benefit of following Jesus without the inconvenience. But great things never emerge from comfort zones. Loving people is hard work. Serving people is hard work. Forgiving people is hard work. There are no shortcuts. Prepare to be inconvenienced. Why? Because there are times when followers of Jesus are called upon to act on their beliefs. The way of the cross calls us to selfless acts of service. The path of self-denial (Luke 9:23) and rebirth (2 Cor. 5:17) to which God calls us does not leave room for personal comfort and easy performance. It never has. From all indications, Abraham lived at home with family and was well off. God commanded the future patriarch to leave his entire life behind for a land he had never seen. Moses was living in exile with his in-laws, working as a shepherd far away from the problems of the Israelite people in Egypt. In this state, God called Moses from the burning bush, sending him to confront Pharaoh and lead God's people out of slavery. Peter, Andrew, James, and John were doing just fine as fishermen, as was Matthew as a tax collector. Jesus called them to drop all they knew and follow Him. Of course, we could explore many other lives from the Bible – Gideon, Elisha, Amos, Jonah, Paul, and the list goes on – all of which drive home the same point: if God is going to use us in His service, we must be prepared to be inconvenienced. Often, a call from God comes from the cry of other people. But take heart. God is with us, and He does not ask us to make any sacrifice He has not made in far more significant ways.

The challenge for us is to reject the popular framing of Christianity that casts God as our biggest cheerleader, who comes into our lives and helps us with whatever plans, dreams, and goals we have. God always uses people who are willing to give up their preferences for His cause. The calling I am talking about goes beyond accepting the gift of salvation. I'm talking about taking up our cross and following Jesus (Luke 9:23). Answering an inconvenient call is about God manifesting His glory in and through us! Abraham demonstrated his faith through obedience, and God rewarded his obedience with blessings (Gen. 15:5). Like all the saints before us, we will find that we are far better off inconvenienced by God than in a comfortable life of our own making. Every call has a cost, but the reward of obedience is far greater than anything you may give up along the way. What is God calling you to do? How will you answer the call? Heavenly Father, open our hearts to hear and obey all the ways the Holy Spirit leads us into your will and purpose. We pray in Jesus' name. Amen.

The Season for a
New Beginning

A SEASON IS OFTEN CHARACTERIZED BY A PERIOD ASSOCIATED WITH A specific activity during which something grows and is harvested. A new beginning can be any number of things. It may be a transition period for starting a degree program, launching a business, getting promoted, moving to a new city, getting married, or reconnecting with an old friend. Seasons bring fresh starts and new beginnings. Autumn starts with the falling of vibrant leaves, winter with a blanket of cold snow, spring with the emergence of new life, and summer with hot, sunny days. In Ecclesiastes 3:1, we read, "To everything, there is a season and a time to every purpose under heaven." There are seasons of joy and sorrow. Seasons of labor and rest. Seasons of calm and storms. We serve the God of strength (Job 12:13), who will change the seasons according to His wisdom (Dan. 2:21). Every life experience allows us to see God in a new dimension. It isn't easy to loosen our grip on what we know for something unknown. But changing circumstances should not cause our confidence in God to falter (Ps. 1:3). Hope dwells in new enterprises, and faith thrives in a desire to experience more of Him. Any new endeavor will challenge us to give more, so we should prepare ourselves, asking the Holy Spirit to help us meet the task. Someone is waiting to be inspired and transformed by your story of God leading you into another season of Christian service (Rom. 10:14-15).

By definition, 'new' is having recently come into an unfamiliar existence, something other than the former or something different than before. God gives us new vision, strength, hope, and faith. And when we trust Him fully, we will embrace everything He has in store for us! There is no limit to what God can do. He is the God of new beginnings (Isa. 43:18-19), and we should look forward with great anticipation. When the Israelites crossed over the Jordan River into the land of Canaan, they had not passed that way before (Joshua 3:4), and every day was an unforeseen territory. Significant accomplishments for the Lord require incredible energy, but an encouraged person awakens to the challenge with, "Good morning, God!" The people of Israel had a remarkable history of God's victories. You recall how He brought ten plagues against Egypt, saving them from slavery (Ex. 7-11). As the Egyptian army went to recapture them, God opened up the Red Sea, and the Israelites crossed on dry land. God closed the sea when the enemy gave chase and saved His people. In Exodus 17, Joshua led them to another victory against the Amalekites. Then, there was the defeat of Jericho, where the walls crumbled, and the conquest of the promised land began (Joshua 6). The God who gave his children these victories is the same God who walked them into their future. Our God has not changed. Seasons of life change, but the Lord of life does not.

Transitions force us into the unknown, but we need not fear. We are not alone. Our Lord says, "Fear thou not; for I am with thee: be not dismayed; for I am thy God: I will strengthen thee; yea, I will help thee; yea, I will uphold thee with the right hand of my righteousness" (Isa. 41:10). Something about the word 'new' screams possibility (Eccl. 3:1). Change is exciting. It's not always comfortable, but it's exciting. When we get married, life is exciting but not always comfortable. When a child is born, life is exciting but not always comfortable. When our children go off to college, life is exciting but not always comfortable. To accept something different, we must be willing to see things in a new way and understand that change is an inevitable part of life. The passage in Ecclesiastes 3 concludes, "He hath made everything beautiful in his time..." (v11). His time. His purpose. His season. "And let us not be weary in well doing: for in due season we shall reap, if we faint not" (Gal. 6:9). When we follow our Father in love, we will accept His work in us. Let's step into our future together and see the perfect will of God performed. Keep walking forward with faith. The same God that performed miracles in the past is with us to do more incredible things in the future. This is our time for a new beginning. Dig deep and embrace what God is doing.

Someone said, "A mind once stretched never returns to its original shape." This is true of our faith as well. God leads us into experiences that require more confidence, dependence, humility, and surrender. Every time we depend upon God to a greater degree, we overcome our former level of self-sufficiency. He is in control to accomplish His purpose (Dan. 4:35). Remember that God's Kingdom is a seed, process, and harvest system (Mark 4:26-29). In the pages of Scripture, we read of many who stepped out of their familiar places and followed God's voice. Abraham is an incredible example of someone who left his home, heading for an unknown promised land. Our church is positioned for an exciting time of spiritual growth that will mark the extension of a familiar pathway. How can we navigate this? The 'father of faith' embarked on an extraordinary journey when he listened and obeyed God's call. He trusted in the promises of God! Just as Abraham left what was known to him, we must relinquish our fears, doubts, and attachments before we can appreciate new possibilities. The Christian life is not static comfort. It is an ongoing adventure where God's faithfulness remains. Trust in His promises, even when the path ahead seems unclear. Beauty is on the horizon, so step out and leave anything that would hold your spirit captive.

In the first six verses of Joshua 3, the Israelites were called to move forward under the leadership of Joshua. God wanted His people to take possession of the promised land. Undoubtedly, they felt uncertain and uneasy about what was before them. This is why the Lord, in His mercy, told them that He would go first, and then they would follow. He will do the same for us. God is one step ahead, and He sees our way. From Joseph, Naomi, Noah, and Esther to more modern stories of faith, new beginnings are a theme woven throughout the Bible. By faith, Joseph used every occasion of life to glorify God. Naomi demonstrates how new beginnings are realized when we trust God to provide. Noah was obedient to God's commands and, with his family, was able to build a new world. Esther's story illustrates how we can experience new things by taking advantage of divinely orchestrated opportunities. Each of these stories demonstrates renewal, hope, and faith in God. The Psalmist says He is acquainted with all our ways (Ps. 139:3). He walks ahead to fight the battles we fear we can't win. He calms the seas and softens the blows we worry will take us down. He knows our road. And, oh, what a joy to partner with the One who makes everything new! Ecclesiastes 3:1 is not merely a description of what happens in life; it is a description of what God sends. The words of the wise man Solomon, "To everything there is a season and a time to every purpose under the heaven," remind us that our circumstances will change according to God's timetable (Eccl. 3:11). Therefore, we must anticipate the ebb and flow. For believers, seasons of sorrow and joy will lead to a more meaningful relationship with Jesus. Regardless of what we face, the Almighty is the author of our days, and joy is found in embracing a sovereign God!

What does the Bible say about new beginnings? First, we are a new creation in Christ (2 Cor. 5:17), and He has caused us to be born again to a living hope through His resurrection from the dead (1 Pet. 1:3). We are told the Lord has a hopeful future in store for us (Jer. 29:11). Isaiah 40:31 promises that the Lord will renew our strength if we wait on Him. In Lamentations 3:22-24 we are told of a love that never ceases and of mercies that never end. According to Romans 8:28, God works all things for our good. Proverbs 3:5-6 says that if we acknowledge the Lord in everything, He will make our path straight. In Psalm 18:2, we understand that God is our fortress and deliverer. Jesus Christ is the same yesterday, today, and forever (Heb. 13:8).

Today, another season begins for our church, and each one of us can participate in the new beginning. We will never experience all the blessings, growth, relationships, protection, and effectiveness of God's Kingdom unless we are united in the Lord's house. The local church is where God displays His glory (Eph. 3:21). Gathering together in the local assembly is God's plan for His people (Heb. 10:25). Community is the heart of God; the Church triumphant (Matt. 16:18). God is sovereign, and our ministry will be effective only as we rely on His wisdom, timing, and goodness. Trust God's foreknowledge in placing you under the leadership He has given you. Discover how you fit within God's harmony and flow. Joyfully anticipate what He will do for us personally and collectively. Your first reaction to change may be to draw back, saying, "I am saved, and I'm quite comfortable right where I am." God has indeed brought us thus far on our journey through life. But new experiences await, and we can gain new spiritual ground by reading our Bibles daily and listening to what the Holy Spirit has to say to us. We can go forward through prayer. We thank God for our private devotions, that secret place of worship where we are shut in and alone with Him. But we also have the opportunity to kneel around the altars of prayer with brothers and sisters who want to help us walk more closely with God (Rom. 12:1). It is human nature to be afraid at times, but read the words of encouragement that God spoke to Joshua. He said, "Be strong and of a good courage; be not afraid, neither be thou dismayed: for the Lord thy God is with thee whithersoever thou goest" (Joshua 1:9). Let's ask for a renewed determination to go forward with God. He offers new spiritual territory if we step out in faith and obedience. His plans are abundantly better than anything anyone can imagine. And if we trust Him, He will lead us to higher places and accomplish beautiful and marvelous things through us. What a privilege it is to serve our wonderful Lord!

Father, we are thankful for the experiences that have influenced our lives and brought us to this place. And now, we confess that our times are still in Your hand (Ps. 31:15). We do not know what the future holds, but we know You are in our future! Jesus, You are a Shepherd who graciously leads the sheep, and You know the way (Acts 15:18). Dear Lord, help us embrace the journey ahead and understand that we are forever walking in your loving care. We pray these things in Jesus' name. Amen.

All Things Come of Thee

IN 1 CHRONICLES 29, WE READ OF THE INCREDIBLE GENEROSITY IN ISRAEL for the collection to build the temple in Jerusalem. It is an occasion where God's love and provision are revealed in His people. The people rejoiced, "with perfect hearts, they offered willingly to the Lord." In the spirit of worship, King David said, "O Lord our God, all this store that we have prepared to build thee an house for thine holy name cometh of thine hand, and is all thine own" (v16). In Psalm 50:10-11, God makes a forceful ownership statement, "For every beast of the forest is mine, and the cattle upon a thousand hills. I know all the fowls of the mountains, and the wild beasts of the field are mine." The Bible says, "The mighty God, even the Lord, hath spoken, and called the earth from the rising of the sun unto the going down thereof" (Ps. 50:1). David said, "Thine, O Lord, is the greatness, and the power, and the glory, and the victory, and the majesty: for all that is in the heaven and in the earth is thine; thine is the kingdom, O Lord, and thou are exalted as head above all. Both riches and honor come of thee, and thou reignest over all: and in thine hand is power and might; and in thine hand it is to make great, and to give strength unto all" (1 Chron. 29:11-12). David's public outpouring of generosity was so incredible that the people were compelled to share their possessions and lives for God's holy purposes.

Estimates of what David's gift would be worth today range from $200 to $800 billion. Yet, he is not best remembered for his net worth. He is recognized as the "man after God's heart" (1 Sam. 13:14). R. C. Sproul said, "All truth is God's truth. For example, the laws of logic and mathematics are ultimately rooted and grounded in the one source of all truth, God Himself. Aristotle didn't invent logic any more than Columbus invented America. He discovered the laws of logic that were already there." Sproul said, "Whether in nature or grace in this world, we discover things that exist because of the light of God's revelation." All wealth, power, and strength originate with God. The same is true for any gift or talent we are given (James 1:17, 1 Cor. 12:1-11). We cannot provide God with anything that is not already His. The idea that everything belongs to God is a standard we must recognize and incorporate into our decisions. We are only managers of what God has allowed us to use (Ps. 89:11). Apostle John said, "He made all things, and without him was not anything made that was made" (John 1:3). God has made everything for a purpose, and that universal purpose of every creation is that He would be glorified (Ex. 9:16, Ps. 67:10, Rev. 4:11). Romans 11:36 tells us, "For of him, and through him, and to him, are all things: to whom be glory for ever. Amen." God created the universe according to His will as a dwelling place where he would make His power and wisdom known (Ps. 19:1), and each of us exists for such purposes as He designed (Eph. 2:10).

Early in life, we learn about possessions and ownership. The word "mine" goes beyond the toddler years and into adulthood, where we desire to stake claim to something. The concept of ownership is not permanent, for we all leave this world with nothing. Everything in our custody is temporary. And, short of settling the issue of 'ownership vs. stewardship,' we will struggle to surrender ourselves to God. But when the matter is resolved, we can live for His glory. God owns the heavens and the earth (Deut. 10:14). He said, "The world is mine, and the fulness thereof" (Ps. 50:12). If God owns it all, what am I doing with it? Yes, money is on everyone's mind these days. It was no different two thousand years ago. Knowing that money was significant to most people, Jesus talked more about it than any other subject. Do we understand the financial responsibility of what it means to live for Christ? The key is not to identify what we have but to use what we've been given. Living in the light of eternity will color how we handle every relationship, task, and circumstance. The closer we live to God, the smaller everything else appears. Stewardship is the use of God-given resources for the accomplishment of God-given goals. Jesus said, "For where your treasure is, there will your heart be also" (Matt. 6:21). Our testimony is not about poverty or prosperity but how we view our possessions. Do you find yourself gripping things, money, investments, influence? Too many of us are owned by the things we have. The apostle Paul said, "We brought nothing into this world, and it is certain we can carry nothing out" (1 Tim. 6:7). Psalm 24:1 says, "The earth is the Lord's, and the fulness thereof; the world, and they that dwell therein." As such, we manage God's treasures His way, for His purposes, and always for His glory.

Someone said, "There are no inspiring stories of accumulation, only stories of sacrifice." Howard Hughes (1905-1976), aviator, investor, filmmaker, business tycoon, engineer, and entrepreneur, was one of the wealthiest men in American history. During his life, he amassed a fortune of over $2.5 billion. Despite this tremendous wealth, he suffered terribly with his physical and mental health. He pushed everyone close to him away and became a loner. Hughes died miserable, sad, and alone. In many ways, his wealth had become his prison. George Müller (1805-1898) is one of the most well-known Christian missionaries ever. After beginning life as a deviant, he became a Christian and set out with a mission to serve God. He and his wife became affected by the plight of the orphans in Bristol, England, and so they opened an orphanage. Initially, they determined they would never ask anyone for money. They resolved to pray. The stories of God's provision are legendary, and the Müllers were able to care for over 10,000 orphans as God provided them with more than $1.5 million in donations during their lifetimes. Whenever an orphan would reach adulthood and leave the orphanage, George would sit down with him and place a Bible in his right hand and a coin in his left. He would tell him to cling tightly to what was in his right hand, and God would always make sure he had something in his left hand. Howard Hughes is remembered as a man of vision, wealth, and power. George Muller is recognized as a man of great faith and impact for all things eternal.

I cannot give anything to God, who has everything. I don't have a right to get angry when God does not give me what I want or takes away what I possess. Job rightly said, "Naked came I out of my mother's womb, and naked shall I return thither; the Lord gave, and the Lord hath taken away; blessed be the name of the Lord (Job 1:21). The Bible says, "In all this Job sinned not, nor charged God foolishly" (v22). When I have done all God has commanded, God still owes me nothing. I have only performed my reasonable service (Rom. 12:1). To understand the principle of Christian stewardship, we must recognize the difference between possession and ownership (Acts 4:32). We do not have anything we have not received from God (1 Cor. 4:7). The idea that God owns everything makes perfect sense. After all, He created us and the earth we inhabit (Gen. 1). We had no right to exist outside of God's sovereignty, so why would we think we have any right to own anything beyond what His sovereignty allows? The confession that God owns everything, including us, requires that we live a life ordered by the power of the One on whom our life depends. When God said, "Bring ye all the tithes into the storehouse" (Mal. 3:10), he is not just interested in the ten percent but in how we manage the other ninety percent. The belief that God holds it all will affect how we handle our resources. It means every dollar we spend and every minute of prayer and study in Scripture will be done with heaven in view. Every action and behavior will communicate our love for Him. It would be impossible to live apart from God, for in him we live and move and have our being (Acts 17:28). One of the most marvelous teachings in the Bible is that we are the children of a wonderful Father who is always ready to provide good things to us (Matt. 7:9-11).

A small boy who lived in an ocean village made a little boat and took it to the seaside. Soon, the waves carried it out to sea. The boy's efforts to recapture it were unsuccessful. But some days later, he saw his little boat in a store window. It was for sale. With great effort, he gathered enough money and bought it. Weeping with happiness, the boy exclaimed, "Now you are twice mine because I made you, and I also bought you!" In precisely the same way, we belong to God because He created us and redeemed us. Our God sustains and cares for us (Rom. 8:32, 1 Pet. 5:7), for we belong to Him (1 Cor. 6:20). Oh, praise His name! What a wonderful owner God is! He is the owner of all, but at the same time, He gives all (Acts 17:25). In Romans 8:32, we read, "He that spared not his own Son but delivered him up for us all, how shall he not with him also freely give us all things?" We give thanks because He allows us access to everything He has. Could we say this about anyone else? Stewardship is a concept that includes all areas of life:

our health, our mind, our gifts, our abilities, our money, our family, our time, and our possessions. If God is our sovereign owner, the most sensible thing we can do is to submit to Him and say, 'Thou art the Potter; I am the clay. Mold me and make me after Thy will.'

What do you have that you did not receive? Look around you and imagine this label attached to everything you have: "On Loan From Almighty God." Consider your bank statement, recent promotion, marriage, children, grandchildren, spiritual gifts, and salvation. After all, who can bestow on themselves the gift of life? Martin Luther said, "I have tried to keep things in my hands and lost them all. But what I have given into God's hands I still possess." Africa's great missionary David Livingstone said, "I place no value on anything I have or may possess, except in relation to the kingdom of God." Cheerful giving can only come from a heart set on things above (Col. 3:1). Understand that your life is a gift from God to share with others as you wait for the Lord's return. A person's heart is tied to what they value most in life. We reveal what we love most by how we spend our time and energy. Jesus explained the foolishness of accumulating earthly treasures that will rust, unravel, and eventually fade away (Matt. 6:19). Worldly wealth seems dull in comparison to the riches of knowing Jesus (Eph. 3:8). We who believe will live unselfishly and joyfully declare, "All things come of Thee!"

Obedience Without Hesitation

CONFORMITY IS BEHAVIOR INTENDED TO MATCH THAT OF THE MAJORITY. But obedience is faith in action, regardless of the outcome. From Genesis to Revelation, the Bible has much to say about obeying without hesitation. The Psalmist said, "Thou art my portion, O Lord; I have said that I would keep thy words. I made haste, and delayed not to keep thy commandments" (Ps. 119:57, 60). Think of a time when you heard from God through Scripture or a conviction by the Holy Spirit. What was your immediate response? When the angel of the Lord told the shepherds the good news of Jesus' birth, they didn't let any questions we might have asked keep them from quickly responding to God. The Bible says, "They came with haste" (Luke 2:16). When Jesus said to four men, "Follow me," they "straightway left their nets and followed him." When He called James and John, they "immediately left the ship... and followed him" (Matt. 4:17-22). In John 14:15, Jesus said, "If ye love me, keep my commandments." In Luke 9:23, He said, "If any man will come after me, let him deny himself, and take up his cross daily, and follow me." What does God require of us? To do justly, to love mercy, and to walk humbly with Him (Micah 6:8). Our Lord is still seeking an immediate response today, and the mark of a Christian is the practice of obedience without hesitation or reservation.

The writer of Acts 5:29 tells us, "We ought to obey God rather than men." This is most clearly demonstrated by the confidence of Shadrach, Meshach, and Abednego when facing a fiery test that threatened their lives (Dan. 2-3). While their story is often told using those names, it's their Hebrew names we should remember. Hananiah means "Yahweh is gracious," Mishael means "who is what God is," and Azariah means "whom Yahweh helps." Deported to Babylon along with Daniel in

605 BC, King Nebuchadnezzar changed the names of these boys in an attempt to get them to conform to pagan worship in the court of the king. He gave each a new name with a new meaning that included the name of a Babylonian god. Hananiah became Shadrach, which means "may Bel protect his life." Mishael became Meshach, which means "command of Aku." Azariah was given the name Abednego, meaning "servant of Nebo." What a mockery against the Lord. Remaining faithful to their God, they refused to bow down before the statue and responded with some of the most inspiring and faithful words in all of Scripture (Dan. 3:16-18): Their simple and straightforward response was: 1) My God can... 2) my God will... 3) but if not ...I will worship my God and not bow to another. Nebuchadnezzar could change their names, but he could not change their hearts! These young men knew the risk involved and had no guarantee of deliverance, but their actions showed they were so committed to the Lord that even their lives took second place in honoring Him.

If we were to prioritize the things declared in the Bible, obeying God's voice would be at the top of the list. Why? Because all of Christianity revolves around obedience. We are not saved by obedience, but there will always be evidence of true salvation in our obedience (Matt. 7:15-23). At the marriage in Cana of Galilee, Mary's words come to mind: "Whatever he saith unto you, do it" (John 2:5). We are talking about a daily, living relationship with God through Jesus Christ by the power of the Holy Spirit (John 10:3-4). Deuteronomy 28 describes many blessings of obedience. It also tells us of the curses of disobedience. I recognize that this passage was a command to Moses and the nation of Israel. Still, the entirety of Scripture is also given to us as a roadmap for our journey (2 Tim. 3:16). Abraham experienced the blessings of God because of his faithfulness and obedience (Gen. 22:1-18). Moses heard the voice of God through a burning bush, which changed his life forever (Ex. 3). The moment Samuel knew and obeyed the voice of God, his ministry became a powerful force for righteousness (1 Sam. 3, 9). Elijah demonstrated his love for God through his obedience to the word of the Lord. John the Baptist testified of the joy of knowing the voice of Jesus (John 3:29).

For the individual who has not trusted Christ as Savior, the first act of submission is to repent and, by faith, trust in Jesus as the only

Savior. To trust in Jesus is God's first and great commandment of salvation (Acts 16:31, 1 John 3:23). Obedience is at the heart of our redemption, for we cannot share in fellowship with God unless we obey Him. Obedience shows that our love runs deep, and our surrender is demonstrated by the degree to which we follow the Bible. The apostle James said, "Let every man be swift to hear... and receive with meekness the engrafted word, which can save your souls." Obedience to God's Word requires ongoing action (James 1:19-25). Jesus said those faithful to Him in love will do what He commands (John 14:15). The promised blessing is the honor God receives through our obedience. Delayed obedience is disobedience. When we wait, we're questioning God. We're asking, "God, do you really know what's best?" Jesus linked obedience and worship when He said, "If you love me, you will keep my commandments" (John 14:15). The apostle Paul writes, "I beseech you therefore, brethren, by the mercies of God, that ye present your bodies a living sacrifice, holy, acceptable unto God, which is your reasonable service" (Rom. 12:1). Obedience and worship go hand-in-hand to prove a person's unyielding commitment to the Lord.

When Jesus said, "Launch out into the deep and let down your nets for a draught," Peter faced a life-changing decision (Luke 5). He said, "I will do as You say and let down the nets." The apostle's journey into obedience began with simple action, and he received the reward. Abraham left his home at God's instruction, not knowing where the Lord would lead. He "departed, as the Lord had spoken unto him" (Gen. 12). Moses went back to Egypt without knowing all that his new role as deliverer would involve (Ex. 4:19-20). Esther approached the king, not knowing if she would lose her life (Esther 5). Rahab hid the spies who came to view the promised land (Joshua 2). Mary heard the angel's voice and said, "Behold the handmaid of the Lord; be it unto me according to thy word" (Luke 1:38). Obedience without hesitation is the essence of discipleship. We worship God because He is worthy (Rev. 4:11). We trust Him because He is faithful (Ps. 111:7-8). We love Him because He first loved us (1 John 4:19). The Psalmist said, "Blessed are the undefiled in the way, who walk in the law of the Lord" (Ps. 119:1). The prophet Samuel called King Saul out on his foolishness when his desire for the praise of men offset God's priority of obedience. He said,

"Behold, to obey is better than sacrifice" (1 Sam. 15). God gives us explicit commands in Scripture, and our sacrifice of time, talent, and treasure will not substitute for obedience. Proverbs 21:3 says, "To do justice and judgment is more acceptable to the Lord than sacrifice." Saul "rejected the word of the Lord" when he tried to spiritualize his partial compliance. From God's perspective, even minor points of disobedience are not without consequence (Prov. 11:21, Rom. 1:18-32).

In the eleventh century, King Henry III of Bavaria grew tired of court life and the pressures of being a monarch. He asked to be accepted as a monk and spend the rest of his life in the monastery. "Your Majesty," said the spiritual leader of the abbey, "Do you understand that the pledge here is one of obedience? This will be hard because you have been a king." "I understand," said Henry. "For the rest of my life, I will obey you as Christ leads you." "Then I will tell you what to do," said the abbot. "Go back to your throne and serve faithfully in the place where God has put you." When King Henry died after returning to his royal duties, a statement was written: "The King learned to rule by being obedient." Oswald Chambers said, "The counterfeit of obedience is a state of mind in which you work up occasions to sacrifice yourself." God is looking for men and women who will respond with instant, complete, wholehearted, and joyous obedience each time He speaks. Simon Peter illustrates what can happen when we say yes to God (Luke 5:5). The soon-to-be disciple chose to obey the Lord and notice what happened. Jesus demonstrated His power and sovereignty in Peter's life, but also in the lives of those gathered there: "For he was astonished, and all that were with him, at the draught of the fishes which they had taken" (Luke 5:9).

We will learn more about God through immediate obedience than a lifetime of Bible conversations. Our Father doesn't owe us an explanation for everything he asks us to do, and every parent knows that delayed obedience is disobedience. Understanding can wait, but obedience cannot. Scripture is full of examples of commands that seem unreasonable. Consider what God told Joshua to do in capturing the city of Jericho (Joshua 6). Since when is blowing trumpets and shouting considered a reasonable military strategy? Too often, we try to offer compliance with reservations. We want to pick and choose which commands we will obey. We list those we like while ignoring the ones we think are unreasonable, complicated, expensive, or unpopular. Everyone struggles to make sense of life's purpose and meaning. But one step forward in obedience is worth a lifetime of learning about it.

By yielding to God, we understand two things: one, that what the world offers is hollow, and two, that what Jesus offers is a release from sin and death's iron grip. We are refreshed and recharged through the worship of obedience, ready to return to the most important business: loving God with all we are and loving our neighbors as ourselves (Matt. 22:37-40). In the New Testament, Jesus cut to the law's core, showing that our heart's attitude goes hand in hand with our deeds. We, like Peter, must recognize that obeying God is always the wisest course of action. There is always a line to be drawn somewhere; obedience is the golden key to a life of joy and excellence. William Booth once said, "If there is anything of power in the Salvation Army today, it is because God has all the adoration of my heart, all the power of my will, and all the influence of my life." When we obey God, we will never be disappointed. The ultimate Lord of our lives will only do amazing things with our lives if we are entirely under his control. Obedience is the golden key to a life of joy and excellence. The gospel impacts the attitudes of our hearts, and Jesus Christ becomes our patience and joy. He who is worthy of praise is our hope for all eternity. Therefore, let us obey our God without hesitation or reservation!

The Unnamed Boy

IN JOHN 6:1-14 WE READ OF A GREAT CROWD OF PEOPLE FOLLOWING JESUS because they saw the miracles He was performing. And, indeed, they were blessed. But according to John 20:29, exercising faith is the most incredible blessing. Jesus told Thomas, "Because thou hast seen me, thou hast believed: blessed are they that have not seen and yet have believed" (John 20:29). Some are filled with awe at God's mighty works, yet not convinced or converted, for we walk by faith, not by sight (2 Cor. 5:7). Signs and wonders are not required to please God, but faith is (Heb. 11:6). Therefore, we understand that even more than seeking a new miracle is taking God at His word. Now, let's consider someone who demonstrated his trust in God by giving what little he had to the Lord before there was any miracle. Several people in the Bible are never identified by name, yet God used them powerfully. One such person is the little boy recorded in the sixth chapter of John's Gospel. This lad was carrying a lunch of five loaves and two small fish. We don't know if his name was written on his lunch basket, but if it was, apparently, no one noticed. And although the boy's name was not revealed, God blessed his willingness to give everything he had to the Lord. And likewise, with us.

No other miracle of Christ is recorded in all four Gospels but this one. Jesus fed the multitudes that came to hear Him teach, and satisfied families went home, never knowing the little boy's name. Nor do we, but the characteristics of his life are impossible to miss. His faith and generosity touched the lives of thousands of people. Of all sitting on a hillside, the Bible speaks only of one who thought ahead and prepared for the day. Too often, we look forward to the performance moments of life but spend little time in preparation for those moments. We want

God to use us to influence others without preparing our hearts and minds through prayer and studying God's Word. But our performance will only be as good as our preparation. President Nixon once told Sir Winston Churchill's son how much he admired the prime minister's remarkable ability to give "extemporaneous" speeches. Churchill's son replied, "Oh, yes. I've watched my father work for hours preparing those impromptu speeches." When we delight in the Scriptures and associate with God's people, we put ourselves in a position where the Lord can use us for His purposes (Prov. 13:20).

What can we learn from this story? First, the boy gave willingly. The outcome would have been entirely different if the boy had withheld his lunch or if he had insisted on being promised a return on his investment. But God blessed his cheerful giving. The apostle Paul commended the churches of Macedonia who were in deep poverty yet had a willing heart to be used by God to meet the needs of others (2 Cor. 8:1-3). Selfishness has a bitter end. But God's goodness and blessing await the Christian who has a willing heart. The boy gave wholly. He could have given three loaves and one fish, and the Lord could have fed the multitude with this lesser amount. But Deuteronomy 6:5 says, "And thou shalt love the Lord thy God with all thine heart, and with all thy soul, and with all thy might." The boy gave wisely. What a great decision this turned out to be for him. God will always do more with what we give Him than we could have ever done with it ourselves. This biblical principle applies to everything we possess (Luke 6:38). We all have a "lunch." We can keep it for ourselves or give it to the One who provided it in the first place and watch Him bless us and the multitudes around us. We often fail to do the little things in search of big things. But when what we have is given willingly to the Lord, a miracle will occur for which only God can receive the glory.

When the boy shared his lunch, he demonstrated that the Holy Spirit's power can work through us when we offer all we have to God. If the child had held onto his lunch, he would have been the only one fed. Instead, his generosity and faith made it possible for all to be fed. Can you imagine how he felt watching everyone eat his fish and bread? A child reminds us to offer ourselves to God, share, and understand the blessing of giving all. I ask myself, "Have I brought my lunch to Jesus?

Have I allowed Christ to multiply things of eternal value in my life? Am I partnering with the Lord in bringing the Bread of Life to those who desperately need it?" When we bring our simple resources to Jesus, and they pass through the hands of our Creator, they become more than enough. God transforms them into abundance, and the blessing of growing the kingdom of God will come when we become broken bread in the hands of the Master. Little becomes much when God is in it! What's in your lunch box? In such a big world with so many people, it's easy to feel insignificant. It's easy to feel like we don't matter much. We're tempted to believe we can't make a difference. We're tempted to think we have little to offer in the grand scheme. We're not heroes. We don't draw crowds. But remember, God uses the insignificant, the overlooked, and the small. Jesus loves to see how we respond to unexpected events. The most unlikely people are the ones who usually do the most for God.

At just 12 years old, Bill Wilson was abandoned by his mother on a street corner. He sat and waited for her in that spot for three full days, but she never returned for him. Countless people walked by this young boy sitting out on the street corner. Finally, a man on his way to see his son in the hospital stopped and asked him if he was okay. After learning of his situation, the man got him some food and made some calls, and within five hours, he was on a bus headed to a Christian summer camp. In 1980, Bill established Metro World Ministry in Brooklyn, one of New York's toughest neighborhoods, known for gang violence, crime, drugs, and poverty. Armed with a bullhorn, Bill went through the streets, inviting and driving children to his fun, welcoming Sunday School program. During this ministry, a woman from Puerto Rico came to Bill with an urgent request. She didn't speak English, so she told him through an interpreter, "I want to do something for God, please." "I don't know what you can do," he answered. "Please, let me do something," she said in Spanish. "Okay," Bill said, "I'll put you on a bus. Ride a different bus every week and love the kids." So, she rode a different bus every week, and she loved the children. She would find the worst-looking kid on the bus, put them on her lap, and whisper the only words she had learned in English: "I love you, and Jesus loves you." After several months, she became attached to one little boy in particular. "I don't want to change buses anymore. I want to stay on this one bus," she told Bill. The boy didn't speak. Every week, he came to Sunday School with his sister and sat on the woman's lap, but he never made a sound. And each week, Rosa would tell him all the way to Sunday School and all the way home, "I love you, and Jesus loves you." One day, to her amazement, the little boy turned around and said, "I love you, too." Then he put his arms around her and gave her a big hug. That was 2:30 in the afternoon. At 6:30 that evening, the boy was found dead in a garbage bag under a fire escape. His mother had beaten him to death and thrown his body in the trash. "I love you, and Jesus loves you" were some of the last words this boy heard in his short life – from the lips of a willing woman who could barely speak English. The story is unbearably tragic - except in knowing that if the child knew nothing else, he knew he was indeed loved by at least two people: Jesus and Rosa! With love, Rosa had offered her limited abilities, and she prayed that it made an eternal difference in that little boy's tragic life.

The days of religious rhetoric are over. People must experience the reality of the gospel. And, for some, we are the only scripture they will read. We are the only sermon they will ever hear. We are the only Jesus they will ever see. When Jesus asked the disciples how they might satisfy the hunger of the multitudes, Andrew said, "There is a lad here." Not a warrior, not a king, not a millionaire, just a boy. A child who was willing to obey God. The apostle Paul tells us in 1 Corinthians 1:27-29 that God has chosen the foolish things of the world to confound the wise. Why? So that none would glory in His work in the world. C. H. Spurgeon said of faith, "Faith sees the invisible, hears the inaudible, touches the intangible, and does the impossible."

Although the young boy in the sixth chapter of John is unnamed, we understand that he was the right boy in the right place that day. The thing I find fascinating is that Jesus chose to associate with a young lad to do something huge. Together, they fed a multitude numbering in the thousands! I can see Jesus as He took the bread and fish; the Bible says He blessed them. Perhaps Jesus then looked at the little boy with a gleam in His eye that said, "Watch this!" And as the boy watched in wonder, a miracle occurred. The story leads me to ask if God needs our resources to accomplish His work on earth. The answer is no. And yet He chooses to use them. What a privilege it is to be used by God! That boy had a story to tell for the rest of his life. I'm sure he told his friends and family about the day he partnered with Jesus to feed a hungry multitude. May we follow his example and do the same. It's a big world, and the multitude is waiting.

Celebrate Your Church Family

IF YOU BELONG TO A BIBLE-BELIEVING CHRIST-CENTERED CHURCH, YOU know the joy of being in a community of people who love, learn, and lean on each other. God's church is a body of believers united in Christ, making an eternal difference in people's lives. It is a safe harbor for the lost and hurt. It is a place of healing and redemption. It is a place to celebrate spiritual victories won through the power of the Holy Spirit. Family conveys a sense of belonging; collectively, we are loved, cherished, celebrated, and fully forgiven. A local church gathering is where we use our talents and provision to spread the gospel of Jesus (1 Cor. 3). The key to recognizing the Church's importance is understanding its ownership (Col. 1:18). Before the foundation of the world, Jesus chose to have a family for Himself "in whom we have redemption through his blood, the forgiveness of sins, according to the riches of his grace" (Eph. 1:4-7). We are children of God by faith in Christ Jesus (Gal. 3:26). The Bible says, "Behold, what manner of love the Father hath bestowed upon us, that we should be called the sons of God…" (1 John 3:1). As followers of Christ, we praise the One who gave himself for us. And what better place to worship than in the congregation of the redeemed? Evangelist Billy Graham says, "Amazing things can happen when the family of God bands together." Are you praying for the church's mission and ministry? Do you support it in active service or only in passive presence? God has always had a people who believe by faith and choose Him as Lord. Indeed, the Church belongs to God, and the gates of hell will never prevail against it!

I think about those with a history of attending a Spirit-filled church. What was your impression of the church when you first heard the sweet hymns and powerful sermons of the Lord's anointing? Perhaps you were a child in awe of what you saw. Do you remember how your heart was stirred? Do you cherish the memories? This was where you discovered that people believed in God with all their hearts. They became a part of your life. You saw them every week. You laughed, cried, and worshiped together. And because of them, life was good. When someone entered your crisis and said, "I understand," it was usually someone at your church. Chances are good that a godly friend said, "I will help you because I love you." These are the people who surrounded you and gave you hope. They had experienced pain like yours; therefore, they could bring light to your darkness. Remember that person who loved you regardless of whether your day was good or bad? Remember those who said, "We are here for you, and we're not leaving?" In the good times, they believed in you and made your celebration their own. These are the people who challenged you and put purpose in your life. Think about the time when you decided to give your heart to God. What if there had never been a church for you? When I hear people say, "I've had it with the church," I am saddened because I realize how much they have lost. From the very beginning of time, relationships with others have been a part of God's plan for mankind (Gen. 2:18). When we see the members of our church as members of God's family, our reasons for pulling away from the fellowship begin to crumble. Dear friend, despite weaknesses and flaws, the people of God are to be celebrated as the most significant demonstration of God's love in the world. And it will continue to be so until Jesus Christ returns!

Are you disheartened and adrift because of how someone in the church treated you, perhaps even years ago? The enemy works as we serve the Lord, even in a church ministry. Then, the cares of life have a way of gradually loosening us from our moorings and little by little; we are affected by the adverse forces. I have a scar like that, so I want to encourage you. If you are a Christian, the church is not a place you attend. It is who you are. You cannot withdraw from the church any more than you can disassociate from humanity. You *are* the church, a "fellow citizen with the saints, and of the household of God" (Eph. 2:11–22). You have been washed by the blood of Jesus and adopted into the family of the Almighty. Worship Him for that! Second, the church was not a human invention. It is God's idea, and it must be regarded as such. Neglecting the church is missing out on evangelism, exhortation, and encouragement. The writer of Hebrews tells us to consider one another unto love and good works, assembling together (Heb. 10:24-25). Most of the New Testament is about what Jesus ordained, and He is the chief cornerstone (Eph. 2:19-21). Christ is foundational to our service and singing. He is our standard of measure and alignment. I recognize that the imperfections of the Christian community have caused some to despair. And it might be a long road to healing, but it's always worth the journey. Dig into Scripture. Seek wise counsel. Pray and ask God to reveal the next steps to you. That our Lord uses flawed people to accomplish his divine purpose is a sign of his grace, not his absence.

You were created to belong. God never intended you to base your identity on accomplishments or performance. He made you for His glory. How? By loving everyone called by His name (Isa. 43:6-7). Our world has trained us to think like consumers, considering what we want from a particular situation, product, or event. This mindset can make its way into the church. But when we accepted the gift of salvation, we gained new identities as children of God. We became members of the household of God, called to love and care for one another. We need to participate in church life and not simply choose what we want to do. Yes, we will harm – and we will be injured. We will disappoint others – and we will also be disappointed. We will experience awkward situations. The solution isn't to withdraw but to continue to love those God has put in our lives. And as distorted as it gets at times, the church's story is a beautiful narrative of God's grace, power, and redemption. The church is where we grow spiritually, nurtured in our faith. If the Apostles visited your church, would they recognize it as true Christianity, or has a rule book compromised the Biblical design? The gospel can be summarized in John 3:16, "For God so loved the world that he gave His only begotten Son, that whosoever believeth in him should not perish, but have everlasting life." His unfailing love is the heart of the entire gospel message! The apostle John said, "I have no greater joy than to hear that my children walk in truth" (3 John 4).

Let me ask you: Can you think of anything more worthy of your time and treasure than those who gather in the name of Jesus in the house of God? Scripture is very clear about the importance of relationships among God's people (Ps. 133:1-3, Rom. 12:10, 1 Pet. 4:8). Why would anyone not want to participate fully with His people on earth? After all, Heaven is a community, too. I love my church. It is a fellowship of people where the Bible is honored, upheld, and never compromised. We come thirsty. We leave filled with God's love, mercy, and truth. We are better together. We are a family of hope in a place where everyone is welcome. I have learned from gifted people who have studied God's Word. We share stories. We pray for God's wisdom and blessing as we seek to do His will. In the first chapter of Philippians, the apostle Paul expressed some feelings that I find easy to identify. He said, "I thank my God upon every remembrance of you; always in every prayer of mine for you all making request with joy, for your fellowship in the gospel from the first day until now... that ye may approve things that are excellent; that ye may be sincere and without offense till the day of Christ." He prayed that love would enable them to recognize, test, and prove things that are excellent without causing others to stumble. Paul was thankful for his fellow believers in Christ. He was grateful for the times when the Lord would bring them to his mind. He would think about their faces, words, and the time they spent together, joyfully supporting the work of God. When he thought of them, his heart was warmed. He was convinced that the Lord, who began a good work in them, would continue strengthening them and developing their faith up until the day He returns. Paul loved them with the love of Jesus, and he held them close to his heart. I have similar emotions for my church family. Without fanfare or drama, they show up when the need arises. Someone asked a pastor whose church was characterized by goodwill and cooperation, "Jim, you just think these people are perfect, don't you." Jim replied, "No. I don't think they're perfect. I just love them."

We are children of God through faith in Christ Jesus (Gal. 3:26). As in all families, we are different in many ways. We must learn to accept and celebrate our differences to function correctly. In the book of Acts, everyone was not always in agreement, but enduring love and respect was the source of unification. All labored for the cause of Christ. Their motives for action were faith, love, and hope in Jesus. Often, God works in us through other people, and He wants us to grow and mature through relationships. Let's look for reasons to unite as the family of God! Let's learn to celebrate our diversities and appreciate our differences! Let's love one another as Christ loves us. Indeed, we want those around us to see His love operating in our family. In John 13:34-35, Jesus tells us to love one another as He has loved us, for by this, all will know that we are His disciples. It is Christian love in a church that draws hearts to desire the salvation of God. The command of Jesus Christ is "Go ye into all the world" with the gospel, and nowhere else is the grand vision of God displayed than in those who labor in His church. We find comfort in sharing daily life with those who know us well and love us anyway. I am grateful that God lets me spend my life loving and serving wonderful friends with whom I will spend eternity!

Wisdom From Above

EARTHLY WISDOM IS OFTEN DEFINED AS THE SOUNDNESS OF AN ACTION based on knowledge or experience. Wisdom from above, or Godly wisdom, is the knowledge of Scripture applied to everyday life. Biblical wisdom influences our decisions and is demonstrated through a God-honoring lifestyle. In Proverbs 9:10, we read, "The fear of the Lord is the beginning of wisdom." This verse is best understood as an attitude of respect that begins with a relationship with God (Phil. 3:10). The Bible says wisdom is more precious than rubies and pearls (Prov. 8:11). And if we desire it, we can have it (James 1:5). In May 2012, the final auction price of a 32-carat Burmese ruby and diamond ring ended at $6.7 million. It is believed to be the most expensive ruby ever sold. As valuable as rubies are, no earthly treasure can compare to God's wisdom because nothing else offers the same blessing (Prov. 4:6, Eccl. 7:11-12). In the Book of Proverbs, knowledge and wisdom are closely associated but not the same (Prov. 3:5-7). Knowledge focuses on the understanding of Scripture. Wisdom takes the best course of action based on that understanding. Knowledge is education, ability, and intelligence. Wisdom is insight, discernment, and judgment. Knowledge is knowing where the quicksand is. Wisdom is walking around it. Knowledge is gained through intellectual means. Wisdom is found in obedience to the Word of God.

King Solomon said, "Wisdom is the principal thing, therefore, get wisdom: and with all thy getting, get understanding" (Prov. 4:7). The Old Testament patriarch Job reveals that wisdom "is not found in the land of the living" but in the mind of God. Job 28 employs mining for precious jewels as the connection for searching for wisdom. With poetic words, Job looked throughout the land of the living, in the sea, in the marketplace. "It cannot be bought with the finest gold," he said, "Nor can its price be weighed with silver" (Job 28:12-15). Gold and silver are for the body and time. Wisdom from above is for the soul and eternity; it is God-centered. Knowledge is abundant in the world. Indeed, we know more, but are we making better choices? Our problem is not a shortage of information but a lack of wisdom. We have learned to travel faster than sound, but we're going in the wrong direction. We know more about our world than ever before, yet we know less about how to live in it. We can acquire knowledge without God, but wisdom is determining God's perspective, discovering His purpose, and depending on His plan. Wisdom is the ability to discern God's hand in earthly situations and apply heavenly judgment (Phil. 1:9-10). It is realizing that life is short and then choosing to live every moment for the glory of God.

How do we become wise? We bow before God and acknowledge that we depend upon Him for our existence. Job finishes chapter 28: "Behold, the fear of the Lord, that is wisdom; and to depart from evil is understanding." The foolish person navigates through life based on feelings, instincts, and knee-jerk reactions. Wisdom is the behavior that results from surrender to the sovereign God. It is living God's way in God's world. A young company president instructed his secretary not to disturb him because he had a necessary appointment. The board chairman said, "I want to see Mr. Jones." The secretary said, "I'm sorry, but he cannot be disturbed; he has an important appointment." The chairman became very angry. He banged open the door and saw the president of his corporation on his knees in prayer. The chairman softly closed the door and asked the secretary, "Is this usual?" She said, "Yes, he does that every morning." The board chairman responded, "No wonder I come to him for advice."

If God's desired purpose is to be accomplished in our lives, biblical truths must reside within us. We have all inherited a corrupt nature at birth from which we cannot recover on our own (Eph. 2:1-10). Therefore, our first instruction of wisdom is applying this knowledge to our lives by receiving the saving grace of Christ through faith (Acts 2:21). We should approach Scripture to understand the heart of God. In Matthew 7:24-27, Jesus compares two men whose houses are identical. The rains that fall, the floods that rise, and the winds that blow are the same. But the foundations are very different. The difference between the two types of people this story represents is that while both hear the words of Jesus, only the wise put them into practice. In his book 'Malcolm Forbes: The Man Who Had Everything,' Christopher Winans tells of a motorcycle tour that Forbes took through Egypt in 1984 with his Capitalist Tool motorcycle team. After viewing the burial tomb of King Tut, Forbes seemed to be in a reflective mood. As they returned to the hotel in a shuttle bus, Forbes turned to one of his associates and asked, "Do you think I'll be remembered after I die?" Indeed, Forbes is remembered. He is recognized as the man who coined the phrase, "He who dies with the most toys wins." That was the wisdom of Malcolm Forbes. That was his ambition. That's why he collected scores of motorcycles. That's why he would pay over a million dollars for a Fabergé egg. That's why he owned castles, hot air balloons, and countless other toys he no longer holds. The Lord Jesus Christ gave us words of superior wisdom when he said, "For what is a man profited if he shall gain the whole world and lose his soul? Or what shall a man give in exchange for his soul?" (Matt. 16:26).

A father and his small son were walking one day when the boy asked him a question. "Dad, how does electricity go through the wires stretched between the utility poles? "I don't know," said his father. "I never knew much about electricity." Further along, the boy asked what causes lightning and thunder. "That, too, has puzzled me," came the reply. The youngster continued to ask about many things, none of which the father could explain. Finally, as they neared home, the boy said, "Dad, I hope you didn't mind all those questions." "Not at all," replied his father. "If you don't ask, how else will you learn?" If you have questions, our Heavenly Father knows the answers – and He wants to share them with you. In James 1:5, we read, "If any of you lack wisdom, let him ask of God... and it shall be given him." Our Lord gives generously to those who trust Him - without reproach or fault finding. In other words, He doesn't look at our previous foolish choices and decide we are not worthy of receiving wisdom from Him. God is willing to give abundant wisdom to those who ask based only on their trust and confidence in Him, not their track record. Thank the Lord for that!

Abraham Lincoln said on more than one occasion, "I have been driven many times to my knees by the overwhelming conviction that I had nowhere else to go. My own wisdom and that of those about me seemed insufficient for the day." If you are unfamiliar with the Book of Job, it is a sad story with a critical lesson. Job is a man who is faithful to God and to whom God is faithful. God blesses Job with a fruitful family and then gives Satan permission to destroy it all, which was to be a process of testing (Job 23:10). In chapter 38, Job gets to approach God with his grievances. His whole life was ruined without any wrongdoing on his part. He has legitimate questions for God about all that had happened to him. God speaks to Job in the following four chapters, asking questions like: "Where were you when I laid the earth's foundation? Have the gates of death been opened unto you? Who set the measurements of the universe? Have you ever commanded the morning or made the dawn know its place? Can you create rain and lightning? Can you make a hawk fly or an eagle mount up?" Throughout all the intense questioning, God reveals His glory, and Job realizes that his perspective is wrong. Job responds, "I know that you can do all things and that no purpose of yours can be thwarted. I have uttered what I did not understand, things which I did not know. I had heard of you by the hearing of the ear, but now my eye sees you; therefore, I will repent" (Job 42). And in doing so, the good man of God gains heavenly wisdom.

What is the value of Godly wisdom? We accept the challenges and unexpected turns of life. We can face obstacles by turning them into ministry. Wisdom from above gives us vision and a purpose for living. We will walk by faith – both on familiar and unfamiliar roads. With Godly wisdom, we see our hopes, dreams, and sufferings from God's point of view instead of our own. We live with less anxiety. We no longer know each success or failure as a make-or-break situation but as one more step toward everlasting life in Heaven. We live with more hope and less fear because we know God is not surprised by tragedy and turmoil. We are nicer to ourselves because the Holy Spirit sees our imperfections and still walks with us to make us holy (Rom. 15:16, 1 Thess. 5:23). We are kinder to others because we recognize that God loves them more than we ever will (John 15:13) and works in their hearts just as He works in ours. Popular fads or ideologies do not sway us because we know that the spirit of the age is passing, but God stays the same. And so, I ask you, where do you land? Are you seeking God's wisdom or letting temporary circumstances form your permanent understanding of the world?

The first question is, "What is the right thing to do?" You can ask what is helpful, meaningful, gratifying, and so on, but only after you've asked, "What is the right thing to do?" Take time to search the Bible. Some decisions are much too permanent an answer for your temporary problem. Bring your questions to the Lord; spend time with Him searching out His ways, and He will give you His wisdom. Examine your vantage points with an awareness that you may see things from the wrong angle. The Bible says, "Ponder the path of thy feet, and let all thy ways be established" (Prov. 4:26). Indeed, our spiritual sight is impaired on this side of heaven, and seeing "through a glass darkly" is our fate (1 Cor. 13:12). But our weak and distorted vision can be corrected through the lens of prayer and Scripture. Human philosophy is driven by envy and selfish ambition. But James said wisdom is pure, peaceable, gentle, reasonable, full of mercy, unwavering, and sincere (James 3:17). These are the characteristics of the wisdom from above.

Heavenly Father, we thank you for being the source of all wisdom. Thank you for giving us your Word as the perfect roadmap. Give us the desire to pursue wisdom as we would a priceless treasure. We want to live in a way that you will be glorified. May we hide your Word in our hearts and apply the principles of Scripture to all we say and do. We ask these things in Jesus' name. Amen.

The Heart of Our Message

THE CENTRAL THEME OF THE BIBLE IS GOD'S FORGIVENESS THROUGH THE death, burial, and resurrection of Jesus Christ (1 Cor. 15:3-4). And when He becomes the heart of our message, people are compelled to respond to the tidings of great joy (Luke 2:10-14). Jesus said, "And I, if I be lifted up from the earth, will draw all men unto me." The apostle John added a comment in the next verse to clarify that Jesus said this, signifying what death he should die (John 12:32-33). Indeed, the lifting up of Jesus would be literal. Our Lord would be raised on a cross and die by crucifixion. Therefore, His first reference was to the Cross. But the death, resurrection, and ascension are all linked to His glorious exaltation and the drawing of sinners to Himself (Rom. 6:9-10). Why? Because the finished work of Calvary is the most beautiful manifestation of love the world has ever known! When the people of Israel suffered from a terrible plague, they could only be saved by looking at a bronze serpent lifted high on a pole (Num. 21). This Old Testament experience foreshadowed the eventual salvation received by those who look to the New Testament Messiah hanging on the cross. Jesus said to Nicodemus, "And as Moses lifted up the serpent in the wilderness, even so, must the Son of man be lifted up" (John 3:14). The ministry of every believer is to point others to the truth that only the cleansing blood of Jesus can remove the deadly curse of Satan (Heb. 9).

Too often, our opinions and traditions are interwoven into the simple message of the Bible. We want others to wear our logo and speak our lingo. We tend to value activity for God over a relationship with God. Recently, I had a conversation with a Christian man who was disheartened over what he described as the constant drumming of a denominational mantra at his church. We discussed the importance of teaching and preaching all of Scripture, not just a few favored topics punctuated by overused verses. I thought of Acts 20:27, where the apostle Paul said, "For I have not shunned to declare unto you all the counsel of God." We cannot choose only those passages of the Bible that merely produce an emotional response. In 2 Timothy 3:16, we are told that all Scripture is inspired and profitable. Every thought in the Bible is divinely empowered (2 Pet. 1:3-4). Every word is purposeful, and each is there for a reason. Every verse leads to a course of action. As the rain produces an earthy harvest, the Word of God will not return void (Isa. 55:10-11). God said, "Let thine heart keep my commandments… write them upon the table of thine heart" (Prov. 3:1-8). The wisdom of Scripture is the refreshment that will sustain us. When we are focused on the message of Christ, the philosophy and rudiments of man-made religion become immaterial.

The joy of the Bible is understanding and worshiping the Author. In John 12, the request of many who gathered to celebrate the Jewish Festival of Passover was to see Jesus. We are told that standing behind the pulpit of the historic Church of the Open Door in downtown Los Angeles and looking out on the massive crowd gives the speaker a feeling of importance. But the sermon to be delivered comes into narrow focus when the minister looks down at a little plaque fixed to the pulpit with the words of John 12:21, "Sir, we would see Jesus." Our objective is not to win arguments about Jesus but to win people for Jesus. Opinions do not transform lives. Jesus does. The message of John the Baptist was, "Behold the Lamb of God" (John 1:29). When we focus on the Cross, the trappings of Christianity and religion grow dim. When we see Jesus in His beauty, things that once consumed our time and energy will give way to being in His presence. The whole story shifts when Jesus is the subject of our conversation.

The wise men who traveled to Bethlehem saw a great light. The star was historical, and it was their privilege to see it. But it was not enough. They wanted to experience the One whom the light represented: the One who had come to redeem all humanity. May we be inspired by more than intellectual curiosity or blessing. May we experience the presence of God made real by the precious blood of Jesus Christ! In Colossians 4:4, the apostle Paul asks people to pray that he proclaims the gospel of Christ in truth and with grace. Then he tells us to make the most of every opportunity to point people to Biblical truth. To the Corinthians, Paul came not with "excellency of speech or of wisdom" but with a resolve to preach "Jesus Christ, and him crucified" (1 Cor. 2:1-2). He made this the central point and essence of all his knowledge. He counted all things of no effect, save only the "excellency of the knowledge of Christ Jesus my Lord" (Phil. 3:8). Paul had no one else to promote, no doctrine to protect, no protocol to preserve, and no organizational structure to uphold. Being rules-oriented is a characteristic of pride, but a believer follows Christ in total surrender.

In Matthew 15:18, Jesus tells of those who pay tribute to God with their words, but their hearts are far from Him. Salvation is a matter of a heart that loves because it is loved, a soul whose treasure is Jesus Christ. The entirety of the Gospel is the Person and the work of Christ, the Holy Spirit, who is allowed complete control. In 2 Timothy 4:3, Paul warns the church as he urges Timothy to keep preaching sound doctrine. He knows that people will want sermons that charm rather than challenge, messages that entertain rather than enlighten. Today, more than ever, churches are abandoning sound doctrine for progressive Christianity and the prosperity gospel. God is not concerned with scratching our itches but transforming us into the image of His Son (Rom. 12:2, 2 Cor. 4:4). The Bible is the mind of God revealed, and if we would know God's mind, we must know what His Book says. The Bible is a book like no other. It is a letter of love that tells us how we can be saved from eternal damnation (Matt. 19). It is our instruction on how to have a personal relationship with Jesus (Rom. 3). It is our direction for this life and all eternity (Ps. 32). Charles Spurgeon said, "It is the whole business of the whole church to preach the gospel to the whole world." It is a privilege to love, learn, and live the entire counsel of God!

Paul testified to the grace of God practically and effectively. He proclaimed the kingdom of God with nothing left unsaid, yet he did not go beyond the Scriptures. Our words are only authoritative as they are evidenced from the biblical text, not of man, but of God. John Newton declared, "If I venture beyond the pole of the Bible, I am on enchanted ground and subject to illusions and distortions." The Pharisees were notorious for adding to, subtracting from, and twisting what God said. Jesus confronted them in Mark 7:9, 13, saying, "Ye reject the commandment of God, that ye may keep your tradition... making the word of God of none effect through your tradition." Our society hates authority, and nothing is as authoritative as the Bible. Some passages of Scripture are hard to understand, and some are hard to believe. But, regardless of how uncomfortable, we must also deal with the problematic verses and how they apply to our lives. Satan desires nothing more than to hinder God's work. And one of the best ways he can accomplish this is by restricting our knowledge of the Bible or altering our understanding of it. Christianity is an active faith (Mark 16:15). The way we show ourselves "approved unto God" (2 Tim. 2:15) is to be doers of His Word, not merely hearers (James 1:22). When we study, teach, and preach all of God's word, we serve and worship Him more completely. We honor God by loving the "lamp unto our feet and the light unto our path" (Ps. 119:105).

We do not bring our agenda to the pulpit. On every page of the Bible, from Genesis to Revelation, the overarching theme is Jesus Christ. Diving deep into Scripture, you understand its timeline and context. You begin to see the story and the glory behind every passage. You know that these events happen to real people, and you will develop a love for the Bible. I cannot think of anything more worthy than understanding Scripture more fully. Pray for the Holy Spirit to illuminate what you read. Jesus said, "Follow me" (Mark 8:34), and the key to following Him is gaining a more precise knowledge of who He is. As we read Scripture, two defining characteristics of Jesus will stand out: faith and love. If we want to become like Him, faith and love must also become our defining characteristics. In Romans 10, we read that faith comes by hearing and hearing by the word of God. Our love for God will increase as we read of His love for us. Jesus is the source of deliverance and salvation, for "there is none other name under heaven given among men, whereby we must be saved" (Acts 4:12). As we become more like Christ, God works through us to share His love and grace with the world. Adrian Rogers says, "When you have said Jesus, you have said it all." People who encounter the risen Christ are transformed. Their outlook on life is altered forever. Through faith, they do not hesitate to face hardship, persecution, and even death. The power of Christ knows no boundary of time or space. Only the blood of Christ can free the soul of man from the bondage of sin and the wrath of God (Heb. 9:13-13, Eph. 1:7). Therefore, Jesus Christ is the heart of our message to the world!

His Burden is Light

THE SCRIBES AND PHARISEES WERE IMPORTANT RELIGIOUS AUTHORITIES of Jesus' day. They were recognized as the champions of God's law, acclaimed for defending the Jewish culture from the influences of Rome. They promoted their ideals in the local synagogues, covering themselves in robes of religious activity. It was a performance to be noticed by men. But observe how these pious leaders came into their role. They seated themselves. God did not call them as He did Moses (Ex. 3:1-14). Theirs was a corrupt authority of hypocrisy and double standard. They opposed anything that threatened their position among the people. In Matthew 23, Jesus warns us about those who sit in the chair of authority to manipulate God's rules. He reveals how the Pharisees imposed suffocating restrictions upon the people while basking in their moral superiority. In Matthew 7:15-17, Christ taught us to examine the teaching and conduct of others to see if they align with God's Word. He said, "Beware of false prophets, which come to you in sheep's clothing, but inwardly they are ravening wolves. Ye shall know them by their fruits." Jesus rejected the Pharisaical lifestyle. He taught a higher law of love, inviting all to come unto Him in humility (James 4:6).

Still today, many teach that the essence of Christianity is following a burdensome set of rules. They promote an image of holiness, contending that allegiance to statutory guidelines is the foundation for righteous living. Very often, their motivation is to enhance their following and status, usually within an organizational structure. But in Acts 15:10, Peter told the legalists, "Now, therefore why tempt ye God, to put a yoke upon the neck of the disciples, which neither our fathers nor we were able to bear? But we believe that through the grace of the

Lord Jesus Christ we shall be saved, even as they." In Matthew 23, the religious leaders' zeal for evangelism did not prove they were right with God. Indeed, they were courageous and energetic messengers. But they were preachers who obsessed with superficial cleansing and ignored the more important principles of justice, love, mercy, and humility (Micah 6:8). If you say something loud enough and long enough, people will start to believe it. Be wary of lively sermons that paint the colors of human opinion. The two most common ingredients in any religion are rules and rituals. We live with a harmful drive to achieve, but God's grace does not demand that we jump through religious hoops or get everything right.

If you are weary and weighed down, the message of hope is that Jesus died in our place, taking the punishment we deserve. He raised Himself from the dead to demonstrate the all-sufficient sacrifice, once - and for all (Rom. 5:8, 2 Cor. 5:21). Let the Scriptures come alive in a brand new way. Understand that the Gospel of Jesus is not about performance but the undeserved favor of God! It is not necessary to have perfect faith for God to answer our prayers (Mark 9:13-42). The image of a hen protecting her brood in Luke 13:34 tells us something about what Jesus wants to do for those living under the legalism that crushes spirits. He wants us to experience His love. He calls us to the righteousness of his holiness, truth, and compassion (2 Cor. 5:21). The Bible says, "Not by works of righteousness which we have done, but according to his mercy he saved us, by the washing of regeneration, and renewing of the Holy Ghost, which he shed on us abundantly through Jesus Christ our Savior" (Titus 3:5-6). And if we receive Jesus as Savior, trusting His death as the entire payment for our sins, we are forgiven, saved, redeemed, reconciled, and justified with God (Rom. 10:9-13, 2 Cor. 5:17-21, Gal. 2:16-21).

The words, "My yoke is easy, and my burden is light," are part of a larger passage (Matt. 11) in which Jesus offers to relieve the system of works laid on the backs of the people. No amount of law-keeping can bridge the gap between our sinfulness and God's holiness. Some may reason there is no difference between the commandments of Jesus and the Old Testament Law because the same God is responsible for both. They may even argue that the commands of our Lord are more burdensome because His sermon on the mount (Matt. 5-7) goes beyond mere outward conformity and deals with the intents of the heart. But what makes Jesus' burden light is that He carried the weight of God's wrath for us (Rom. 5:1-11). His sacrifice at Calvary was the substitution for our sin (2 Cor. 5:21). The Holy Spirit working in our lives is a great exchange of our burdens for the peace of God. And if we live under the power and influence of the Spirit, we no longer carry the burden of figuring out life and eternity on our own. Proverbs 3:5-6 says, "Trust in the Lord with all thine heart, and lean not unto thine own understanding. In all thy ways acknowledge him, and he shall direct thy paths." As we do this, we will receive God's guidance in every situation. He's waiting right now to offer you His yoke. I tell you from experience that laboring under the religion of human philosophy is tiresome, exhausting, and unending. It is also unnecessary. The powerful meaning of Matthew 11:28-30 is that we are liberated from the yoke of death, yielding ourselves to the Lord's good and perfect yoke of life and freedom. Let Jesus take your burdens, fears, and stress. Align your thinking with His and live in the light of God's Word. Let the Bible be your refuge in a world of many opinions. Choose the words of Jesus today. Walk in obedience and experience God's rest for your soul.

The time was the late 1700s. The place was India. The missionary was William Carey. He was a shoe repairman. He had a world map on his wall. India became a burden to him. He left for India, spent forty-two years there, and translated the Bible into twenty-five languages. He became the Father of Missions. What was the secret of William Carey's life? He had a bedridden, crippled sister in England. William wrote his sister daily and shared his missionary heart with her. And, every day, she would take these things to the Lord in prayer. To cast our burden upon God is to rest upon His providence and promise. Cooperate with God's plan for your life. He who bore the responsibility of our sorrows knows what is best for us and will provide it accordingly. Live with an awareness of His presence, and you will find that the sense of companionship lightens your burden. Through prayer, David begins Psalm 55 by expressing a storm of emotions. Then, he desires to escape the intense anxiety of life. Later in the psalm, he emphasizes that God will hear our prayers. Finally, David entrusts it all to God when he says, "Cast thy burden upon the Lord, and he shall sustain thee…" (v22). The song's message is learning to trust that God rescues, saves, and redeems us. Why do we not trust Christ to govern those He has redeemed? What do we do with these circumstances, these stresses, these anxieties? Cast whatever has been given to you on Him, for He cares for you (1 Pet. 5:7).

We pray "Thy will be done" countless times, but do we mean it? Sometimes, these words are hard to say. Why? Because we're not sure how God will answer. We think, "What if His desire doesn't match mine?" We can say the words, but in the end, any misgivings are always a failure to trust. Like Eve in the Garden, we are tempted to doubt. We sometimes listen to lies and entertain them. We doubt God's goodness. We question His love. We listen to a slithering serpent who suggests that God might not want good things for us (Gen. 3). But we must surrender. Surrender is the shattering of our self-will – the unconditional release of our mortal desires to the supernatural will of God. We say, "Yes, Lord!" – no resistance, chafing, or stubbornness – simply submitting ourselves to His direction and authority.

Why do we insist on hanging onto that which our Creator better handles? Nothing falls outside the scope of God's sovereignty, providence, wisdom, and goodness. Therefore, we can trust that His burden is light. Do you believe your past keeps you from the future God has for you? Have you ever thought, "I have forever forfeited the kind of life that could have been mine?" If you have accepted Christ as your Savior, recognize who you are. You are a child of the King! Ignore the unrealistic standards put upon you by others and acknowledge that you belong to Him. Know Whom you're trying to please, make a habit of personal prayer, and give your stress to the One who loves you the most. Until you deal with these issues, you will be hindered by the hesitation of uncertainty. Hear the invitation and the promise of Jesus in Matthew 11:28-30: "Come unto me, all ye that labor and are heavy laden, and I will give you rest." He said, "My yoke is easy, and my burden is light." The collective promise throughout the history of Israel is that God would give rest to His people if they would trust and obey. Unfortunately, they could never enjoy much rest because of their lack of obedience. But now, Jesus enters the picture, and the peace we have longed for has become a reality. God offers to do for us what we are incapable of doing for ourselves. He frees us from the weight of mere religion by offering us a relationship with Jesus Christ.

The yoke of Jesus, as understood by Matthew, was not one of allegiance to a rulebook but of dedication to God. To follow Jesus does not mean we are released from all responsibility. Our love for Christ demands obedience. Jesus said, "If ye love me, keep my commandments" (John 14:15). He came to deliver us from unnecessary burdens. The oppressive yoke of self-righteousness expectations will weigh us down. To live out the agendas of others is burdensome (Acts 5:29). But Jesus' yoke is easy. Not effortless, but appropriate. It is the yoke of repentance and faith followed by a commitment to obey the Holy Spirit. Jesus offers each of us a well-fitted yoke to protect and guide us. He promises a life tailored to our frame, individual needs, strengths, and capabilities. We come to him weary and heavy-laden. He removes those crushing burdens that would destroy us and replaces them with a yoke of appropriate design. The apostle John said, "For this is the love of God, that we keep his commandments: and his commandments are not grievous... and this is the victory that overcomes the world, even our faith" (1 John 5:3-4). In a world of toil, demands, and expectations, God has a better way for His people. His way allows us to experience life's fullness; after this, we are granted eternity in His presence! Today, there is hope if your burdens are too much to bear. Pour out your heart in prayer to our Heavenly Father, holding nothing back. Then, thank Him for His faithfulness; He has always been there, just waiting to help. Dear Lord, your burden is light. Please help us to trust only in you. Make us humble, and may your will be done on earth as it is in heaven!

He Leadeth Me

PERSONAL DEVELOPMENT COACHES OFTEN USE LIFE MAPPING, DRAWING from left to right a timeline of your life. They will record the high points, low points, significant events, etc. They aim to improve specific areas of your life by assessing your strengths and weaknesses. Documenting the past is easy, but predicting what comes next is difficult. We are never sure of the future, but God is (Ps. 90:2). He will give us the direction we need. The Bible is filled with stories about God presenting a course of action based on His goodness and love. The Holy Spirit guides a variety of ways. The first is, through Scripture, the roadmap for every child of God. Then there are prayer, godly counsel, discernment to evaluate circumstances, and peace when decisions are made in faith (Phil. 4:6-7). Abraham was 75 years old when God told him to leave his home and travel to a distant and unknown land he would later receive as his own (Gen. 12). Traveling over 1,500 miles from Ur to Canaan, this righteous man of God listened carefully and obeyed God's directions because his life depended upon it (Heb. 11:8-10). God called Abraham to leave his old life and led him to a new life and future. He promised to bless Abraham and make his descendants into a great nation. Though childless and with no obvious path to becoming a father, Abraham journeyed through the land, worshiping and building altars to God. He praised God in advance for the promises he knew would become a reality! Whatever the situation, the invitation from God is usually the same: "Will you step away from what you know and trust me with what you don't know?"

Psalm 23 describes a journey, not a standstill. Even when the sheep lie down in green pastures, it's a temporary rest for the weary. Our Lord's leadership is always filled with purpose, goodness, and mercy.

He leads His lambs away from the peril of evil and into safety and blessing, for He is righteous in all His ways (Ps. 145:17). The Bible emphasizes God's absolute sovereignty in the work of salvation, but it never downplays human obedience. The Shepherd leads, but the sheep are not passive. God's children follow Him for His name's sake; that is, to demonstrate His character, power, and glory (Ps. 106:8, 1 John 2:12). Wherever we go, we carry our family name. We exist to glorify God's name, not our own. And if we wander from the righteous path, we exhibit a distorted view of who He is and what He does. May we always remember that people learn something about our God through us. His name is made known by the way we live. The word 'path' refers to a course of conduct. The Bible describes what sort of paths are righteous. In the original language, the word for 'righteousness' means adhering to moral standards like honesty, justice, and uprightness. The ways of righteousness are the avenues of safety, wisdom, fairness, integrity, and eternal blessings (Prov. 4:10-18, 11:3). How does God light our paths? The Bible is the foundation of instruction for all of life, and the Holy Spirit will illuminate our minds (Rom. 12:2) to a remembrance of what we have read in Scripture. He will bring to our memory what verses we need – when we need them (John 12:16, 14:26).

Before His ascension back into heaven, Jesus taught many things to His disciples. Then He told them, "When he, the Spirit of truth, is come, he will guide you into all truth" (John 16:13). The Holy Spirit will never instruct more rapidly than we can receive the lessons. The great promise of the New Testament is that all believers will be taught by God (Eph. 1:7; Col. 1:10) according to our state of condition and our measure of understanding (Eph. 4). There are promises of strength in the Bible that we will never understand until we are weak; words of protection that we can never know until we face times of danger. There are consolations for sickness whose comfort we can never grasp so long as we enjoy good health. Promises of our Lord's companionship will never be fully appreciated until we are alone. And how can we ever apply the words of comfort for old age when we are yet in our youth? Many things in Scripture had little meaning to me in my earlier years because I had no experience preparing my heart to receive them. But now, they are the rod and staff I lean upon. I have been through enough to know He will take good care of me!

What happens in a Christian's life is nothing short of the mercy and glory of the Almighty God. Only as we walk with Him, step by step, will he reveal his plan for us. If we could look into the years and see all that is to come, perhaps seeing great prosperity would rob us of our dependency on God. Maybe the impending sorrows would overwhelm us and steal our courage to endure. The Lord leads, and we can watch Him work in ways that only He can (Act. 12:1-17). Experiencing God's closeness and knowing how much God loves us is essential! We can be confident that God will show us the path of life. God's way is the best, but it's not always the easiest way. People often get confused when they start following Christ because they are told their lives would be fantastic if they put their faith in Jesus. Indeed, our lives will be extraordinary if we follow Jesus, but the Bible is clear that our lives will not be effortless, calm, or unopposed. God never causes temptations in our lives, but he does allow them to test our faith and bring glory to Himself. God never wants our circumstances to trump His work! James 1:11 tells us, "Blessed is the man that endures temptation: for when he is tried, he shall receive the crown of life, which the Lord hath promised to them that love him."

Proverbs 3:5-6 says, "Trust in the Lord with all thine heart, and lean not unto thine own understanding. In all thy ways acknowledge him, and he shall direct thy paths." This may be one of the most frequently quoted Scripture verses about God's guidance. However, when it says God will "direct thy paths," what does it mean? Is it a general assurance that faithful believers will be shown godly directions? Or is this a promise that each individual will receive specific instruction for their life choices? The idea of a general assurance seems to fall short in light of the rest of Scripture. Indeed, an all-knowing and all-powerful God can encourage us along righteous paths. But He can also precisely guide our decisions since He knows the best choice among several possible pathways. A shepherd doesn't just send the sheep off in a general direction, hoping things go well. He goes ahead of them and guides them along the specific paths that he knows will be best for them. The author of the twenty-third Psalm learned a lot about caring for sheep.

Under the inspiration of the Holy Spirit, David went beyond the basic model of a shepherd leading his flock to emphasize God's guidance for individuals. Jesus, speaking of Himself, said this about His care for us: "The sheep hear his voice: and he calleth his own sheep by name, and leadeth them out. And when he putteth forth his own sheep, he goeth before them, and the sheep follow him: for they know his voice. And a stranger will they not follow, but will flee from him: for they know not the voice of strangers."

So, are specified outcomes included in God's plan for your life? This is where many Christians get confused, believing He will reveal it all to them like a road map, highlighted with all the right turns to make. Well, God does have a plan for our lives, but He does not reveal it to us as a highlighted map. He may not tell much (or any) of it ahead of schedule. The "way of wisdom" referred to in Proverbs 4:11 is simply living according to God's Word. We walk in obedience in the areas where God has revealed His will for us in Scripture. In the places where God has not explicitly made His thoughts known, we rely on the Holy Spirit dwelling within. We ask for advice and counsel from godly believers and pray for insight to analyze our circumstances properly. Study the life of Jesus. Why? Because God desires us to become more like Christ (Rom. 8:28-29), correct choices will lead in that direction. This sovereign God knows our abilities, shortcomings, and limitations and controls all the events and circumstances we encounter. Our responsibility is to obey Him in all we do. Then, we can be sure that whatever unfolds is God's plan for our lives. In all of God's leading, He wants to fill the earth with the knowledge of His glory (Hab. 2:14). Therefore, before making any significant decision, the question is, "Will my choice glorify God?" In Romans 11:36, Apostle Paul said, "For of him, and through him, and to him, are all things to whom be glory forever. Amen." As born-again Christians, we no longer exist to serve our agenda. We cannot claim the right to follow our path to our goals. Instead, Christ redeemed us, meaning He paid for us (1 Cor. 6:19-20). As Paul puts it, "Whether we live therefore, or die, we are the Lord's" (Rom. 14:8).

The God with infinite wisdom and knows everything from beginning to end promises to be our counselor. Psalm 32:8 declares, "I will instruct thee and teach thee in the way which thou shalt go;

I will guide thee with mine eye." If one of my children asked me for guidance and wisdom, I would give them the best advice possible. I want my children to be blessed and happy. I want them to make the best decisions. How much more, if we ask our generous heavenly Father to guide us, will he give us wisdom and guidance? On every long journey, there are many moments when we get tired, impatient, fearful, or disoriented, and we wonder if we've lost our way. Following Jesus takes us beyond what's familiar or comfortable. But God promises to keep us on the right path through life's challenges. He only asks that we let go of our ideas and assumptions of what's right and good and give Him complete control (Ps. 56:3). When we delight ourselves in the Lord, He will establish our steps (Ps. 37:23). If we humbly seek Him in prayer and reading Scripture, we will find our way. When we believe in Jesus, He not only saves us but also takes up residence within us by his Holy Spirit. He is continually with us. He never lets us go; he holds our right hand. He promises to guide us throughout this life and receive us to heavenly glory (Ps. 73:24). Our wonderful Lord will get us safely to our eternal destination!

Lift Jesus Higher

ANCIENT ISRAEL WAS A NATION WAITING FOR THE COMING OF THE Messiah. God had chosen Israel to be his people and promised He would be their God. But, because of their sin, the people suffered. Conquered, plundered, and their temple destroyed, they ended up in captivity. Psalm 85 is the prayer of a sorrowful nation. In verse 7, the Psalmist asks for mercy: "Shew us thy mercy. O Lord, and grant us thy salvation." God answered David's prayer. He did not abandon His people forever into exile. Amid its national tragedy, Isaiah speaks of hope. God tells the prophet to comfort His people, to go up to the high mountain and proclaim the good tidings (Isa. 40). "Prepare ye the way of the Lord; make straight in the desert a highway for our God," was the voice of one crying in the wilderness (v3). Foretelling the Messiah's coming and bringing hope to Israel during a challenging time, the prophet Isaiah played an essential role in God's plan; more than 700 years after Isaiah's prophetic vision, the voice of one in the wilderness reappears. In the New Testament, we find John the Baptist preaching the baptism of repentance for the forgiveness of sins (Mark 1:1-28). John humbly acknowledged his inferior position as only "a voice." When John said, "There cometh one mightier than I," he admitted that his speaking part was not worth mentioning compared to the work of Christ. This man of God was chosen not to gain a reputation for himself but to preach Jesus. He understood that he was not the focal point of his ministry. These days, many desire to hear a word of comfort from God's messengers. As one preacher said, "Preach to broken hearts, and you will never lack an audience." Today, we join our voices with his, proclaiming the message of salvation to a lost and dying world. To what end? That the glory of the Lord may be revealed (Isa. 40:5).

163

John the Baptist is an amazing man. He was set apart from his mother's womb for a holy purpose. His parents were Zacharias and Elisabeth, both from the priestly family of Aaron. The Bible says, "They were both righteous before God, walking in all the commandments and ordinances of the Lord blameless" (Luke 1:6). Elisabeth was barren. She and her husband were advanced in years. Still, God demonstrated He is the One who does great and mighty miracles (Luke 1:11-20). What can we learn from the life of John the Baptist? First, we realize that God does the impossible to fulfill His purpose. We see humility, zeal for God's work, and passion for delivering the message of God to the people. We find in Matthew 3:1-2 that John was enthusiastic and motivated to preach the Kingdom of God. He was unafraid to stand for righteousness, even in death (Matt. 14:1-12). His ministry pointed others to the Savior of the world. And when it was time for Jesus to enter the scene, John was humble enough to step aside and let the ministry of his Lord begin. He knew his mission; it was to prepare the people for the coming of One Greater (Matt. 3:11). John the Baptist was "a burning and a shining light" for his season (John 5:35), and he teaches us what it means to live wholly devoted to God.

Influential people were giving the preacher a lot of attention, and if John wasn't operating within the power of God, how would he have responded to the question of who he was? There are several things he could have truthfully said. "Well, gentlemen, I am the son of a well-known priest named Zacharias. I'm sure you have heard of him, and it's apparent that you have heard of my ministry. I've been preaching in the desert and baptizing multitudes of people, perhaps even more than any other man. I am not the Messiah, but he is my cousin. I have many things to say in my sermons, so I hope you all will listen and learn." John could have heaped accolades upon himself more than anyone else. He was related to the Lord. He was a fulfillment of Old Testament prophecy. He had a band of disciples who followed his teaching. In today's world, it would have been easy for the Baptizer to place an improper emphasis on celebrity, pageantry, denominational affiliation, size, and numbers while neglecting spiritual development. Yet, the cry of his heart was, "Make straight the way of the Lord." In other words, 'It's not about me; the King is coming; prepare your hearts to receive Him.' We are instruments through which the Word of God flows to the world. Whether we realize it or not, hardly a day goes by when we aren't asked in one way or another, "Who are you?" John sought to turn men's attention away from himself to the Lord. The messenger insisted that all sufficiency exists in the God of heaven! He didn't claim to be who he was not. He didn't exalt himself beyond what he had been called to do. He was not distracted. In John's interactions with the religious leaders, he didn't call attention to himself but to the "Lamb of God, which taketh away the sin of the world" (John 1:29). John was not perfect, but his love for the Lord was perfect. Jesus was the center of his life. What an incredible servant of the Lord.

Our message to the world isn't to give God a passing glance. No, we invite people to "behold your God" (Isa. 40:9). Behold His strong hand, gentle leadership, and power to the faint. Exalt the Almighty who has measured the waters in the hollow of His hand. Worship the One who measured heaven with a span, calculated the dust of the earth in a measure, and weighed the mountains in a balance (Isa. 40:12). We speak of the greatness and character of Jesus Christ. Without question, Paul was a man who could reason and debate persuasively. But he didn't use that approach in preaching the gospel. He determined to emphasize the crucified Christ (1 Cor. 2:2). Paul did not reject preaching, even persuasive preaching. His sermon before Agrippa in Acts 26 is a remarkable example of compelling sermonizing. Still, Paul rejects confidence in the preacher's ability to persuade with human wisdom. Many Bible scholars believe Paul had the equivalent of two doctorate degrees in theology by the time he was twenty-one. He studied at the feet of a chief Jewish rabbi. Paul was brilliant, and he spoke several languages. He was a man who wrote with great insight into the full scope of theology. Nevertheless, he said the focal point of his teaching, preaching, and ministry was "Jesus Christ and Him crucified." Paul was saying that in all of his education, in all of his preaching, in all of his missionary activity, the central point of importance was the cross of Christ. The testimony concerning Jesus and His salvation is so supremely excellent that it cannot be conveyed with mere human eloquence, rhetoric, intellect, or philosophy. The gospel message must be delivered in the divine power of the Holy Ghost (1 Cor. 2:10). This is the voice of one crying in the wilderness of sin.

It wasn't enough for the shepherds to see the angels. They wanted to know the One who sent the angels. Consider John and Andrew. For them, it wasn't enough to listen to John the Baptist. And when they saw Jesus, they followed Him. As for Simeon, seeing Jesus was enough. He said, "Lord, now lettest thou thy servant depart in peace, according to thy word: For mine eyes have seen thy salvation" (Luke 2:29-30). All who sought Jesus found Him. He wanted to be seen and known. That's the reason He came to earth! God is a rewarder of those who diligently seek Him (Heb. 11:6), and the reward goes to those who settle for nothing less than Jesus himself. How do we lift Jesus higher? How do we lead souls to a saving knowledge of Christ? What is our part in the process? A common phrase in Christian circles comes to mind: Exalt the Lord. To exalt means to praise, acclaim, worship, magnify or glorify. It also means to raise, heighten, or elevate. In essence, it means to lift the Lord. To magnify his name. To praise him. To glorify him. The phrase "lift/exalt the Lord" refers to a state of worship. Christ's character becomes evident to others when He is lifted high. The world doesn't read the Bible. The world reads Christians. When onlookers saw the boldness of Peter and John, they "took knowledge of them, that they had been with Jesus" (Acts 4:13). Many of the wise men, scribes, and debaters during the apostle's day were appealing to signs or utilizing the wisdom of that age. But Paul hid himself and his preaching behind the cross. Today, we preach the responsibility of man's sin and the righteous demands of God concerning man's sin. We preach His resurrection and the necessity of a response to God through Christ alone. On July 9, 1876, Charles Haddon Spurgeon declared in his sermon, "A sermon without Christ in it is like a loaf of bread without any flour in it. No Christ in your sermon, sir? Then go home, and never preach again until you have something worth preaching." Presbyterian minister Mark A. Matthews (1867-1940) often prayed before preaching: "Lord, hide me behind the cross, lift me out of self, and teach me to speak the truth."

The author of Hebrews gives sound doctrine when he says, "Consider Jesus." "Looking unto Jesus, the author and finisher of our faith" (Heb. 12:2) is continuous guidance for every day and at any moment. There is peace, joy, and salvation in a Christward gaze. "We would see Jesus" (John 12:21) should be our cheerful refrain before any prayer or study of Scripture. Imagine these words coming from non-believers: "Sir/Madam, we wish to see Jesus." As Moses lifted up the serpent in the wilderness, even so, must the Son of man be lifted up (John 3:14). The purpose of teaching and preaching is to point others to Christ and to make God's glory known. Charles Spurgeon was probably the most famous preacher of his time. A visitor from America eager to see the famous 'prince of preachers' traveled to England to hear him. Afterward, the American stood in the church lobby, talking with his friend. Not knowing Spurgeon was standing nearby listening, the Englishman asked what his friend thought of the sermon. He replied, "What a preacher!" According to the story, Spurgeon began to weep. A church member asked him what was wrong. Spurgeon replied, "I wish he had said what a Savior!" Jesus said, "And I, if I be lifted up from the earth, will draw all men unto me" (John 12:32). When Jesus spoke these words, the Bible tells us that he was speaking of how he would die. Therefore, our mission is to "preach Christ crucified" (1 Cor. 1:23) to a world that desperately needs Him. Lift Jesus higher!

Loving the Next Generation

CHILDREN COME INTO THE WORLD AND START ASKING QUESTIONS AS soon as they can talk. As adults, we use our knowledge and experience to help them understand their world. In time, they get better at interpreting things for themselves, for we all grow into a place where we can figure things out independently. Yet I can recall times when, had I talked to an older, wiser Christian, I would have seen more clearly what was happening and made better decisions. In Psalm 78, the writer Asaph knew that what the older generation had received, they needed to pass on to the younger generation. He was concerned about teaching them three things: the praises of the Lord, the strength of God, and His wonderful works (v4). Asaph knew the importance of telling the next generation that God is worthy of our adoration and thanksgiving. He recognized the obligation of telling them that His power is above all and that He is active in the lives of His people (Rev. 4:11). Oh, how we must speak of these things often!

The purpose of discipleship is captured in the first eight verses of the second-longest Psalm, where we are commanded to teach "the generation to come" about the wondrous works of the Lord. Notice how remarkably honest the psalm is about instructing younger people to avoid some things. What Asaph had in mind were sins that displeased God. Namely, ingratitude, testing God, and doubting His power and care. Therefore, he began by describing one of the greatest of God's wonderful works – the written Word. I believe the responsibility of every Christian is to help people love the Bible and then share their own stories. We who have learned from our experiences should help others enjoy the victories of life while avoiding the mistakes we have made. We need to help those coming behind us to make sense of life

168

and understand the God who loves them. We must help them avoid what separates us from God and all He has for us. The purpose of communicating to the next age group is that they will learn to trust God for themselves, obey His commandments, and claim His promises. God wants to use us to help others. Love those around you and engage them in honest conversations. Challenge them to see themselves honestly and confront the truth about their lives. Cast a vision for them. And when God does His work in them, you will have helped make a disciple! Men and women who take time to invest in younger people are rare. But when we connect by sharing, we collectively grow to be more like Jesus.

The psalmist wanted the younger population to understand God and believe He would provide for His children in all circumstances. In 1933 – the middle of the Great Depression – a young Irishman named J. Edwin Orr left a good-paying job, and, with no fixed source of income, he trusted that God would provide for him and his mother. He planned to travel around Great Britain with the message of prayer, salvation, and revival. He left Belfast with 2 shillings and 8 pence – about 65 cents. He had a bicycle, a change of clothes, and a Bible. He spent the next year traveling to every Great Britain county, organizing 300 prayer groups dedicated to praying for revival. He wrote a book about it all and finally convinced a publisher to take it – after being rejected 17 times. That first book, titled 'Can God—?', was based on Psalm 78:19 and published in 1934. It sold hundreds of thousands of copies and was a tremendous inspiration to Christians in that day. Orr's book and his life were remarkable demonstrations of the fact that God can prepare a table in the wilderness. When Israel crossed the Jordan into the land the Lord promised to give them, Joshua took twelve stones from the river and set them up on the west side. He did this so that "When your children shall ask their fathers in time to come, saying, What mean these stones? Then ye shall let your children know, saying, Israel came over this Jordan on dry land… that all the people of the earth might know the hand of the Lord, that it is mighty: that ye might fear the Lord your God forever" (Joshua 4:21-24). The elders were to tell them the miraculous works God had done for them in the past. It is the privilege and responsibility of every follower of Jesus Christ to faithfully pass along the truth about God - His will, His work, His ways - to the next generations. Psalm

78 is a narrative of God's wonderful works for the ancient Israelites, how ungrateful they were, how God justly punished them for their sins (v62), and how graciously He spared them with compassion and mercy (v72). What is shown throughout the psalm is God's faithfulness to his people despite their unfaithfulness. Today, we know, love, and trust God because people in every past generation were committed to fulfilling the Psalm 78 mandate.

We all tend to forget, which leads to doubt and ultimately to unbelief and rebellion. But if we remember who God is and all He has done, we will remain faithful, even in difficult times. As athletes pass the baton in a relay race, we must pass biblical principles on to our kids. This begins in the home (Eph. 6:4). But the church's role is also essential. As believers, we are part of a community of faith. And the local church is the vital, local expression of that community. The church can never replace the task of the family, but the family cannot do it alone without the church. If we fail to teach our children and nurture them spiritually, then we are refusing to make known what God has given to us. If we hide the revelation of God from our children, we do them a severe injustice. Spiritual nurture is their due. It is their right. It is their proper inheritance from us. What parent would hide his children's inheritance from them? Someone nurtured us in our faith, and now we owe it to the next generation to teach them the works of God. We must share with our children the wonderful things God has done (Deut. 11:18-22): commendable things, powerful things, and things of wonder. We should be amazed at God's faithfulness, as should our children!

Share personal stories of how God has answered prayer in your life. Let them see God's influence in your response to everyday struggles and trials. Most of all, share with them what God has done by sending his Son Jesus to bring us salvation (John 3:16). Teach your children to praise God for his mighty deeds. Our greatest hope for the next generation is that they will fully trust in God. There is a battle going on for the spiritual lives of our children, and we must not turn our backs on them. God has given us a story to share. Lead them to a saving knowledge of Jesus Christ. Tell of His provision, His faithfulness, His love. Recount the story of your conversion. Asaph taught in a way that caused him to examine his own heart. Be honest with younger people about your struggles and tell them how God brought you through. Teach the truth so that young people will put their hope in God. A changed life is the goal of our testimony, not just more knowledge. Keep your stories pointing to God's goodness, who He is, and what you've seen Him do in your life. The aim of passing on a heritage of faith is that those taught might set their confidence in the Holy Spirit and be brought to prayerful reliance on the Word of God. The Bible contains stories of the Lord's faithfulness that span many generations. God always takes care of His people. His love is boundless and unending. He has not changed. He is our provider, and He keeps His promises. Tell the next generation about the promises God has fulfilled in your life!

Stories are powerful, and anyone who has encountered Christ has a powerful story. Sharing how you came to know Jesus and what he has done in your life will encourage others seeking to draw closer to God. Your spiritual story, whether it's about you coming to Christ or something God has done for you, is one of the most effective ways to share the love of Jesus. The apostle Paul never shied away from sharing his conversion story. He started with his life before Christ. He spoke about the moment of his conversion. He told how the transformation changed his outlook on life (Gal. 1:11-24). Whenever you tell of how you came to have a personal relationship with Jesus Christ, you give honor and glory to God. Your testimony, regardless of how ordinary or spectacular you think it is, is a story about God's character. It is your eyewitness account of how God rescued you from sin and death through Christ and changed your life. When you share your story with others, you help them understand what God is like and what He can do. Pray for younger people who may be facing experiences similar to yours. The intentional, specific prayers of older people are a powerful connecting influence. A remarkable woman in my life has wonderfully helped a child of mine, and I am so thankful for her. Invest in the lives of others. Give them space. Remember, our role is to take a step of faith and leave the results to God. The world is changing, and the generation gap is getting wider. But despite all the changes, the Biblical constants of faith, grace, and love remain. These are the things that we should be teaching the next generation. Our goal should be to instill in them a love for God.

We who cherish the old, rugged Cross should want our kids to love it, too! And if they have a strong foundation of faith, they will be better equipped to handle life's challenges. We can help them develop this foundation by teaching them about God's grace with words and a lifestyle. Never forget that the power of love is the most significant influence in changing lives. By showing our kids how much we love them, we give them something tangible to hold onto when life gets tough. Your story is unique, and it has the power to reach someone who may be searching for answers. When you share your testimony, you're giving someone a glimpse into who Jesus is and what He can do in their life. Be genuine in your faith. Don't be afraid to share your struggles and triumphs. As we teach young people about Jesus and His love, we are helping them grow into compassionate and caring adults who will make a difference in God's world. Pray for an opportunity to share with someone this week. Why? Because the next generation needs to hear your story – and the gospel of Jesus Christ!

God Orders My Steps

W<small>E</small> <small>GET UP IN THE MORNING AND VISUALIZE THE ACTIVITIES OF THAT</small> day. We have an idea of how the day will go and hope it matches our expectations. According to Proverbs 16:9, we make our plans, but God ultimately determines what happens. There are many lessons that God's people must learn, and often, it takes a lifetime to pass the various tests the Lord sets before us (James 1:2-3). Learning to trust God and wait upon the Lord is rarely easy, but it is always best. Sometimes, we are deficient and nearsighted, but God, in His grace, leads us to the most beautiful destination. If we trust the Lord's guidance, He will get us to a place of fulfillment we could not have thought possible – not only in this world but in the eternal ages to come.

I have always been intentional with scheduling my day. Maybe it's because I need a sense of control in an otherwise chaotic world. But I must ask myself: What happens when my schedule is interrupted? How do I react when the Holy Spirit prompts me to speak with someone or do something not on my list? Can God trust me to follow what seems like a detour? Does He have enough confidence that I will trade my will for His? I pray He does. The apostle James wrote, "Go to now, ye that say, today or tomorrow we will go into such a city, and continue there a year, and buy and sell, and get gain: whereas ye know not what shall be on the morrow…" Instead of proudly assuming that our plans are absolute, we ought to follow the counsel James gives next. He says, "For that ye ought to say, If the Lord will, we shall live, and do this, or that" (James 4:13-15). God has a plan. Reading the creation story, you see His plan in action (Gen. 1:1- 31). When the fracturing of the world happened through the sin of mankind (Gen. 3:1-24), God would have a plan for our salvation through the coming of Jesus to earth. God gave detailed instructions to Moses, Joshua, David, and others. He provided clear instructions for all offerings, documented in the book of Leviticus, and the law was given with a specific purpose in mind. There are plenty of examples of people in the Bible creating God-inspired plans. Nehemiah took a strategic approach to reconstructing the walls of Jerusalem. He evaluated the situation, calculated the cost, and appointed others to join him. In short, he prayerfully followed God's plan. The life of Jesus was all part of God's plan to bring redemption to humanity (Luke 19:10). Proverbs 16:1-9 reflects on the heart's intention to make plans and the Lord's rule over that plan.

Life doesn't always go as we intend, and we are tempted to take matters into our own hands. But Proverbs 3:5-6 tells us to "Trust in the Lord with all thine heart; and lean not unto thine own understanding." Jeremiah 29:11 has brought me much comfort in times of uncertainty: "For I know the thoughts that I think towards you, saith the Lord, thoughts of peace, and not of evil, to give you an expected end." I have found that God will bring good out of a hopeless situation. Allow the Spirit to move in and through your daily schedule. Begin with prayer and Bible study. As we spend time with God, we become more sensitive to His voice and leading. We learn to recognize His direction, and we sense His peace. Expect the unexpected and trust the Lord in all things. He loves and cares for us so much that He takes pleasure in guiding our actions (Ps. 37:23). God is operative in all that comes to pass. His hands may be hidden, but His rule is absolute. His will extends to all places and all occurrences, and He is working all things for His purpose and glory (Eph. 1). Christian friend, you can take comfort in the knowledge that all your days unfold in the care of a loving Father. And once you get this melody in your heart, you will sing it repeatedly.

The average American walks 3,000 to 4,000 steps daily, roughly 1.5 to 2 miles. For a believer, each one is ordered by God, another way of saying that nothing is governed by the hand of fate. God guides events according to His eternal purposes (Eph. 1:11). What appears to be mere circumstance is the outworking of God's plans. We don't have the big picture of what God is doing and why He is doing it. (How unsearchable are his judgments and unfathomable His ways - Rom. 11:33). Life is untidy by its very nature. We are not in charge. Emotionally, we are often overwhelmed and find that things we thought we had control over have unraveled before us. Left to ourselves, we are confused. We wonder why God doesn't do something about the evil in the world, the problems in our families, or the illnesses in our bodies. Indeed, the prophet Habakkuk bemoaned injustice, violence, strife, and conflict in the land because the wicked seemed to win above those seeking to do the right thing. He was concerned about God's timing and apparent tolerance of evil and injustice: "O Lord, how long shall I cry, and thou will not hear... and thou wilt not save?" (Hab. 1:2). But in the following verses, God's point is clear: "You may not like my answer, but I am in control, and I will take care of the problem. I am not indifferent to sin." How should we respond to this reminder of God's sovereignty? Notice the tone of the book shifts from bewilderment to praise. In chapter 3, we discover that the complaints with which the prophet had begun – "How long and why?" – are now replaced with waiting patiently in fervent prayer. The majesty of God has brought Habakkuk to his feet. You see, the God of the Bible demands attention, and the display of his sovereign power causes men and women to stand in awe and put their hands over their mouths. This is the proper response. It is vitally important for us to keep our faith concerning God's activity. Finally, the prophet of God rejoices (3:18-19), not because the circumstances are fixed, but because he gained eternal perspective. God orders our steps by securing our footing. The Psalmist says God set his feet upon a rock and established his goings... and "blessed is the man that maketh the Lord his trust..." (Ps. 40:2- 4).

Commenting on Psalm 37:23-24, Charles Spurgeon says that for the godly man: "All his course of life is graciously ordained, and in loving-kindness, all is fixed, settled and maintained. No reckless fate; no fickle chance rules us; our every step is the subject of divine decree." Spurgeon compares God's delight in a righteous relationship to a parent who is "pleased with the tottering footsteps of their babies." He said, "All that concerns a saint is interesting to his heavenly Father. God loves to view the holy strivings of a soul pressing forward to the skies." God promises to direct my path (Prov. 3:5-6), guide my way (Ps. 48:14), and lead me on my path (Ps. 25:5). My steps are ordered to a deeper faith and trust in Him; a greater revelation of Him and greater obedience to Him.

Two scrolls with Chinese characters graced the mantel of Hudson Taylor's (1832–1905) home. The calligraphy depicted two names that reminded Taylor of God's provision: Ebenezer and Jehovah-Jireh. The first comes from 1 Samuel 7:12: "Then Samuel took a stone and set it up between Mizpah and Shen, and called the name of it Ebenezer, saying, Hitherto hath the Lord helped us." The second is found in Genesis 22:14: "And Abraham called the name of that place Jehovah-Jireh: as it is said to this day, In the mount of the Lord it shall be seen." Ebenezer is a depiction of God's past provision. Jehovah-Jireh is a designation of God's provision promised for the future. The verses are often cited as among Taylor's favorites. Together, they shape an overarching narrative of God's salvation story in Scripture and give us insight into Taylor's conviction to live by faith. The truth is I cannot live a victorious Christian life, or any part of the Christian life, without the help of the Holy Spirit. I can look back over my life and see a trail of failed attempts to do things with my strength. The Lord defines who - and Whose - I am. Romans 8:14, "For as many as are led by the Spirit of God, they are the sons of God." My most significant efforts to live a godly life will always fall short. But if the Spirit leads me, I am not under the law (Gal. 5:18). The book of Acts is filled with examples of men and women being led by the Spirit. He actively led every aspect of their lives, helping them make better decisions. The Holy Spirit's leading will always align with Holy Scripture. If the impulse to do something does not align with God's Word, you can be sure it is not of God. If I outrun Scripture, I will have to come back again. If I go beyond the boundaries of the right road, I will lose my way.

The Lord ordered Job's steps so that He might be glorified. Job's appointed trials were not a result of God's neglect nor a reflection of Job's transgressions. It was a process of refining with a purpose. We are better equipped to face the purifying furnace of affliction in the knowledge that God is working all things for our good (Job 23:9-10, Rom. 8:28). The apostle Peter said, "Wherefore let them that suffer according to the will of God commit the keeping of their souls to him in well doing, as unto a faithful Creator" (1 Peter 4:19). Free thinking and free living are the desires of ungodly people. But when the grace of God has renewed the heart, the soul finds its true freedom in obedience to Christ's commands. Just as God arranges the universe and the stars keep their appointed courses, so we take our proper places and are kept in them, joyfully obedient to the will of the Almighty. It is one of the marks of God's grace when we willingly put ourselves under his command. According to Luke 10:31, a biblical definition of coincidence would be "what occurs by God's providential arrangement of circumstances." What appears to us as random chance is overseen by a sovereign God (Matt. 10:29, Luke 12:7). Citing happenstance is how we explain unexpected events and surprise meetings. But just because we are surprised does not mean that God is. In ways known only to God, He takes even our mistakes and unplanned events, weaving them together to fulfill His purposes (Prov. 16:33, 19:21). When the Psalmist prayed, "Order my steps in thy word and let not any iniquity have dominion over me" (Ps. 119:133), I believe he was asking the Lord to turn the everyday actions of his life into a holy service for God. I want to live the same way.

Dear Lord, thank you for pastors, friends, and family members who played a specific role in my life. You have ordered my steps, and I am so thankful. May your commands become a conviction of my heart. And may that conviction be demonstrated by how I live. In Jesus' name, I pray. Amen.

A Home, Eternal
in the Heavens

THE APOSTLE PAUL TOLD THE BELIEVERS IN CORINTH, "FOR WE KNOW
that if our earthly house of this tabernacle were dissolved, we have a
building of God, a house not made with hand, eternal in the heavens" (2
Cor. 5:1). He describes our existence in this fallen world as a temporary
dwelling place that is not built to last forever. Jesus told His disciples,
"In my Father's house are many mansions: if it were not so, I would
have told you. I go to prepare a place for you. And if I go and prepare
a place for you, I will come again, and receive you unto myself, that
where I am, there ye may be also" (John 14:1-3). What an incredible
promise for all who have chosen to follow Christ (Matt. 16:24)! Life on
earth is a momentary assignment described as a vanishing vapor (James
4:14), withering grass (1 Pet. 1:24), a shadow that declines (Ps. 102:11),
burning smoke (Ps. 102:3), a wind that passes through (Ps. 78:39), and
a flower that fades (Isa. 40:6). The Bible uses words like alien, pilgrim,
foreigner, stranger, visitor, and traveler to describe our brief stay on
earth. God's Word is straightforward about the danger of embracing
the values, priorities, and lifestyles of the world around us (Matt. 16:25).
We are ambassadors for Christ in a foreign country. We must not betray
the King and kingdom to which we belong (2 Cor. 5:20). The greatest
heroes of faith view this life as a temporary shelter while anticipating
their promised reward (Heb. 11). We are not satisfied here because we're
not supposed to be. We were created for something better!

He was an elderly missionary who spent his life in Africa
establishing medical outposts and caring for the people. Eventually,
the time came for him to retire and return home. His health had been

strained by years of deprivation and hard work. Because he had never accumulated any resources and had no pension to draw upon, he barely managed to scrape together the money necessary to buy passage aboard a ship sailing to New York City. As they entered the harbor, the old missionary could see a tremendous fanfare in the distance. A band played, and people lined up to wave and watch. As the boat neared the American shore, he became even more saddened, for he could see a massive crowd of admirers waiting for another man traveling on his vessel. The band blared its welcome as the city's mayor and many other dignitaries lined up to honor this man. Of course, no one was there to meet the old missionary. He had neither family nor friends left to greet him. So, he slipped off the ship and found a cheap place to rest for the night. But that evening, the man's spirit broke. He decided to kneel and lay his deep disappointment before God. He told the Lord he had spent an entire lifetime in Africa with nothing to show. He told God he felt especially bitter about the other man's homecoming. The President of the United States had merely gone big game hunting and was welcomed home with a grand celebration. But when the missionary arrived home, no one even cared. In the quietness of his heart, a gentle, loving voice whispered, "My child, you're not home yet." Whose approval are you seeking? Whose applause and welcome do you most hope to receive? "We are troubled on every side, yet not distressed; we are perplexed, but not in despair, persecuted, but not forsaken, cast down, but not destroyed... for our light affliction, which is but for a moment, worketh for us a far more exceeding and eternal weight of glory" (2 Cor. 4:8-17). Brothers and sisters, we are not home yet!

How does a traveling pilgrim sing and serve? Where does his heart belong, and how does he live? Having no lasting city here, he looks for the heavenly city to come (Heb. 13:14). He does not become so fond of this world that he's indifferent to the needs of others. This foreigner will tell you that everything is held loosely in an open hand. He will speak of another city that is coming, one that God is building, one that will last forever, one in which he will dwell eternally with his Lord. Friend, we are looking for another city, and we need help getting there. We can only approach the heavenly Jerusalem with the One who abides there (John 10:1-5). Just as Jesus went out of Jerusalem to suffer beyond the city walls and outside the gate, so must we bear the reproach of the crucified One (Heb. 12-13). The Cross, that gruesome last stop, is the means of salvation and access to our eternal home. The Bible says the sinless Lamb of God who knew no sin became sin for us that we, through Him, might become the righteousness of God (2 Cor. 5:21). The way to that heavenly City begins at Calvary, for Jesus Christ will lead us there in resurrection power! Just as His natural body merged with the spiritual body that left earthly burial clothes lying neatly (John 20:1-10), "we shall be also in the likeness of his resurrection" (Rom. 6:5). While Jesus left His grave attire behind, Lazarus came forth bound by his (John 11:44). Notice the corresponding difference: Lazarus returned to the same life as before; Jesus did not. The Almighty God, our resurrection life (John 11:25), had risen from His tomb!

Temporary housing has challenges. Our earthly accommodations have never been under as much pressure as today. We suffer emotional distress and restlessness. We experience social isolation, sleep disturbances, economic burdens, and health issues of every kind. This worldly environment is unsuitable for a child of God. I remember singing with the church congregation in my younger days:

> I'm longing for home, for the sun's going down.
> I want to go where sweet rest can be found.
> I'm just about through with this old house of clay.
> I'm leaving this world for Glory someday.

The unsettled nature of temporary lodging causes stress and anxiety. But living with Heaven in view is a source of strength and encouragement. Focus on the everlasting joy of the Lord. Your permanent home will be far greater than anything this world can offer! When my wife passed away on August 19, 2020, she did not leave home – she went home. I desire to help others relocate to that eternal place by pointing them to the Savior of the world.

If the bus for Heaven pulled up to your house today, would you get on? That seems like an easy one. Who wouldn't get on that bus? But it's not that easy. It only takes a few seconds, and we start to think about things we would like to do before we go. There is a balance to strike. In 2 Corinthians 4, Paul wrote as a man who felt the strain of living on earth and longing for Heaven. Then, in chapter 5, he confesses hope. Job felt the same way. Remember his words? After revealing his faith in his living Redeemer and the resurrection from the dead, he speaks of a yearning heart (Job 19:27). We all think this way when we experience the struggle of living in a flimsy tent. But God's ways and timing are perfect, and He will decide when we go to Heaven. And until the day when we are clothed with the heavenly, we will make it our goal to please God. Live each day knowing that heaven is real – and that the blood atonement of Christ is sufficient to get you there. Hebrews 10: 14 says, "For by one offering he hath perfected forever them that are sanctified." We imagine something better because there is something better. I am very thankful for the life I have been given, and the Lord is teaching me to be content with each day. At the same time, I look forward to a place where my life will be even better. Our souls are made for God's eternity (Eccl. 3:11). He is in our emptiness, longing and searching for more. We who have been raised to new life in Christ can come into the presence of God, into the presence of angels, into the presence of just men made perfect, into the presence of the general assembly on high (Heb. 12:22-29). Indeed, we can enjoy a measure of heaven on earth, but we cannot be satisfied until we enter our Lord's eternal embrace. Knowing that God will wipe our tears away makes the sorrow of this world worthwhile (Rev. 21:4). And in that faith, we can live in a tent and long for a mansion.

Stuart Hamblen (1908-1989) was an entertainer. Radio's first singing cowboy was saved at a Billy Graham Crusade and began writing songs that glorified God. As a growing Christian, Stuart realized he couldn't answer all of life's questions. But in 1958, he wrote:

> My heart can sing when I pause to remember
> A heartache here is but a stepping stone.
> Along a trail that's winding always upward,
> This troubled world is not my final home.
> But until then, my heart will go on singing,

Until then, with joy, I'll carry on,
Until the day my eyes behold the city,
Until the day God calls me home.

Evangelist Billy Graham was said to have stated, "Most of life is filled with valleys." Scripture tells us that as believers, we are to talk about heaven. Apostle Paul said, "For our conversation is in heaven; from whence also we look for the Savior, the Lord Jesus Christ" (Phil. 3:20). Later, he declared, "Henceforth there is laid up for me a crown of righteousness, which the Lord, the righteous judge, shall give me at that day: and not to me only, but unto all them also that love His appearing" (2 Tim. 4:8). This world is not our home; we're just passing through. A few weeks ago, I went to the doctor to get checked out for pain in my upper abdomen. Because of the location of the pain and some things I was told, my mind went into overdrive with worst-case scenarios. But I think of countless individuals dealing with agony that I can't comprehend. And then I pray that, in every circumstance of life, I will set my affections on the land of 'no more.' No more pain, guilt, shame, sorrow, or death—just peace and unspeakable joy in a place of divine splendor. But the greatest of the joys of Heaven will be the absence of sin. Imagine being in a sinless place where justification is perfected by glorification. Oh, how I long for a city where the Savior awaits, for Jesus Christ will be the most precious treasure in my home, eternal in the heavens!

The Family of God

When was the first time you heard about the concept of adoption? For me, it was sixty years ago on the Jefferson Elementary School playground. I was informed by someone there that one of our friends had been adopted. I knew little about adoption but was told I wasn't supposed to repeat that information. It was almost as if adoption was scandalous when it was beautiful. Adoption is a biblical concept spoken well of in the Scriptures (Esther 2:7), and if you have faith in Jesus as your Savior, you have been adopted into the family of God. He loves us enough to take us for His own and not abandon us. All who the Spirit of God leads are children of God (Rom. 8:12-14), set free from sin and death through Jesus Christ. Please consider for a moment the nature of adoption. When someone adopts a child, they choose to bring that child into their family forever. They are willing to bear the significant cost, take the risks of raising a child, give that child their family name, invest their life, and then make that child an heir to all they own. That's precisely what God has done for us through Christ. He has adopted us into His family, bore the cost for our redemption at the cross, taken the risk of being grieved with our decisions, given us His name, made continual investments in our growth, and designated us heirs of His kingdom. What an incredible expression of divine love!

In John 1:12-13 we read, "But as many as received him (Jesus), to them gave he power to become the sons of God, even to them that believe on his name; which were born, not of blood, nor of the will of the flesh, nor of the will of man, but of God." The phrase translated "born again" can also be translated as "born from above." It is a spiritual transformation that can only come from God (2 Cor. 5:17, Titus 3:5). Using the words of a song written by Bill and Gloria Gaither, "Washed in the fountain, cleansed by His blood (Eph. 1:7); joint heirs with Jesus" (Rom. 8:17). Twice in His conversation with Nicodemus, Jesus emphasized the truth that one must be born again to enter the kingdom of God (John 3:3-5). Faith in Jesus Christ, the One who paid the penalty of sin when He died on the cross, delivers us from eternal punishment in hell (2 Cor. 5:21, Matt. 25:46, Rev. 21:8). And, having been redeemed (1 Pet. 1:18-19), we are children of God by right of the new birth (Rom. 6:4-6). We who have been adopted into God's family through faith in the sacrificial death and resurrection of Jesus (Gal. 6:10) belong to a grace-based, Christ-centered, Bible-believing community (Eph. 2:19-20) where our differences should never divide us. Healthy families communicate, interact, and participate in fellowship. Therefore, may we celebrate our diversity and unite as the family of God. Jesus modeled kindness, compassion, and forgiveness for all, and as His children, we should commit to doing the same.

Family conveys a sense of belonging. To be in the family of God means to be accepted for who we are: loved, cherished, celebrated, and fully forgiven (2 Cor. 5:17). The Greek word for 'one another' occurs one hundred times in the New Testament and over half are specific commands teaching us how to relate to each other. For example, the command to love one another occurs sixteen times (John 13:34). We are commanded to be devoted to one another (Rom. 12:10), to exhort one another (1 Thess. 5:11), to care for one another (1 Cor. 12:25), to serve one another (Gal. 5:13), to bear one another's burdens (Gal. 6:2), to forgive one another (Col. 3:13), to be patient with one another (Eph. 4:2), to submit to one another (1 Pet. 5:5), and to pray for one another (James 5:16). God has given each of us talents and abilities to become a channel of love to our siblings (Eph. 2:19-22). We are "laborers together" to accomplish the purposes of God (1 Cor. 3:9, Eph. 1:3-5). Billy Graham said, "Amazing things can happen when the family of God bands together." Paul encouraged the Corinthians to be steadfast, always abounding in the Lord's work (1 Cor. 15:58). Our common salvation in Christ is the basis for spiritual unity in a family where we have fellowship with our heavenly Father (Eph. 4:6). This blessing belongs only to those who have come to Him by faith. The most wonderful blessing of adoption is the promise of a glorious inheritance.

The riches of God belong to us for all eternity (Eph. 2:7, 3:8). One day, we will fully grasp how great and awesome God's mercy is to us, for He has granted us access to His family as treasured sons and daughters!

In Romans 12:10, Paul writes, "Be kindly affectioned one to another with brotherly love; in honor preferring one another." We need God's wisdom and the power of the Holy Spirit to give us patience, gentleness, and self-control (Gal. 5:22-23). Jesus loved people who were devoted to Him and those who were different from Him. Love is patient and kind, even when someone does not meet our expectations (1 Cor. 13:4). Some will avoid the church when they discover its imperfections. And, usually, the farther from the fellowship, the more critical they become. Few things place us at risk of leaving the local assembly more than unresolved problems and festering conflicts. The enemy will do all he can to disrupt unity. Indeed, we are saved by grace, not church attendance. But our motivation matters (Heb. 4:12), and we should constantly evaluate the reasoning behind our actions. The mark of spiritual maturity is to learn to love a messy family. Why? Because God does (Eph. 5:25-27)! The early church set the standard for us as Acts 2:42 tells us, "They continued steadfastly in the apostles' doctrine and fellowship, and in breaking of bread, and in prayers." God's design for his people is rich fellowship, and having opportunities to minister to others should be one of the priorities of Christianity. If healing needs to take place in the life of a brother or sister, we can have a part in that restoration through fervent prayer and encouragement. I thank God for the many who have prayed for me in times of disappointment and confusion. The Bible says the effectual fervent prayer of the righteous is profitable (James 5:16). Prayer is a gift that speaks of our relationship with God. We glorify Him by loving others, and as we grow in discernment, we will develop the ability to sense the most loving stance in every situation. Building relationships takes effort and sacrifice.

Jesus is our role model (John 15:12-15). He tells us not to do life alone (Luke 10:1-2) but to put others' needs before our wants (Matt. 14:13-21). Rather than seeing people as projects to improve, God wants us to love the way He loved and serve the way He served — personally and unconditionally. The necessity of loving one another is emphasized thirteen times in the New Testament. God desires the

Christian community to be a place where love and good deeds can be lived for His glory (Heb. 10:24). Until the day the church is presented to Christ "holy and without blemish" (Eph. 5:27), God calls us to worship and serve together with the beautiful, imperfect saints of God. The Lord continues to teach me much about the importance of the fellowship of the saints (Gal. 6:10). The emphasis throughout the Bible in our interaction with other Christians is not judgment, but love (John 13:34-35, 1 Pet. 4:4), encouragement (Heb. 3:13), and forgiveness (Eph. 4:31-32). How we treat other Christians says much about our relationship with God. One of the most common needs among believers is emotional healing. There have been times when I needed the Lord to heal my injured spirit, and He often did it through wonderful, caring people of God. May we never be too busy to help those with a wounded heart. This is the will of God, for He has given us the ministry of reconciliation (2 Cor. 5:18).

Pastor Karl Stegall tells of two brothers who entered the first grade. One said he was born January 1, 1984. The other said he was born April 4, 1984. "That is impossible," said the teacher. "No," replied the first brother, "one of us is adopted." "Which one?" asked the teacher. "I don't know," he replied. "One day, I asked my Dad, and he kissed us both and said, 'I forgot.'" Christians, never forget that we were adopted into the family of God (Rom. 8:15). Believers in the early church were devoted to one another in friendship, provision, and generosity (Acts 2:42-47). At the same time, we know that wherever there are people, there will be disagreements. When believers in the Philippian church seemed to have issues of self-ambition and conceit, Paul urged them to "be of the same mind in the Lord" (Phil. 4:2). A person who loves God will love God's children (1 John 4:21). Hebrews 10:25 commands us not to forsake the assembly of the saints. Verses like Colossians 3:13 encourage us to forgive and bear with one another. The church needs to be a safe place where we learn biblical truths and apply them to our lives. We are all saved by Christ's sacrifice, and when we recognize the strengths and weaknesses of our siblings, we care for them more. When we understand their difficulties, we can show compassion. We are all a work in progress, ministering grace to each other. Mutual love does not express itself in accidental meetings at the grocery store and sporting events but in the house of God. The disciples of Jesus met in regular fellowship and served one another (Gal. 5:13, 6:10). I have to believe they were more effective in God's kingdom by belonging to a loving community.

In Matthew 16:18, Jesus said, "I will build my church, and the gates of hell shall not prevail against it." According to Scripture, the church exists to exalt God, edify the saints, and evangelize the world. God has called us to live "the praise of His glory" (Eph. 1:12). To exalt God means to give Him first place in every thought, every word spoken, and every deed done (1 Pet. 2:9). Paul said that he aimed to "present every man perfect (mature) in Christ Jesus" (Col. 1:28), "unto the measure of the stature of the fulness of Christ" (Eph. 4:13). To edify is to build up spiritually through teaching and encouragement, helping others to become more like Christ. If we are glorifying God and edifying the saints, we will obey our Lord's command to go into all the world and preach the gospel (Mark 16:15). The mission of the family of God is to share the hope of salvation with others. We are the vessels He uses to spread the "good tidings of great joy" (Luke 2:10) to a lost world. There is a place for everyone in the family of God. Choose to belong. Understand the mission of your family (Matt. 28:19). Revelation 22:17: "And the Spirit and the bride say, Come… take the water of life freely." Brothers and sisters, we are here to glorify God and increase His kingdom on earth (Matt. 22:36-40). Devote yourself to the Lord. Continue to love and serve the body of Christ. As we are obedient to this work set before us (Eph. 2:10), our Lord will continue to add daily to the number of those being saved (Acts 2:47).

Amazing Love

THE LOVE OF GOD IS MORE WONDERFUL THAN ANYTHING WE CAN imagine. His love is beyond understanding. It is limitless, without measure (Eph. 3:19). The Psalmist said, "Because thy lovingkindness is better than life, my lips shall praise thee" (Ps. 63:3). God's amazing love is perfect, steadfast, and unconditional. Because of His love, we can endure pain, conquer fear, forgive freely, avoid conflict, renew strength, and bless others. There is no force more powerful than the love the heavenly Father has for his children. In the light of His goodness, we can rise above insurmountable barriers. His love can heal wounded hearts, transform lives, and free those held captive by sin and shame. I think of the beautiful song written by Frederick Lehman after a camp meeting in a Midwestern state, where he heard a powerful sermon on the love of God:

> O love of God, how rich and pure! How measureless
> and strong!
> It shall forevermore endure: The saints' and angels' song.

God is greater than words can communicate. Job said, "The thunder of his power who can understand?" (Job 26:14). The apostle Paul said, "O the depth of the riches both of the wisdom and knowledge of God!" (Rom. 11:33). We cannot understand His love, but we can accept it! The most significant expression of God's love is in John 3:16, "For God so loved the world that he gave his only begotten Son, that whosoever believeth in him should not perish, but have everlasting life." This is the most incredible love story ever told! One thing I love about the apostle John is that he knew he was not second place to anyone when it came to Jesus. He referred to himself as "the one Jesus loved" (John 13:23). John knew he was the Lord's favorite. And so was Peter, James, Andrew, Phillip and all the rest. And so am I. And so are you. Of all the things people could say about you, "the one Jesus loved" is the only description that matters.

While earning her master's degree, a young woman found it necessary to commute from the university to her home several times a week. Coming home late at night, she would see an older man sitting by her roadside. He was always there, in sub-zero temperatures, in stormy weather, no matter how late she returned. He never acknowledged her passing. The snow settled on his cap and shoulders, and she often wondered what brought him to that spot every evening. Finally, she asked a neighbor of hers, "Have you ever seen an old man who sits by the road late at night?" "Oh, yes," said her neighbor, "many times." "Is he a little touched upstairs? Does he ever go home?" The neighbor laughed, saying, "He is no more touched than you or me. Furthermore, he goes home right after you do. You see, he doesn't like the idea of you driving by yourself on these back roads, so every night, he walks out to wait for you. When he sees your taillights disappear around the bend and knows you are okay, he goes home to bed." When Paul spoke of a love that compels us (2 Cor. 5:14), he described the Spirit-filled motivation that drives born-again believers to share the gospel of the One who loved us first!

During the 17th century, Oliver Cromwell, Lord Protector of England, sentenced a soldier to be shot for his crimes. The execution was to occur at the evening curfew bell ringing. The bell had rung curfew for one hundred years without fail. However, on this day, the bell did not sound. The soldier's fiancé had climbed into the belfry and clung to the great clapper of the bell to prevent it from striking. When Cromwell summoned her to account for her actions, she wept as she showed him her bruised and bleeding hands. Cromwell's heart was touched, and he said, "Your lover shall live because of your sacrifice. Curfew shall not ring tonight!" In Romans 8, Paul reminds us that Jesus Christ endured the agony of the cross to deliver us from our death sentence: "There is therefore now no condemnation to them which are in Christ Jesus, who walk not after the flesh, but after the Spirit."

When the singers of Israel summoned the people to praise God (Ps. 106:1), it was because of His redeeming mercies, His willingness to forbear and forgive. Christ gave His life for us when we were the least deserving. Oh, such incredible love! The Psalmist said, "Whither shall I go from thy spirit? Or whither shall I flee from thy presence? If I ascend up into heaven, thou art there: if I make my bed in hell, behold, thou art there. If I take the wings of the morning and dwell in the uttermost parts of the sea; even there shall thy hand lead me, and thy right hand shall hold me" (Ps. 139:7-10).

Even when our world falls apart, we who have been redeemed (Heb. 9:15) can say, "Lord, I do not understand this, but you have saved me, and I know you love me." We are like the little boy separated from his mother in the department store. He began to cry because everyone was a stranger, and everything around him was confusing. When his mother found him and picked him up, she wiped away his tears. He didn't stop crying because his surroundings were changed but because of whose arms he was in. God is our refuge and strength, a very present help in trouble (Ps. 46:1). When Karl Barth, the famed German theologian, visited the United States, a student at a seminary asked, "Dr. Barth, what is the most important truth you have learned as a theologian?" Barth replied, "The most important thing I have learned is this: 'Jesus loves me this I know, for the Bible tells me so.'" God loves us. The cross of Calvary has made it plain for all to see! Innocent of any wrongdoing, Jesus was crucified, taking upon Himself the punishment for our sins. In Ephesians 3:18-21, it seems as if Paul invites us to look at the limitless sky above, to the infinite horizons on every side, and say, "The love of Jesus is just as vast as that." We cannot put the love of God into a box of our understanding. When our Father speaks of us, he calls us his children (Rom. 8:15, 9:26, Gal. 3:26). Therefore, we understand that nothing will invalidate the covenant of our adoption (John 1:12-13).

God loves me. I have always known it. Growing up in a faith-filled home, accepting Jesus very early, spending summers at camp, Sundays and Wednesdays on a church pew, and Fridays at youth group, I knew God loved me. Yet, I think I lost sight of it somewhere along the way. It seemed like God's powerful love became something I knew, not something I lived. I was drowning in questions: Who to please? What to do? How do I walk this chaotic tightrope of life? Did I do enough? Did I word that right? The questions were a weight I never intended to carry. The truth is, I can give Him my cares, worries, and fears and then leave them there. I can express my heart and know He hears me and works daily. I do not know where you are on your journey of faith. Your story might not be my story. But I know that sometimes, we need to be reminded of a simple truth. God loves me. God loves YOU. Have you ever doubted that God loves you? Have you ever faced circumstances that caused you to say, "How could God love me when He has allowed circumstances such as these?" Maybe you didn't verbalize it, but in your heart, you allowed the thought to resonate. The question of God's goodness eventually confronts everyone. Try to base your understanding of God on His Word rather than on circumstances, feelings, and emotions. Ephesians 3:19 speaks of love that surpasses knowledge. Jeremiah 31:3 says God's love is everlasting. Psalm 103:7 says His love is steadfast, "from everlasting to everlasting upon those who fear Him." On the banks of the River Clyde in Scotland is a little stone church where a young pastor, because he was going blind, was rejected by the young woman he loved and wanted to marry. He wrote, "O love that will not let me go; I rest my weary soul in Thee; I give Thee back the life I owe; that in Thine ocean depths its flow; May richer, fuller be." George Matheson (1842-1906) discovered that God's love is unending, and so can you.

The realization that God continually thinks of us should awaken a fresh enthusiasm in everything we do (Ps. 139:17, Isa. 49:16). In Christ, God's love is forever settled. He rejoices over us (Zeph. 3:17), and nothing we do or say can remove the assurance of His love (Rom. 8:38-39). He sees us at our worst and loves us to our best. How? Through His infinite patience and willingness to forgive (Eph. 1:7). What are the effects of God's love in a believer's life? We love Him because He first loved us (1 John 4:19), and we love others unconditionally (Mark 12:31). God's love is shown in answers to prayer, comfort in sorrow, provision in need, protection in danger, and wisdom in times of uncertainty. When they first met, Edwin Stanton slighted President Abraham Lincoln personally and professionally, even referring to him as a "long-armed creature." However, Lincoln appreciated Stanton's abilities and chose to forgive him, eventually appointing him to a vital cabinet position during the Civil War. Stanton later grew to love Lincoln as a friend. Edwin Stanton sat by Lincoln's bed throughout the night after the president was shot at Ford's Theater and whispered through tears on his passing, "Now he belongs to the ages." As wonderful as friends are to us, God's love is so much greater! His love is unfailing (Ps. 86:15). It is eternal (Jer. 31:3), sacrificial (John 3:16), and inseparable (Rom. 8:38). Spend some time with the Lord today. Cast your cares upon him (1 Pet. 5:7). Trust His Word (Ps. 62:8) and believe He holds you to the day of eternal salvation (Ps. 121:7-8). David said, "Whom have I in heaven but thee? There is none upon earth that I desire besides thee" (Ps. 73:25). Dear Lord, we do not walk alone. Lead us in strength and courage today. You have forgiven our many sins, and our hearts are filled with gratitude for your amazing love!

Lord, Increase My Faith

THERE IS NO QUESTION THAT THE BIBLE ENCOURAGES US TO BE STRONG in faith, implicitly trusting God and His promises (Heb. 13:7). Abraham stood firm in his faith to the glory of God (Rom. 4:20). The Roman officer (Matt. 8:5-13), the woman with an issue of blood (Mark 5:25-34), and the Gentile woman (Matt. 15:21-28) showed such exceptional faith that even the Lord Jesus was outspokenly happy with them. Many in Israel had faith, and Jesus said the man in Matthew 8:10 had more. But, in Luke 17:5, where the apostles said, "Lord, increase our faith," Jesus said a grain-sized faith would accomplish impossible things. The Lord seemed to suggest that what matters most is not the magnitude of our faith but its object. Friends, we are secure in God by the power of the One in whom we have placed our trust, and faith counts for nothing unless its object is Jesus Christ. Living a victorious life requires more than human ability. It requires a godly belief system that endures in every situation. If we don't have confidence in the character of God, we will default to our abilities instead of acting on the truth of Scripture. Oswald Chambers said, "Faith means, whether I am visibly delivered or not, I will stick to my belief that God is love." We must trust our Lord to be everything he says he is. Faith is essential for righteous living; without it, we cannot please God (Heb. 11:6).

Faith will change the way we live. James speaks: "Even so faith, if it hath not works, is dead, being alone. Yea, a man may say, Thou has faith, and I have works; shew me thy faith without thy works, and I will shew thee my faith by my works" (James 2:17-18). Faith is more than logic. Mere reasoning can be a tool of Satan to cause confusion and doubt. Why? Because knowing about the Lord Jesus is not the same as trusting Him as the only sacrifice for sin. Knowledge alone does not equate to salvation. It is possible to be close to the Cross and far from Christ (Matt. 7:21). Jesus said, "Not every one that saith unto me, Lord, Lord, shall enter into the kingdom of heaven; but he that doeth the will of my Father which is in heaven" (Matt. 7:21). We must turn our knowledge *about* God into the knowledge *of* God. How? Through prayer and study of the Word. Faith is more than an intellectual experience. We will become proud and arrogant if we pursue theological learning for its own sake, considering ourselves a cut above other Christians because of our interest in and grasp of it (1 Cor. 8:1-3). Knowing about God is a necessary precondition of trusting in Him, for Paul said, "How shall they believe in him of whom they have not heard... (Rom. 10:14). But information alone is not a measure of faith (Gal. 2:16). J. I. Packer said there is no spiritual health in doctrinal knowledge if sought for the wrong purpose and valued by the wrong standard. Salvation comes from the grace of God through our faith in the sacrificial work of Christ on the Cross (Eph. 2:8-9). Eternal life is inherited by trusting in the redeeming blood of Christ for the forgiveness of sins (Eph. 1:7). Our redemption exists only in Jesus, "for there is none other name under heaven given among men, whereby we must be saved" (Acts 4:12).

Faith is living with the assurance that we are a part of God's greater plan, for "in him, we live, move, and have our being..." (Acts 17:28). Faith believes the truth of the Bible entirely. We must free ourselves from the entanglements of nature, science, and human logic, all of which are creations subject to their Creator. The laws of reasoning, chemistry, planetary motion, physics, science, mathematics, and the uniformity of nature exist because the Creator has imposed order on His universe (Ps. 19:1, 95:4-5, Job 12:7-12). Jonathan Edwards said, "Nature is God's greatest evangelist." Paul wrote, "Your faith should not stand in the wisdom of men, but in the power of God" (1 Cor. 2:5). Children of God walk by faith (2 Cor. 5:7), accepting Scripture for what it says and presents. We receive God's Word at face value, recognizing that God is deliberate and intentional in what He says. Too often, we discredit the promises of God when things aren't going our way. But we must not confuse or complicate the teachings of Christ. Believe that what God said is true. The Psalmist said, "I have chosen the way of truth" (Ps. 119:30). The apostle James said, "But be ye doers of the word, and not hearers only, deceiving your own selves" (James 1:22). We read in Psalm 18:30, "As for God, his way is perfect; the word of the Lord is tried; he is a buckler (a shield of defense) to all those that trust in him." Jesus said, "Blessed are they that hear the word of God, and keep it" (Luke 11:28). Faith is more than academic agreement or mental assent. It is accepting the Word of God and allowing it to impact our lives. One night, a house caught fire, and a little boy was stranded on the second floor. All the boy could see was smoke and flames. However, he could hear his father's voice telling him to jump. The boy said, "Daddy, I can't see you." His father replied, "But I can see you, and that's all that matters." God's promises will only be meaningful when we believe He will fulfill them.

The apostle Peter says the testing of faith produces an assurance that it will stand (1 Pet. 1:7). During an especially trying time in the work of the China Inland Mission, Hudson Taylor wrote to his wife, "We have twenty-five cents—and all the promises of God!" Faith jumps where it cannot see. The African impala can jump over 10 feet and cover over 30 feet. Yet these stunning creatures can be kept in an enclosure in any zoo with a 3-foot wall. Why? Because the animals will not jump if they cannot see where their feet will fall. Faith frees us from the flimsy enclosure of a fearful life. Charles Spurgeon said, "I recommend you either believe God up to the hilt or else not to believe at all. Believe this Book of God, every letter of it, or reject it. There is no logical standing place between the two. Be satisfied with nothing less than a faith that swims in the depths of divine revelation." He said, "Faith that paddles about the edge of the water is poor faith at best. It is little better than a dry-land faith and is not good for much." Believing God's words is essential to a relationship with Him (Heb. 11:1-3). The Psalmist said, "What time I am afraid, I will trust in thee" (Ps. 56:3). Notice that David never claims to be immune to fear. In Psalm 55:5, he was shaking in fear! He said, "Fearfulness and trembling are come upon me, and horror hath overwhelmed me." But through all, David resolved not to lose faith because of his anxiety. I am praying for this kind of confidence in the coming days. Virginia Whitman said, "Faith is the bucket of power lowered by the rope of prayer into the well of

God's abundance. What we bring up depends upon what we let down." Friend, we have every reason to use a big bucket!

God always speaks truth (Num. 23:19). "He is the Rock; his work is perfect... a God of truth and without iniquity..." (Deut. 32:4). When God makes a covenant, he keeps it (Ps. 89:34, Heb. 10:23). When He makes a statement, He means it (Isa. 46:10). And when He proclaims the truth, we can believe it (John 16:13). Faith involves complete trust in God. It is the assurance of prophecies and promises yet unfulfilled. Faith is the cornerstone of our salvation, and to doubt God is to short-change ourselves of His richest blessings. What blessings? Faith in God brings peace and hope (Rom. 15:13). Faith gives us the strength to survive challenging times (Phil. 4:13). Faith prevents us from sinning against God. When we have faith in God, we will not seek solutions elsewhere or rely on our understanding; instead, we will look to Jesus for guidance and provision. Trials enable us to grow in our knowledge of God, but we cannot pass any test without confidence in Him (James 1:12). Our faith in God can strengthen the faith of others. God has called us to be a light in a dark world, to share the gospel through our actions and behavior (Col. 4:5-6). The storms of life can shake our confidence and cause us to question God. Doubt and fear are strategies of Satan, but faith will help us overcome both (Matt. 14:28-31). We read in 2 Timothy 1:7, "For God hath not given us the spirit of fear; but of power, and of love, and of a sound mind." Faith makes the impossible possible. It is the key to moving the hand of God (Matt. 9:22). Faith helps us reject the lies of the enemy. God loves us, and He has a plan. God has the final say, and He never fails! There is nothing like the peace of those who have full assurance that they know God and God knows them! This is the peace of which Paul speaks in Romans 5:1, "Therefore being justified by faith, we have peace with God through our Lord Jesus Christ." So, place your confidence in the goodness of God, for He knows what is best for you. God will prove Himself faithful if we cling to Him and seek His ways better than our own. Lean on Him and trust Him to get you through.

The world desperately needs to see what faith looks like, and the only place they will see it is in the lives of those who follow Christ. This kind of faith will undoubtedly result in people saying, "Who is this

Christ that inspires such love, trust, and sacrifice? I want to know Him!"
Faith is a relationship of trust and love through which we manage the
circumstances of life. Faithfulness means that no matter where we go or
what we face, we do so in relationship with the One who created, loves,
sustains, and redeems us (2 Tim. 1:10). The Bible says we are justified
and made righteous by faith. We have peace with God by faith (Rom.
5:1-11). In Christ, we are no longer separated from God by sin. We have
been placed in eternal union with Him by trusting in His forgiveness
(Rom. 1). Faith drives the powers of darkness away and brings the
authority of God into every situation. We are not perfect, and neither
is our faith. But when we recognize our weakness, God will provide
strength. He always does.

Heavenly Father, deliver us from our fear and anxiety, for you
know what we don't. Please give us the strength to release our will and
embrace yours. Help us to believe and act upon all you have written
in your Word. We ask that you forgive us the sin of disbelief (Rom.
10:4) and increase our faith. Have your way in our lives, and may you
be glorified through us. In Jesus' name, we pray. Amen.

A Loving Father

CHARLES FRANCIS ADAMS, SON OF PRESIDENT JOHN QUINCY ADAMS and grandson of President John Adams, kept a diary. He entered one day: "Went fishing with my son today—a day wasted." His son, Brook Adams, also kept a diary, which still exists. On that same day, Brook Adams made this entry: "Went fishing with my father—the most wonderful day of my life!"

I was born into a Christian household where my parents faithfully served God for many years. I will forever be grateful to have been raised in such an environment! I was not born a Christian. No one is (Psalm 51:5). But as soon as I could know names, I knew the name of Jesus. I was raised in a home of love and discipline. My sisters and I felt secure. Despite the frayed circumstances of life, my parents walked upright with the Lord. They reflected the light of Jesus through their interaction with others. Dad was dependable, and he expected the same from me. My father was a happy man who served God faithfully. He was a pastor's friend. His focus was on his God, his family, and his church. Dad lived according to biblical principles (James 1:22–27). He could see all sides of an issue and then act with uncompromised integrity. He would never let the actions of others govern him. He demonstrated his love through the things he did every day. My father suffered some physical setbacks that would have broken the spirit of most men, but I never heard him complain. He prayed for God's wisdom, trusting that He does all things well (Mark 7:37). My Dad displayed a solid and wonderful spirit I can still visualize. I am now persuaded to say, "Great is Thy faithfulness" (Lam. 3:23) because I witnessed God's faithfulness in his life.

I am speaking to fathers who have influenced their families according to the will of God. I am talking to sons and daughters who are thankful for the influence of a godly father. But some among us have not known a loving earthly father. A young lady writes, "The word 'father' has always been difficult to grasp. When I hear it, I don't recall any good memories. The word 'father' meant broken, scary, and hurtful things. How was I supposed to call God by a name like that? My wounds never seem to heal fully. I still yearn for memories of running to greet my daddy after he comes home from work. It wasn't that way for me. But God's love exceeds all the abandonment and disappointments in my past. Now that I'm a Christian, I have a relationship with my Heavenly Father. Instead of looking at my dad and then back to God, I learned to look to God first. I realized that if God wasn't my first source of fatherhood, I was always going to be off-balance. I feel privileged to understand love and respect for the one dad who will never leave me." In Ephesians 1:3–6, the apostle Paul shows us what kind of father we have in heaven. First, He has blessed us with spiritual blessings far more valuable than any material blessings. He has chosen and adopted us because of His love for us. And, because of His mercy, we love Him in return.

General Douglas MacArthur said, "By profession, I am a soldier and take pride in that fact, but I am infinitely prouder to be a father. A soldier destroys in order to build; a father only builds, never destroys. One has the potentialities of death; the other embodies the creation of life, and while the hordes of death are mighty, the battalions of life are mightier still. It is my hope that my son, when I am gone, will remember me, not from the battle, but in the home repeating with him our simple, daily prayer, our Father Who art in Heaven." Father's Day is a time set aside to honor fathers. And whether our father is living or not, many of us have beautiful memories. But some have a tough time today because they cannot remember their dad with fondness. Maybe your father promised to always be there for you, and he wasn't. Perhaps your dad is (or was) physically present yet emotionally detached. The pain is deep for those who have not experienced a father's love. One day, a New York businessman who commuted to work by ferryboat noticed a new passenger, a young boy with a shoeshine kit. The man spoke kindly to him and paid him to shine his shoes. From that day on, the boy always approached him with a happy smile whenever the businessman boarded the boat. He would offer to carry his briefcase and brush off his clothing without expecting any reward. After a week or two, the man asked the youth what made him so attentive. "Sir," he replied, "The first time you met me, you called me 'my boy.' Until then, I didn't think I belonged to anyone because my parents were dead. But you are so kind, and you always call me your boy. There's nothing I wouldn't do for you!" If we have trusted in the Son of God for salvation, we belong to a heavenly Father who sees every pain and struggle. He knows where we have walked and can heal each wounded heart and broken place. He promises never to make us figure things out on our own. He forgives, and He helps us to forgive.

God is a Father to the fatherless, and He will help you forgive the one who has done you wrong. He gives us the power to let go of resentment and bitterness. If we have been redeemed through Christ, we are loved by an amazing God. He is kind and compassionate (Eph. 2:7–8; Ps. 103:8). He is giving and gracious (John 3:16; Ps. 116:5). He is faithful and merciful (Lam. 3:22–23; Eph. 2:4–5). He is the One who makes all things new (Rev. 21:5). He is patient and approachable (Ps. 106:1; Heb. 4:16). You will never have to earn His love. You will never fail enough to lose His love (Rom. 5:8). We praise Him for all these things and so much more. In Him, we find rest and peace, life, and hope. The Bible says, "Behold, what manner of love the Father hath bestowed upon us, that we should be called the sons of God" (1 John 3:1). Psalm 139:7–12 tells us God cares about His children. The Psalmist reminds us that we are not alone in the hard times (Ps. 23:4), and nothing can separate us from the love of God in Christ Jesus (Rom. 8:38-39).

Dear friend, you can give your heart to Him without fear of Him leaving. God is the ever-present, perfect Father. He is faithful every day. His compassions do not fail. They are new every morning, and great is His faithfulness. The prophet Jeremiah said, "The Lord is my portion, saith my soul; therefore, will I hope in him" (Lam. 3:22–24). He is truly a dad who will not leave you! When we are troubled, we need to hear from our Heavenly Father. Remember the biblical account of eleven poor men who were crushed and lonely at the thought of Christ leaving and that if He left them, surely they would lose Him? Jesus spoke to them, "I am going away, and sorrow has filled your hearts. But do not be troubled about my leaving. I will return to get you; there is plenty of room for you where I am going. I have never allured you with false promises, so believe me now. I would have told you if my Father's house of many mansions did not exist. I will not leave you comfortless, but my Spirit will come to you, and your sorrow will be turned into joy." Then, lifting His eyes to heaven, Jesus prayed for his disciples and for all who will believe (John 14–17). Open your Bible to the wonderful promise in John 14:19, "Because I live, ye shall live also." We were not meant for this world alone.

When the telegraph was the fastest method of long-distance communication, a young man applied for a job as a Morse Code operator. Answering an ad in the newspaper, he went to the listed address. When he arrived, he entered a large office filled with noise and clatter, including the sound of the telegraph in the background. A sign on the front desk instructed job applicants to fill out a form and wait until they were summoned to the inner office. The young man filled out his form and sat with several other applicants in the waiting area. After a few minutes, he stood up, crossed the room to the inner office door, and walked right in. Naturally, the others perked up, wondering what was going on. They muttered among themselves that they had yet to hear any summons. They assumed the young man who went into the office made a mistake and would be disqualified. Within a few minutes, however, the employer escorted the young man out of the office and said, "Everyone, thank you very much for coming, but the job has just been filled." The other applicants began grumbling at each other, and one spoke up, saying: "Wait a minute, I don't understand. He was the last to come in, and we never even got a chance to be interviewed. Yet he got the job. That's not fair!" The employer responded, "I'm sorry, but the last several minutes while you've been sitting here, the telegraph has been ticking out the following message in Morse Code: 'If you understand this message, then come right in. The job is yours.' None of you heard it or understood it. He did, and the job is his."

One day, our Father will welcome us home! We will drop our bags of sorrow. Those we know will shout. Those we love will applaud. And, with a nail-scarred hand, Jesus Christ will wipe away every tear from our eyes. My anxiety subsides when I hear Him say, "In my Father's house" (John 14:2). The immediate purpose of what Jesus said was to soothe the fears of a handful of disciples. But more than that, He looked into the future and saw all the unborn millions drawn to Him by faith. Jesus Christ positions Himself as the host of heaven, and there is certainty in His words. He speaks of that unseen world as one who has been there. He is reporting experiences, not opinions. Heaven was his own calm home, his habitation from eternity. He is the Holy One who left a perfect place to live with imperfect people. We are told in Hebrews 12 that heaven is a beautiful city where God dwells with an innumerable company of angels who worship Him continually. What a perfect place for a joyful uniting with our loved ones (Rev. 21:4, 27). So, today, we find comfort in knowing He makes everything beautiful in his time and that he has set eternity in our hearts (Eccl.3:11). Oh, what joy will fill our hearts as we walk into our Father's house to live forever with the One who would rather die for us than live without us. Indeed, He is a loving Father who will never leave us!

God Reigns Supreme

IN THE APOSTLE PAUL'S FIRST LETTER TO TIMOTHY, HE SPEAKS OF THE Messiah, the sovereign Lord, the source of everlasting life, God eternal with endless power, the incarnation of the Almighty, the immortal King who dwells in unapproachable light. Paul said, "Now unto the King eternal, immortal, invisible, the only wise God, be honor and glory forever and ever. Amen." (1 Tim. 1:17). This is not just an expression unrelated to life. God is not whatever we conceive Him to be. He is not a "higher force" or a "cosmic notion." He is the Creator and Sustainer of the universe. The Old Testament prophet Isaiah comforted God's people by revealing the glory and majesty of God. He said the God who holds the earth's waters in one hand and measures the heavens with the other was with them in strength and power (Isa. 40:12). Likewise, He is with His children today! There is no kingdom or authority, but that which God has established (Rom. 13). He has no rival. He exists in self-sufficient life, eternal and infinite. He is not limited by time or space. God reigns supreme!

Do you wear your badge of honor and accomplishment proudly? Are you anxious for the world to see your robes of righteousness? Well, before you answer, consider the words transcribed on the garments worn by Jesus Christ: KING OF KINGS, AND LORD OF LORDS (Rev. 19:16). Rulers of this world may have inscriptions on their vestments that reveal their prestigious rank, but none have ever rightfully bore a classification as impressive as the one on God's robe! Augustus Caesar ruled in the first century, but God was in charge. He used Caesar's edict to move Mary and Joseph eighty miles from Nazareth to Bethlehem to fulfill His Word (Luke 2:1-4). The Psalmist asks, "Who is this King of glory?" Then he answers, "The Lord strong and mighty, the Lord mighty in battle... he is the King of glory" (Ps. 24:8-10). God reigns over all because He is the Maker of all! We who follow Christ have the marvelous news of a victory to share: The battle for our souls was won by the sacrificial Lamb of Calvary (Matt. 27:45-50; Rom. 6:23). Therefore, if you have accepted Him as Savior, be encouraged - and live in this truth.

King Nebuchadnezzar was a ruthless man who let nothing get in his way of subduing people and conquering lands. However, he was merely an instrument in God's providential plan. Read Daniel chapter four: In arrogant tones, the king proclaimed, "Is not this great Babylon that I have built for the house of my kingdom by the might of my power, and for the honor of my majesty?" To which the King of all kings answered (v32 paraphrased), "Until you acknowledge that I am the Ruler of the universe, you will dwell with the beasts of the field and eat grass like oxen." Thus, he did. Moreover, after God humbled Nebuchadnezzar, he rightfully proclaimed, "Now I Nebuchadnezzar praise and extol and honor the King of heaven, all whose works are truth, and his ways judgment" (v37). Notice how this stricken man completes his submission statement, "And those that walk in pride he (God) is able to abase." That is, to 'bring low.' God alone is perfect and immortal. When I kneel in prayer, only God, by His grace, allows me to stand back on my feet again. The Psalmist said, "Unto thee, O Lord, do I lift up my soul" (Ps. 25:1). He said, "Not unto us, O Lord, not unto us, but unto thy name give glory. Our God is in the heavens; he hath done whatsoever he pleased" (Ps. 115:1-3). David was indeed a king, but he was humble enough to praise the One in control of heaven and earth. Heaven is God's throne, and the earth is His footstool (Isa. 66:1).

The remedy for the sinful conduct of humanity is the knowledge of and obedience to God's Word. What I know of God will impact how I live. I will see the world through the lens of His mercy (Rom. 12:3). My priorities will change, and I will be at peace. Through faith and humility, the Holy Spirit will convict me of sin and guide me in righteousness (John 16:8). At the end of King Uzziah's reign, when moral darkness began to gather over the kingdom, the prophet Isaiah could say, "I saw also the Lord sitting upon a throne, high and lifted up, and his train filled the temple" (Isa. 6:1). God revealed Himself as

Jehovah, the Lord of hosts. It may be that in the darkness of this hour, you will turn to God. What an encouragement in these dark days to know that the One "high and lifted up" is our Lord and Savior, Jesus Christ! Let the heavens be glad, and the earth rejoice. Let them say among the nations, 'The LORD reigns!' (1 Chron. 16:31). The LORD has established His throne in heaven, and His kingdom rules over all (Ps. 103:19). All the kindreds of the nations shall worship Him (Ps. 22:27-29). Holy is our God! Far above all principality, power, might, dominion, and every name named, not only in this world but also in the world to come, He has put all things under his feet (Eph. 1:21-23). Nothing is outside or above the authority of Jesus Christ. What does it mean that God reigns on the earth? The reign of God means salvation. God's grace overcomes the evil that holds people in slavery (Rom. 5:20). He delivers people from oppression, bondage, and addiction. God's rule brings freedom. The Holy Spirit breaks the chains of evil, sin, and Satan (Ps. 107:14, Isa. 61:1). The Book of Revelation maps out specific events that tell of an everlasting reign when all violence and conflict will be broken.

Consider the passage of Scripture in Colossians 1:16-17, "For by him were all things created, that are in heaven, and that are in earth, visible and invisible, whether they be thrones, or dominions, or principalities, or powers: all things were created by him, and for him: And he is before all things, and by him, all things consist." Abraham Kuyper said, "There is not one square inch of the entire creation about which Jesus Christ does not cry out, 'This is mine! This belongs to me!'" God proclaims the wonder of the eternal Son who existed before time began and came down in the person of Jesus Christ. The invisible God became visible in Christ. We worship this God, and His fingerprints are all over creation. Our lives are meant to display the sufficiency and supremacy of Jesus Christ. David killed Goliath (1 Sam. 17) in a way that those who saw it said, "God did that!" From any human perspective, the sacrifice of Elijah (1 Kings 18) was an absolute impossibility. Nevertheless, God reigned supreme that day and for all to see! Unless there is a God dimension in my life, unless He reigns supreme, those around me will perceive me as just another religious man. Make Jesus Christ the lord of your life today. If you are discouraged, be of good cheer. God is working out his sovereign plan. It may seem your life is falling apart, but remember that Jesus Christ holds you fast. He cares for all things in creation, especially you. You are the crown of his creation (Ps. 8:1-9). God reigns. No world leader, no natural disaster, no trial or death can wrench control from Him. God's grasp on world events and the details of your life are secure. There comes a point where we leave our limited understanding on the table and raise our hands and hearts in worship (1 Tim. 6:15-16).

Jesus suffered the penalty that our sins deserved, and all who repent – and trust Christ's sacrifice – are forgiven and reconciled to God. Only the blood of the supreme Son can restore the perfect union with God that was always meant to be (Gen. 2:1-25). How will the knowledge that God reigns over all things influence your life? God's sovereignty impacts everyday life by removing all causes for worry. God loves and cares for us (Ps. 55:22). The sovereignty of God affects how we make decisions. And if we make the wrong decision, all is not lost. We can trust God's faithfulness and ability to set us back on the right course. God's sovereign control does not mean we sit idly by and allow life to happen. Some people confuse divine control with fatalism. They believe everything is predetermined, so we have no control over our destiny. This view is contrary to the Bible. The danger of fatalism is that it eliminates accountability for our actions. Just as valid as divine sovereignty is human responsibility. The reality is that as fallen human beings, we are naturally inclined to choose evil over good, thus standing in opposition to God. However, He has provided a way of reconciliation through Christ, and the Holy Spirit enables us to choose what is right (Deut. 30:19, John 14:25-26). God's sovereignty in salvation in Romans 9 is followed by the human responsibility of accepting it in Romans 10: "For whosoever shall call upon the name of the Lord shall be saved "(v11). In John 3:1-10, we have as clear a presentation of sovereign salvation as anywhere in Scripture, and right against it, we have a clear presentation of human responsibility. God is always at work in the believer to produce the fruit of righteousness, but we are responsible for obeying and acting upon His Word. We have a choice. We can carry the world on our shoulders or say, "I give up, Lord; here is my life. I give you my world, the whole world." Jesus Christ is not valued at all until He is valued above all.

The appeal to God's sovereignty is not to foster hope that we will be spared all difficulties but confidence that when those difficulties come, we are not abandoned (Ps. 94:14). In a chaotic world, a child of God can rest in the rule of God. More times than I can count, I have found myself repeating this phrase to myself and others: God is still on His throne. Whether we await the outcome of an election, anticipate a Supreme Court ruling and legislative decisions, or make personal decisions about work and family, it is wonderful to know that nothing surprises God. Acts 15:18 declares, "Known unto God are all his works from the beginning of the world." God is in control, not just sometimes, but at all times; not just with some things, but with all things. We find satisfying rest when we believe there is no boundary to His rule. His authority extends to all of creation, including the circumstances of our day and the outcome of the future. From beginning to end, Scripture reminds us - shows us - what it looks like to rest under the sovereign hand of a loving Father (Isa. 41:10, Ps. 136:12). We will become insecure and indecisive if we do not believe God reigns supreme. Anxiety will rule. Worry and dread will overwhelm us. If we doubt God's wise control, we will fear the future and exhaust ourselves, trying unsuccessfully to control every outcome in life. God's plans cannot be thwarted (Job 42:2, Matt. 2:13-23). His nature is unchanging. Whatever circumstance you face now or in the future, God is there. He is for you. The biblical truths regarding sovereign purpose should lead us to a greater appreciation of God, for He reigns supreme!

Faith in Crisis

WE STAND ETERNALLY RIGHTEOUS BEFORE GOD WHEN WE TRUST CHRIST alone for salvation. His grace justifies us through faith (Eph. 2:8, Rom. 5:1-11). The next step is to yield our lives to Him, receptive to the leadership of the Holy Spirit. In total surrender, we can live out our faith in meaningful and powerful ways (1 Tim. 6:12). Yet, there are occasions when we struggle with doubt and uncertainty. The Greek dictionary defines "doubt" as "to waver or hesitate." The modern English definition is to fear, be apprehensive about, be uncertain or undecided in belief. When the eleven disciples saw Jesus after his resurrection, Matthew tells us, "They worshiped him, but some doubted" (Matt. 28:17). Do you find it remarkable that some disciples doubted? I find it comforting. Why? Because I find myself in good company. Matthew does not tell us what caused the apprehension on the Galilean mountain that day. But apparently, the encounter with the resurrected Christ and the scope of the mission he gave them differed from their everyday life experience. In Matthew 11:2-6, we see a touching illustration of our Lord's kindness intended to strengthen the faith of a surprising doubter, John the Baptist. Jesus knows when to deal gently with the doubts that strike us in the darkness of suffering and isolation. The fight for faith is hard, and doubt is part of the hard fight. When we experience realities different from our view of Christianity, these are the times when taking God at His word can be difficult.

From the beginning of time, Satan's approach has been to interrupt belief by placing uncertainty in the hearts of God's children (Gen. 3:1). Sometimes, we become disoriented and must regain our direction. It has been so in my life. But through the Holy Spirit's power, we can overcome the enemy through faith in - and obedience to - verses like

Psalm 91:2, "I will say of the Lord, He is my refuge and my fortress: my God; in him will I trust," or Isaiah 55:8, "For my thoughts are not your thoughts, neither are your ways my ways, saith the Lord," or Matthew 11:28, "Come unto me, all ye that labor and are heavy laden, and I will give you rest." A faith crisis is often the explosion of questions accumulated over time. But what we need is more than immediate answers. We need shelter in the storm, and Jesus Christ is that haven of rest!

I'm reminded of the little boy who fell out of bed. When his mom asked him what happened, he answered, "I don't know. I guess I stayed too close to where I got in." It is easy to do the same with our faith. It's easy to stay where we got in and never mature through prayer and study of Scripture. Some have said that nearness to God means knowing all the correct answers. I disagree. I have experienced a deeper relationship with the Lord, searching for answers. Doubt is part of human nature. John the Baptist, Thomas, Gideon, Abraham, Sarah, and many others in the Bible illustrate this truth. King Solomon wrote these words of wisdom, "Trust in the Lord with all thine heart; and lean not unto thine own understanding. In all thy ways acknowledge him, and he shall direct thy paths" (Prov. 3:5-6). God will lead us if we put ourselves in a position to hear and receive. Peter and Judas walked with Jesus for the same amount of time. They both received the same blessings, saw the same miracles, and heard the same stories. And yet, their lives ended very differently. Why? Because of their response to a crisis. Judas went out and hung himself (Matt. 27:5). Peter went out and wept tears of repentance (Luke 22:62).

Reading John 6:60-71, we find that some who said they were with Jesus had a decision to make. They were at a crossroads. They had come to understand that everything Jesus said was true, but not everything He said was easy. We generally do not have difficulty understanding the teachings of Scripture, but we wonder if they are too hard to accept. So, we are left with two choices: either look, believe, and come to Christ in humble surrender or continue in life without Him. They didn't want to live according to the prompting of the Spirit because it meant a change of lifestyle and behavior. The body of Christ stands ready to pray on your behalf, but the choice is yours. In this passage of Scripture, those who "walked no more with him" (v66) were not prepared to trust the Lord with their entire life. They were happy to be part of the crowd because being around believers is exciting. It's comfortable to rely on a family legacy or religious tradition or only listen to what is said from the pulpit. But are we listening to the words of Jesus when He says, "Come unto me?" Are you attracted to what Jesus can give but opposed to what He demands? Jesus calls us to a decision, not to an emotion.

To get through a crisis of faith, we need to examine whether we misdirected our trust in the first place. Did we assume that because we love Jesus, no evil, pain, or harm would come our way? It's important that we compare our expectations to the truth of God's Word. We are prone to question God when our world is rocked by unexpected events that throw us off balance. But as an anchor is to a storm-tossed sea, confidence in our Lord will produce steadfastness, character, and hope (Ps. 28:7). Faith is the conviction that God can, and trust is the assurance that He will. When we fully believe in the sovereignty of God, we will follow Christ regardless of what happens (2 Cor. 5:7). Most comforting of all, we know that our Lord will never allow us to be tested beyond what we can handle (1 Cor. 10:13). His grace is sufficient! Life is hard, but God has promised to get us through even the darkest storms. George Mueller, known for trusting God in desperate circumstances, said, "God delights in increasing the faith of His children. I say – and say it deliberately – trials, obstacles, difficulties, and sometimes defeats are the food of faith." He said, "We should take them from God's hands as evidence of His love and care for us in developing more and more that faith He seeks to strengthen us." We all face challenges that put our confidence to the test. But if our faith is worth anything, it will prevail over life's disappointments.

Corrie ten Boom (1892-1983) was a Dutch watchmaker, Christian writer, and public speaker. During the Second World War, she and her family helped many Jewish people escape the Nazi army by hiding them in her home. They were caught. She was arrested and sent to a concentration camp. Corrie wrote a biography recounting her family's efforts and how she found and shared hope in God while imprisoned. Afterward, when speaking to audiences about her horrific experiences, Corrie often looked down while talking. She was not reading notes.

She wasn't even praying. She was working on a piece of needlepoint. After sharing the doubt, anger, and pain she experienced, Corrie would reveal the needlework. She would hold up the backside of the piece to show a jumble of threads with no discernible pattern and say, "This is how we see our lives." Then she would turn the needlepoint over to reveal the design of beautiful colors on the other side and conclude by saying, "This is how God views your life, and someday you will have the privilege of seeing it from His point of view."

Some rarely speak openly about doubt because they fear being judged as "lacking faith" or accused of "backsliding." But keeping our questions secret tends to magnify the struggle instead of bringing us nearer to resolving it. Jesus cares about our sincere questions. Thomas was curious, and he didn't hesitate to speak his mind. His imagination would only stretch so far. He could not grasp something he had not personally experienced and was unwilling to make assumptions. The pursuit of truth demands that we ask tough questions. The disciple asked, "Lord, we don't know where you're going, so how can we know the way?" And, because he did, we have received one of the most wonderful Scriptural truths: Jesus responded, "I am the way, the truth, and the life: no man cometh unto the Father, but by me" (John 14:1-6). This should be a story of thanksgiving for us, that Jesus showed up to cast out all fear and doubt. How? By showing Himself as the way to eternal salvation. There is no trace of fault-finding in what Jesus says to Thomas in John 20:24-31. The Lord only tells him that doubt is not the most blessed state to live in and that there is stronger faith in believing what is not seen. Jesus declares, "Become not faithless but believing."

A television program preceding the 1988 Winter Olympics featured blind skiers being trained for slalom skiing, as impossible as that sounds. Paired with sighted skiers, the blind skiers were taught how to make right and left turns on the flats. When that was mastered, they were taken to the slope, where their sighted partners skied beside them, shouting, "Left!" and "Right!" As they obeyed the commands, they could negotiate the course and cross the finish line depending solely on the sighted skiers' word. It was either complete trust or catastrophe - a vivid picture of the Christian life. As believers, we should expect that God will test us, and we should pray that we will respond correctly.

Testing ascribes the integrity of the creation to its creator, and the testing of our faith is all for God's glory, not ours. Nothing arrests the attention of God like faith. In Luke 7:1-10 we read of our Lord's astonishment at the Roman commander's humility, awareness, and understanding of God's authority. This remarkable man received from God because he believed Him without hesitation!

Above the front door of every church, we should erect a sign: "Doubters Welcome." This should be the church's message: If you have doubts, come inside. If you have questions, come inside. If you are uncertain, come inside. If you are searching for truth, come inside. Job and David repeatedly questioned God and were not condemned (Job 7; Ps. 10). God is big enough to handle our doubts and our questions. Jacob was a man who encountered fear and anxiety, and he struggled with God in the process. The Bible says he was "greatly afraid and distressed." Sound familiar? Here's the lesson for us: Jacob prayed for deliverance, and having seen the face of God, his life was preserved (Gen. 32). We can either live with uncertainty or cling to the reality of the Holy Spirit's sustaining presence in our lives. When we understand that God is on the throne and everything is under His control, the defeating questions are replaced with confidence. God never promised that we would know every answer to every question. But He did promise that He would never leave us nor forsake us (Heb. 13:5). He also promised that if we rely on Him, we would never be overwhelmed by anything that happens to us (1 Cor. 10:13). Hope is in the resurrection of Jesus Christ. For Thomas, doubt moved to joyful worship and a confession of faith the moment he cried, "My Lord and my God!"

Wishing to encourage her young son's progress on the piano, a mother took the small boy to a Paderewski concert. After they were seated, the mother spotted a friend in the audience and walked down the aisle to greet her. Seizing the opportunity to explore the wonders of the concert hall, the little boy rose and eventually explored his way through a door marked "No Admittance." When the house lights dimmed, and the concert was about to begin, the mother returned to her seat and discovered that her son was missing. Suddenly, the curtains parted, and spotlights focused on the impressive Steinway piano on stage. In horror, the mother saw her little boy sitting at the keyboard, innocently picking out "Twinkle, Twinkle Little Star." At that moment, the great piano master entered, quickly moved to the piano, and whispered in the boy's ear, "Don't quit; keep playing." Then, leaning over, Paderewski reached down with his left hand and began filling in a bass part. Soon, his right arm reached around to the other side of the child, and he added a running melody. The audience was mesmerized. Together, the old master and the young boy transformed a frightening situation into a beautiful experience for all to see. What we can accomplish on our own is hardly noteworthy. We try our best, but the results aren't exactly graceful flowing music. But as we yield to God, our work can be beautiful. Listen closely, and you will hear the voice of the Master whispering in your ear, "Don't quit, keep playing." You will feel His loving arms around you and know that His strong hands are playing the concerto of your life.

As I look back, God was with me in very dark days to remind me how faith blossoms in the dark. And through the healing, I have a deeper appreciation for Him. I serve the One who loves me in ways I cannot describe, and His love for me will never end! What is the refuge from the storms of life? The Psalmist declares, "God is our refuge and strength, a very present help in trouble" (Ps. 46:1). Logic, reason, and science will fail you. The Christian faith will require you to believe in something you cannot prove. English poet Dora Greenwell wrote, "I am not skilled to understand what God hath willed, what God hath planned; I only know that at His right hand is One who is my Savior!" From beginning to end, the most wonderful way to live is to have complete confidence in the Word of God. We must be humble enough to let the Lord call the shots and brave enough to follow where He leads.

The Blessing of
Desperate Prayer

A PERSON VERY DEAR TO ME DESPERATELY WANTED HER MARRIAGE TO improve. Kathy's husband had walked out after several years, and a resolution seemed unlikely. Storm clouds were gathering, and she was slipping into a dark valley. She searched for answers in and of herself. Her confidence was shattered, and she hated the idea of being alone. She prayed, "Oh Lord, surely this can't be your plan for my life. Please make yourself known to me in all of this!" Difficult days became a time of reflection, so she prayed the Psalmist's prayer, "Search me, O God, and know my heart..." (Ps. 139:23). Where could she find relief from the painful burden of an uncertain future? Kathy turned to the One who is "nigh unto them that are of a broken heart... and a contrite spirit" (Ps. 34:18). This was the answer! Nothing short of earnest prayer and Bible reading would bring peace to her troubled spirit. At the time of this writing, Kathy remains hopeful for reconciliation and a covenant of marriage by God's design (Matt. 19:4-6). But regardless of the outcome, she will tell you that while her heart is severely bruised, her faith has been strengthened. How is this possible? It is the blessing of desperate prayer!

Are you weary from the anxiety and panic of life? Jesus understands your pain, and He cares! Demanding circumstances are hard to understand, but the redeeming grace of God will hold more than you can see. Hebrews 4:15 tells us, "For we have not a high priest which cannot be touched with the feeling of our infirmities...." For every child of God, there has been - or there will be - a moment of awakening that will change Romans 8:28 from a memorization quote to a belief system. Your prayer will move from "God heal me" to "God use me for your glory and help me cope." And when this happens, you will discover that joy can indeed coexist with uncertainty and confusion. The more we open our hearts to God's love, the better our story becomes. Romans 15:13 tells us, "Now the God of hope fill you with all joy and peace in believing, that ye may abound in hope, through the power of the Holy Ghost." Kathy discovered this truth when she was brought into a situation so desperate that her abilities failed. A storm rocked her world, and the fierceness of the storm caused her to cry out, "For this, I need Jesus!"

The author of Psalm 42 expresses a passionate desire for immediate help from God. He compares his longing for God to a deer's thirst for flowing water. It was not a simple thirst but a desperate need for something vital. He uses a metaphor of an exhausted animal, parched from the heat of the day, exhausted from the pounding pursuit of howling hounds, yearning for a waterhole. This is what the psalmist said, "As the hart panteth after the water brooks, so panteth my soul after thee, O God." When we reach the end of ourselves, we understand that only the refreshing pools of God's love can provide what we need. He is the fountain of life. He is the well-spring of satisfaction for the weary one (John 4:14). Kathy prayed desperately, "Heavenly Father, I realize more today how much I need you to restore my soul. I need the living water from on high to refresh and sustain my spirit. Times are hard, dear Lord, and the pressure is great. Please keep me and those I love under the shadow of Your wing."

A former alcoholic tells his story, "I always thought that religious people were weak-minded. It seemed they were trying to comfort themselves by inventing a supernatural being that would solve their problems. I liked the idea of being able to help other addicts and alcoholics. I could not, however, accept 'the God idea.' I suppose I was missing the key ingredient for a lifestyle change: desperation. Then, after yet another relapse and failed suicide attempt, I found myself in the state mental hospital – again. I clearly remember what happened. I was sitting in the day room, watching TV with the other patients, and feeling sorry for myself. I was reading a copy of the AA Big Book that a friend had sent me, although I couldn't concentrate for long.

Specifically, I was reading Bill's Story, and it seemed like Bill was describing me exactly. At every other paragraph, I would have to stop reading and collect myself before I started crying in front of everyone. Eventually, I was so overcome emotionally that I had to get up and leave. I went into the bathroom and shut myself in a stall – the doors don't lock in a mental hospital. I sat on the toilet and started sobbing. I knew I couldn't go on as I had been, and there was no doubt that I was going to die. Either I was going to drink myself to death, or I was going to wander out into the middle of the interstate and let a bus do the job for me. I cried out for help. I said, 'God, I don't know if you're there. All I know is I can't do this anymore. I'm all out of 'try.' I don't care what I have to do. If you show me what to do, I'll do it.' And the most amazing thing happened. He answered. I don't mean that a moonbeam came down from heaven or that I heard angels with trumpets. I heard God speak to me – not with words, but in my bones. He said only, "I will." An electric current went through my whole body. Please don't misunderstand; I wasn't immediately overwhelmed with happiness, and all my problems didn't miraculously melt away. However, there was undeniable proof that I had been wrong about God my whole life. I knew, beyond any doubt, that if I would only go where I was led, I could be free. It was a desperate prayer that led me to recovery. I remember that day, and I still get chills two and a half years later. When I have doubts or fears, as we all do, I have only to reach out for guidance, and I feel again the voice of God saying, 'I will show you the way.'"

We all face circumstances that seem as if they will never get better. We don't see how things will improve. The odds are against us, and too often, we settle where we are, accepting that better things were not meant to be. Has something died in your life? Is there something you have given up on? The heavens may have seemed silent for a time. But even now, God can resurrect dead dreams. Charles Spurgeon said, "It is when we are at our wits' end that he delights in helping us. When our hopes seem to be buried, that is when God can give a resurrection." There's a lesson here: We must patiently allow God to work things out for His purpose, according to His timing. He is always working for something much greater than we can imagine. Jesus will show up and do something so incredible that we will know the work was far beyond our abilities! Did you come to God because things were going well in your life, or did you come to Him during a crisis? What was it that caused you to seek a deeper relationship with Christ? When the prophet Isaiah wrote, "In the year that king Uzziah died I saw also the Lord sitting upon a throne, high and lifted up…" (Isa. 6:1), it was to say, "I had an encounter with the Lord through the sad ending of a good man." The prophet's spiritual awakening was the demise of a king, for it was only then that he saw the enthroned LORD as greater than any earthly king. Has something in your life died? There is no better time to cry out to God than on your way home from a funeral. Perhaps your loss is not the death of a person. Maybe it's the end of a marriage, a relationship, a dream, or a career. Whatever the case, God will help you cope with the injury. It's safe to say that this Old Testament prophet who left the temple was not the same man who had entered it earlier. He was a different man for having been in the presence of God. Sometimes, the only way out is through. And when your earthly king has been removed from the throne of your life, you can see the real King in His beauty! This is the blessing of desperate prayer.

Those who travel with Jesus will face storms. Those who travel without Jesus will face storms. No one escapes the trials of life. Sometimes, we become so fearful that only our Lord can help us endure. And when He speaks peace to our hearts, we sense the presence of the Almighty One! The wonder of God is His willingness to heal broken hearts and revive wounded spirits! Will you, like those who mourned Lazarus's death, though they cringed at opening an occupied grave, roll away the barrier to your miracle? Will you allow God's glory to manifest in you so that others may know Him? Why do we avoid the crossroads where God said He would always meet our needs? Put your trust in Christ alone, for He is making all things new (Rev. 21:5). A little girl was staying with her grandparents, and when it was time for her to go to bed, her grandfather told her he would come to her room to pray with her. As he went to the doorway, he realized she had already started praying. He overheard her saying her ABCs. As she went through the alphabet, she emphasized each letter. She concluded with a thank-you, an amen, and proceeded to get into bed. When her grandfather came to tuck her in, he said, "Darling, I listened to your prayers. It sounded like you were praying the alphabet." She responded, "Yes, Grandpa, I had so much to pray about, and I didn't know all the words. But I knew if I gave God all the letters, He would put the words together."

What does the Bible say about desperation? Psalm 50:15: "And call upon me in the day of trouble: I will deliver thee, and thou shalt glorify me." Psalm 91:14: "Because he hath set his love upon me, therefore will I deliver him: I will set him on high because he hath known my name." 1 Corinthians 15:55: "O death, where is thy sting? O grave, where is thy victory?" 1 Corinthians 6:14: "And God hath both raised the Lord and will also raise us by his power." There are times when hopelessness looms on the horizon. It's an intensely dark time. Have you ever been there? I have. The condition is so complex that there seems to be no end. But God hears our prayers and answers them according to His will, timing, and purpose. As dire and hopeless as the situation seems, God will draw us closer if we call upon Him. This is the blessing of desperate prayer.

Dear Lord, you are our shelter and high tower (Ps. 18:2), our ever-present help in time of need (Ps. 46:1). The Psalmist said, 'What time I am afraid, I will trust in thee' (Ps. 56:3). Even now, O Lord, you can do all things. Even now, heavenly Father, may you be glorified! Please forgive, cleanse, deliver, and comfort us today. With love and worship, we ask these things in Jesus' name. Amen.

Lessons From A Servant Girl

In 2 Kings chapter five, we are introduced to a teenage girl kidnapped and enslaved during an attack on her homeland. The attack was led by Naaman, the captain of the Syrian army, and this young Jewish girl, whose name is not recorded, became a servant of Naaman's wife. Although she had been taken from her people to become a slave among strangers, she remembered what she had learned from her family and friends about God's faithfulness. Naaman was a wealthy and talented soldier with everything going for him except one thing: he had leprosy. Leprosy is a dreadful disease that begins unnoticed under the skin's surface and eats away the flesh from the inside out. Leprosy was an internal disease, a loathsome disease, a separating disease, and the leprous person could not cure themselves. As such, the Bible portrays leprosy as sin. Sin corrupts someone spiritually the way leprosy corrupts someone physically. At first, sin is unrecognized by those around us. But in our hearts, sin, for which there is no cure outside divine intervention, works to destroy us. Education, psychology, and even religion take turns trying to reform the hearts of men. But the only hope for cleansing is the Word of God received by a humble and repentant heart (1 John 1:9, Rom. 10:13-14).

Our Lord could have cleansed Naaman's leprosy in many ways, but he chose one small girl to set up the pathway to divine healing. This young, unnamed girl was not in Naaman's home by choice. She was taken into slavery as a spoil of war. And we don't know her name because Scripture is silent about that. We know that she lived sometime after Elisha began his ministry in 852 BC and before the death of King Jehoram in the early 840s BC. We know she was an adolescent girl who had been a resident of Israel, the northern kingdom that separated from

Judah in 931 BC. We know she was from a nation of people who had heard God's spoken word and believed in God's promises (Gen. 17:7-8). More importantly, we know that she didn't have to be comfortable and at ease to serve God. She had been taken prisoner, no doubt working in the household as a personal attendant to Naaman's wife. Although she was the private property of her masters, she seems to have had a special relationship with Naaman's wife so that she could make suggestions to her, almost like a child with her parents. She lived in a wealthy and influential household, for Naaman was a great man of military might, highly regarded in society (2 Kings 5:1). But this young lady was not intimidated by worldly trappings. She was a compassionate girl. She felt sorry that her master had leprosy, and, wanting him to be healed, she did what she could to lead her captor to the prophet Elisha. With faith in the power of God, she became an incredible blessing to the household. How so? Her faith generated a hope that resulted in salvation!

We can learn several things from this young maiden. First, we understand that no situation is so dire that we cannot find contentment in serving God. The Bible gives no indication of bitterness or discontent in this young lady. She goes about her tasks cheerfully and diligently – so much so that people listen when she voices her concern for Naaman. What a testimony! Second, we learn that others will be blessed when we share God's truth. Slaves, especially junior high girls in the home of the army captain, are not usually asked their opinion. Yet without this little girl who remained anonymous and powerless, one of the great Bible stories would never have happened. Lastly, we learn that she cared about the ruthless leader who had destroyed her village. Why? Because she understood that God would make Himself known in extraordinary ways to ALL who will humbly seek Him! The apostle Paul spoke about this in Romans 5:8, "But God commendeth his love toward us, in that, while we were yet sinners, Christ died for us." When God's love changes us, our response to others also changes. I ask myself, "Does the love of Christ compel me to have compassion for all people? Does it lead me to speak the truth and share the gospel with them?" This unnamed servant girl so believed in her God that people observed her life and acted on what she had to say. With the Holy Spirit's power, I desire to do the same.

We can also learn much from Naaman. He thought his healing would come on his terms (2 Kings 5:10-14). After all, he was a man of many fine qualities. He was an outstanding military leader, highly successful in his chosen career. He was popular, a king's favorite, with honors lavished upon him. He was rich. He was also courageous, "a mighty man of valor," the Bible calls him. But he was also a leper, and that one additional piece of information changes everything. Naaman suffered from the ancient world's most feared and dreadful disease, a condition without respect for prominence and fame. This man's strength, courage, victories, and money could not save him from leprosy. When we walk in pride regarding our talents and accomplishments, we demonstrate that we do not understand or appreciate God's role in everything we do. Hudson Taylor was scheduled to speak at a large church in Melbourne, Australia. The moderator of the service introduced the missionary in eloquent and glowing terms. He told the large congregation all Taylor had accomplished in China and presented him as "our illustrious guest." Taylor stood quietly for a moment and then opened his message by saying, "Dear friends, I am the little servant of an illustrious Master."

None of us can succeed in our strength or wisdom. The miracle for a famous and powerful military man occurred only when he did things God's way. This is the most crucial discovery anyone can make. Before Naaman could be made whole in body, he had to know himself to be a leper. He had to confront the reality of his disease and ask God to do something about it. Before you and I can be cleansed within, we must know ourselves to be sinners. Unless we confess our sin of pride, there can never be any healing for our souls. Naaman found he was cured only when he conquered his pride, swallowed his anger, and humbled himself to believe in God's promise. He had to obey God's command. Likewise, the gospel is always a word of command and promise. A condition is required, and a blessing is ensured: go and wash, and you will be clean. "Believe on the Lord Jesus Christ, and you will be saved" (Acts. 16:31). The object of belief is the Lord Jesus Christ, the divine Savior chosen by God to accomplish the work for our salvation through His death and resurrection. Those who would be saved, having believed in this Jesus for eternal salvation, should then submit to the Lord's will for their lives. We may not understand the intricate leading of the Lord. Still, we can trust Him because He sees the big picture (Ps. 37:23).

The story is told about Earl Weaver, former manager of the Baltimore Orioles, and how he handled his star player, Reggie Jackson. Weaver had a rule that no one could steal a base unless given the steal sign. This upset Jackson because he felt he knew the pitchers and catchers well enough to judge his play. So, in one game, he decided to steal without a sign. He got a good jump off the pitcher and easily beat the throw to second base. As he shook the dirt off his uniform, Jackson smiled with delight, feeling he had vindicated his judgment to his manager. Later, Weaver took Jackson aside and explained why he hadn't given the steal sign. First, the next batter was Lee May, his best power hitter other than Jackson. When Jackson stole second, first base was left open, so the other team walked May intentionally, taking the bat out of his hands. Second, the following batter hadn't been strong against that pitcher, so Weaver felt he had to send up a pinch hitter to drive in the men on base. That left Weaver without bench strength later in the game when he needed it. The problem was that Jackson saw only his relationship with the pitcher and catcher. Weaver was watching the whole game. We, too, see only so far, but God sees the end from the beginning (Isa. 46:10). Sometimes God doesn't work the way we expect, but He is still working! We try to fit God into a little box that we can understand, but we can never fully comprehend the workings of the Almighty God. Don't let your ego get in the way of your miracle. Don't try to complicate what God has made simple. It's far too simple for our minds to comprehend that the greatest gift is not one we can ever earn or be good enough to deserve. Let us be wise to obey, no matter what we think we know.

While this young servant girl must have had moments of fear, loneliness, anger, frustration, and self-pity, the Bible doesn't record them. Instead, we see her rising above any selfish thoughts and sinful reactions. God need not look further than our attitude to determine our spiritual condition (Prov. 20:27), and our contentment in Christ is not based on our circumstances. Unlike so many others, this girl didn't need her situation to change before she would trust and serve God. She lived as one who believed that nothing ever happens by accident. She knew God planned her circumstances for His glory and her good.

She believed God would use her in the lives of others. Therefore, she was willing to speak out for the Lord regardless of the perceived risk. She lived with faith in God, and as a result, His miraculous power was demonstrated in the world around her. Think about it: Naaman's healing came through the simple witness of an unidentified servant girl! God has also spoken an excellent Word to us about our disease. He sent his Son to the world not to condemn us, but that we might be saved through Him (John 3:17). Jesus died unjustly on a Roman cross under false accusation and rose from the dead three days later (Matt. 27/28). The gospel message that must be preached to everyone, everywhere, is that we can be delivered from the power and penalty of sin. Christ died to heal us from spiritual leprosy (Isa. 53:5, 1 Pet. 2:24), and we are made clean through the finished work of Calvary (Acts 3:19, Heb. 9:14). Truly, there is no other word for grace but amazing!

My Rock, My Refuge

THERE ARE MANY REFERENCES IN THE BIBLE TO GOD BEING OUR ROCK. The Psalmist David said, "He only is my rock and my salvation: he is my defense; I shall not be moved" (Ps. 62:6). Moses said, "He is the Rock, his work is perfect" (Deut. 32:4). In a world of corruption, unprecedented crime, racial tension and breakdowns in the family unit, we need something steady to hold on to. Apostle Paul said, "For other foundation can no man lay than that is laid, which is Jesus Christ" (1 Cor. 3:11). Christ is the eternal foundation that can never be shaken. He alone is the foundation that will never crumble. The prophet Isaiah said, "Trust ye in the Lord forever" (Isa. 26:4). Bible verses like these carry a powerful message of faith and strength. Look to Him for guidance, even when things seem out of control. If you have been redeemed, you can be confident about your place in the world because you are a child of God. Samuel Rutherford responded to a Christian's shaky sense of security, "Your Rock is Christ. It is not the Rock which ebbs and flows, but your sea." Trust the Holy Spirit's power to sustain you in all things. He will strengthen you during these turbulent times. May we never forget the reassuring power of trusting God's Word. It is the dependable rock of our salvation! The last words of the Sermon on the Mount instruct us to build our lives on Christ Jesus (Matt. 7:24). After teaching the multitudes many things, Jesus said, "Whosoever heareth these sayings of mine, and doeth them, I will like him unto a wise man, which built his house upon a rock."

Today, we sing the wonderful hymn written by Edward Mote in 1834,

> My hope is built on nothing less,
> Than Jesus' blood and righteousness;
> I dare not trust the sweetest frame,

But wholly lean on Jesus' name.
On Christ the solid Rock I stand;
All other ground is sinking sand.

More than a century ago, an ocean liner sank off the southwest coast of England, taking many people down with it. A 16-year-old galley boy, tossed up along the rugged shore, survived by clinging to a rock all night. When rescued, he was asked, "Didn't you shake as you clung all night to that rock?" The boy replied, "Yes, of course. But the rock never shook once." The ancient Israelites learned from their experiences in the desert that rocks were more than masses of stone. A rock could serve as shelter from a sudden storm. It could provide a cool shadow from the oppressive heat. Rocks were a stronghold and a place of safety. And, though the storms of confusion and panic rage, our hearts rest in the Prince of Peace. With your day of salvation being the first, remember what the Lord has done in the past. Reflection will sustain your faith in what He will do in the future. David knew firsthand how vital a rock can be in times of trouble. He was compelled to hide in the great rocky caverns of his native land while his enemies passed by his hiding place. Notice how he recognizes God in Psalm 19:14. He did not say "my accuser and my judge," but "my strength and my redeemer." Strength refers to a place of refuge in a world of weakness. Redeemer refers to one who has rescued another from slavery by paying the required price. We find our salvation in the One who saves us from bondage to sin and death through the Sacrifice of Calvary (Eph. 1:7). All sufficiency for this life and eternity is found in Jesus Christ! The Bible says, "O taste and see that the Lord is good" (Ps. 34:8). From His death, burial, and resurrection flows the sweet honey of salvation. When we have accepted Christ as our Savior, we can face the hard places of life with confidence and courage.

It's easy to become so preoccupied with earthly affairs that we shift our confidence from God to our intellect and abilities. Phillip E. Johnson (1940-2019), a gifted lawyer best known as one of the founders of the Intelligent Design movement, suffered a stroke and was likely to have another. Plagued by frightening thoughts during those first few days after his stroke, he was profoundly touched when a friend came and sang, "On Christ, the solid rock, I stand; all other ground is sinking sand." Johnson writes, "What was the solid rock on which I stood? I had always prided myself on being self-reliant, and my brain was what I had relied on. Now, the self with its brain was exposed as the shaky instrument it had always been. I was a Christian, even an ardent one in my worldly fashion, but now all the smoke was blown away. I saw Truth close up." Resolved to keep Jesus at the center of his life, Mr. Johnson became a different man. How quickly we rely on our reasoning, only to find that it is a "shaky instrument." Some make a 'rock' of their wealth, talents, friends, good deeds, and religious observances. In Matthew 7:24-27, we find the Master's famous illustration contrasting two foundations for life: The wise live according to His teachings; the foolish do not. Foundations matter, and only one house will survive a violent storm. The other will fall hard. The mark of true Christianity is not simply hearing but believing and doing. The storms of life reveal the strength of our faith. Faith is not an addition to life. It is a foundation for life that changes the tenor and trajectory of our lives. A person who merely professes to know Christ has only a self-righteous life that is shallow and short-lived. Jesus is the only foundation of truth, and the storms of life are weathered by clinging to the reality of God's Word.

The word 'refuge' is defined as a condition of being safe or sheltered from pursuit, danger, or trouble. The Psalmist said, "God is our refuge and strength, a very present help in trouble" (Ps. 46:1). Martin Luther was inspired to write the great hymn, "A Mighty Fortress is our God," after reading and studying Psalm 46. As a child of God (1 John 3:2), I am not an outcast; I have been grafted in (Rom. 11). I am not forgotten or alone; I am chosen and loved (Eph. 1:4). I am not a product of my past mistakes; I am a new creation (2 Cor. 5:17). My identity does not exist in anyone or anything but Jesus Christ. Charles Spurgeon said, "I have learned to kiss the wave that slams me into the Rock of Ages." I am never more aware of God's love than when I'm overwhelmed by circumstances outside my control. Why? Because through life's hardships, I am pushed into the presence of God. Indeed, the Bible is the bedrock of my faith, yet sometimes I struggle with contentment. And in these moments, God teaches me how His protection and strength can fight all battles. I will say of the Lord; He is my refuge and my fortress: my God; in him will I trust (Ps. 91:2). This is one of the most uplifting messages of Scripture. It speaks of someone wholly secure in the protection and presence of the Most High God. Isaiah 25:4 describes our Lord as a hiding place for those in distress - a shelter from the storm and a shade from the heat. To dwell in the "shadow of the Almighty" (Ps. 91:1) is to find complete rest and safety, no matter what we face in life – even death. I have decided to release my plans and trust God's purpose (Heb. 6:17-19).

Much of the Book of Proverbs is an admonishment to rely on godly wisdom (Prov. 1:7). It also warns us of the consequences of trusting in worldly foolishness (Prov. 3:35). The wise man Solomon refers to God as a strong tower where the righteous can find safety (Prov. 18:10). Our Lord began to unveil His holy name and perfection in the first chapter of the Bible. To Adam, He was a relational Lord (Gen. 1:27). Abraham saw Him as the Almighty God and Provider (Gen. 22). To Moses, God became his Banner and Sanctifier (Ex. 17:15). Gideon found Him to be a perfect Peace that passes all understanding (Judges 6:1-24). David discovered the Lord as the tender Shepherd who laid down His life for the sheep (Ps. 23), and Ezekiel worshiped the righteous God whose name is Jesus (Ezek. 1:26-28). During an earthquake, the inhabitants of a small village were very much alarmed. One elderly woman, whom they all knew, was surprisingly calm and joyous. At length, one of them said, "Mother, are you not afraid?" "No," she replied, "I rejoice to know that I have a God who can shake the world." Indeed, God is a refuge for believers!

Did you know that an emergency shelter is carved deep into the mountainside of West Virginia? Housed under the West Virginia Wing of the Greenbrier Resort, a top-secret, supersized bunker was built for all 535 members of Congress during the Eisenhower era. Construction on the 112,544-square-foot bunker began in 1958. It was built 720 feet into the hillside. Once completed in 1961, the facility was constantly maintained by a small group of government employees working undercover as audio and video technicians. The bunker provided four entrances, a 25-ton blast door that opens with only 50 pounds of pressure, decontamination chambers, 18 dormitories, purification equipment and three 25,000-gallon water tanks, a clinic with 12 hospital beds, medical and dental operating rooms, a laboratory, pharmacy and intensive care unit, a cafeteria, and meeting rooms for the House and Senate. The facility's location, critical to its effectiveness, remained a secret for more than three decades. On May 31, 1992, The Washington Post published an article, "The Last Resort," which exposed the facility. In 1995, the US government ended the lease agreement with The Greenbrier, and later that year, the resort began offering tours of the historic facility. The massive facility was never used—not even in the Cuban Missile Crisis. It was an unused refuge. We can say that God is our shelter, rock, and hiding place. But too often, prayer itself is an unused refuge. Corrie ten Boom said, "The center of His will is our only safety. Let us pray that we may always know it!" According to Psalm 46, this is what we know: Fear exists, waters are troubled, the heathen rage, and kingdoms are moved. This we also know: God rules, He is present, and He speaks, "Be still."

Dear Lord, you are our strength and our safe place. You are the infinite, all-powerful Creator who spoke the world into existence, the One who sees and knows all things. You are not only mighty, but you are also merciful and kind. We run to you as a loving Father, full of kindness, care, and love for your children. Thank you for the promise of eternal life with you. Be near to us in our restlessness and loneliness. You said you would be exalted in all the earth. Thine, O Lord, is the greatness, and the power, and the glory, and the victory, and the majesty: for all that is in the heaven and in the earth is thine; thine is the kingdom, O Lord, and thou art exalted as head above all (1 Chron. 29:11). Be exalted among the nations. Be exalted in our hearts today and always, Lord, for you alone are the Rock and the refuge of our souls!

Beyond Speech and Words

I LOVE THE SONG WRITTEN BY CLELAND MCAFEE THAT BEGINS, *THERE is a place of quiet rest near to the heart of God; a place where sin cannot molest, near to the heart of God.* For most of us, a God-honoring worship song running through our mind will reach places of the heart that conversation cannot. Even more incredible is that we can have an experience with Christ that is beyond speech and words! A few years ago, I began to recognize an inner chaos more unsettling than anything I had experienced. No matter how much I prayed, read the Bible, and listened to Biblical teaching, I could not calm the internal roar created by questions with no answers. I was convinced there was more to Christianity, and I identified with the phrase that was coined by John Piper, "God is most glorified in us when we are most satisfied in Him." I knew there needed to be a transformation of my heart. There were emotions I could sometimes hide but could not control. Then, the most amazing change occurred as I approached God's throne in silence and solitude. I discovered the sweetness of communion with God in the quietness of the early morning hours. I was inviting God into the rest of my day by wiping out the requirements of mere religion and leaning into the relationship. Did I find answers to my questions? Some — but not all. At least I had come to a place of tranquility where I saw life more clearly and experienced God's love more profoundly. Once my eyes opened to the sovereignty of God's grace, I found it on every page of the Bible! Isaiah said, "Thou wilt keep him in perfect peace, whose mind is stayed on thee: because he trusts in thee" (Isa. 26:3). A tranquil mind is a satisfied mind, and a satisfied mind is a peaceful mind (Ps. 37). My God's peace is perfect!

Several passages of Scripture emphasize the importance of silence in our lives. God met people silently (1 Kings 19:12, 1 Sam. 3:3-4). He encouraged the practice of silence (Ps. 62:1, Eccl. 3:7) and even retreated to find solitude himself (Mark 1:35, Luke 5:16). Jesus would withdraw, sometimes abruptly, from the crowds and his ministry of doing his Father's will to "the hills" or a "lonely place" or "the wilderness" or a "high mountain" or to the seashore or the Garden of Gethsemane. Psalm 46:10 tells us to contemplate the God we serve this way: "Be still, and know that I am God; I will be exalted among the heathen, I will be exalted in the earth." The prophet Jeremiah admonished those who were afflicted to sit quietly. He said, "It is good that a man should both hope and quietly wait for the salvation of the Lord" (Lam. 3:1-26). Waiting implies trust. It tells God and others that we believe He will meet all our needs according to His riches in glory (Phil. 4:19). The prophet Elijah encountered God during silent meditation. After he had experienced great success in ministry, Jezebel, the queen of Israel, was so threatened by Elijah's prophetic ministry that she wanted to kill him. Her threat sent Elijah into fear and depression, and he ran for his life. Eventually, he sat down under a solitary broom tree in the wilderness and asked God to take his life (1 Kings 18,19). Several things happened as Elijah withdrew from the busyness of life. He had to face himself, give up control, and receive God's guidance for his next steps. When we quietly release our agendas and our need to control everything, we open ourselves to what God wants to give.

Praying is not so much about expressing our dependence on God but rather experiencing it. Elijah had come to the end of himself. And although his distorted statement was self-centered and born out of despair, it shows he was willing to accept whatever God wanted to do. As painful as it is to relinquish control, this is an excellent place to be. It creates space where God can do and share with us according to His purposes. He wants to convey His loving, ministering presence through the Holy Spirit. God rarely chooses to reveal His whole plan to us in these moments. He didn't even write the Bible like that. Forty different authors penned Scripture over 1,600 years. If God only tells you a little bit, then that's all He wants you to know right now. He often shows just the next step, and this guidance doesn't usually come in audible words but as a gentle, inner voice. As we grow in our willingness to follow God's leading, we will eventually look back on all those seemingly unrelated steps and see a path that only a God of boundless love could have cleared for us. This is beyond speech or words! Today, with enthusiasm, I sing the song written by Frederick Lehman:

> O love of God, how rich and pure!
> How measureless and strong!
> It shall forevermore endure—
> The saints' and angels' song.

The apostle Paul wrote many things, but he did so in the awareness of what he could not express in his own strength. He said, "Thanks be unto God for his unspeakable gift" (2 Cor. 9:15), a presence too incredible to describe! Reflecting on his weakness, Paul saw grace and goodness beyond words (2 Cor. 11:15-33, 12:8-9). Barnabas saw the grace of God and was glad (Acts 11:23). Many things pull at our attention, seeking to distract us. We cannot live a holy life without the Holy Spirit's power. The security of the godly is to dwell in the secret place of the most High, abiding under the shadow of the Almighty (Ps. 91). In Psalm 139, the author's hope rests entirely in the God with whom he has a relationship. In this passage, David speaks of something not material but spiritual, not earthly but heavenly. He says the Lord is familiar with all his ways and that such knowledge is too lofty for him to attain. Having been raised in a Christian family, I understood God knew my name, and I knew He loved me. But even more remarkable is that God has never let me go! I cannot look back over my life without seeing His hand guiding me. And I cannot look to the future without seeing the work of Christ being proved in me. God has me in His embrace. I rest in His love because He always thinks about me (Isa. 49:15-16). I have joy in good and bad days, knowing He will never leave me (Deut. 31:8, Acts 10:34). Words will never express what His lovingkindness means to me. Like the Psalmist David, I have found comfort in something that cannot be described, something beyond speech and words.

Some have asked, "What does the presence of God feel like?" My answer is, "It cannot be described as a feeling because it is so much more! It is a powerful connection with Jesus that cannot be explained." Through the music we sing, the expression of prayers, and even in preaching, we struggle to find the right words to describe the majesty of God and the extent of his love. How do you explain eternal love that reaches from east to west and runs as deep as it is wide? In Romans 8:26, Apostle Paul tells of a divine experience in prayer that cannot be expressed in human terms. He even speaks of the Holy Spirit stepping into our thoughts and feelings to help us pray. Linger in God's promises. Listen to His wisdom. Cling to His truth. God listens to our hearts. He hears the communication that is beyond our words. I have often sought better ways to glorify God and express my love. Sometimes, I pray, but words are not enough. My vocabulary isn't vast enough, and I can't find the right words. These are the times I kneel and hold my hands open before Him. The ancients called this the "giving of the hand." Subjects of a kingdom did this when they came into the presence of their king. Without words, this act of kneeling declared their allegiance and surrender to the will of the one sitting on the throne. Perhaps we need to say less so we can communicate more. Sometimes, looking to God's Word will help us verbalize our feelings. Our words will fail, but God's never will. God has elevated His words above all else that exists. He proclaims His truth as the standard over all things (Jer. 1:12). As you read the Bible, turn God's words into your prayers. Repeat the supplications of those mentioned in the Bible. Sing them in a song. Ask the Spirit of God to highlight a verse or phrase that applies to your situation. Let passages of Scripture stir your spirit and strengthen your faith!

Unfortunately, many view prayer as an escape mechanism rather than a continuous line of communication. A co-worker asked a friend why he got donuts if he was trying to diet. He said, "Well, I came around the corner where the donut shop was. I told God if He wanted me to buy some donuts, he should have a parking spot in the front. Sure enough… on the eighth time around, there it was!" Prayer is more than a request. It is communicating with God as you would with a friend. A great example of quiet prayer is Psalm 63:1-6, "My soul shall be satisfied... when I remember thee upon my bed and meditate on thee in the night watches." Notice what David said in Psalm 5:1, "Give ear to my words, O Lord, consider my meditation." Frequently, we talk to God through audible speech. But often, we cannot find words to communicate our joy (1 Pet. 1:8). More commonly, we run out of words during personal turmoil and struggle. In times like these, can we pray without words? The psalmist David did! He asked God to hear his words and pay attention to his meditations. Allow Biblical truths to flow into your spirit. Delight in Him. Evangelist Gypsy Smith was asked what the secret of revival is. He said, "Go home. Take a piece of chalk. Draw a circle around yourself. Then pray, 'O Lord, revive everything inside this circle.'" D. L. Moody said, "Jesus Christ never taught His disciples how to preach, but only how to pray." Prayer is more than saying words. It is pouring out our hearts to God (Ps. 62:8).

Gracious Heavenly Father, you said if we would seek you with all our hearts, we would find you (Jer. 29:13). Help us to desire your presence more than anything else; more than answers and more than blessings. We are amazed that we can communicate with you. And how wonderful it is that you listen! Thank you for not telling us to go away and come back when we have something more meaningful to say. Forgive us for letting our lives get so busy that we do not prioritize our time together. Words alone cannot express our gratitude for your goodness to us. Father, we know that Calvary's perfect, complete, and sufficient Sacrifice is effective for all who will believe it is your design for redeeming souls (Acts 16:31, Eph. 2:1-10). Thank you for listening when we cannot find the words to say. When our grief is inexpressible, or our joy is unspeakable, you always command peace and hope – and we love you, Lord, beyond speech or words!

The Promise of Paradise

AND HE SAID UNTO JESUS, "LORD, REMEMBER ME WHEN THOU COMEST into thy kingdom." And Jesus said unto him, "Verily I say unto thee, today shalt thou be with me in paradise" (Luke 23:42-43). When Jesus was crucified, His cross was positioned between two others on which hung two criminals condemned to death. The Bible says both men used what little breath they had left to mock Him (Matt. 27:44). They had adopted the same behavior as the religious leaders and other onlookers who witnessed the death of Jesus (Matt. 27:39-43). But one of these two men eventually recognized his sinfulness and wanted forgiveness. It was an amazing transformation. What changed? The apostle John tells us that Jesus died before the robbers did (John 19:32-24). This means they were able to observe everything that happened when Jesus was on the cross, including his cry, "Father, forgive them; for they know not what they do" (Luke 23:34). Perhaps the repentant thief thought, "If Christ was ready to forgive the men who drove spikes into His hands and feet, maybe He will forgive me." This powerful event teaches the gospel of grace and describes one of the most amazing promises of the Bible. The statements made by the thief contain all of the elements of salvation! He perceived his guilt, knew that he deserved death because of his sin, and then prayed to Christ to receive forgiveness. The words and actions of Jesus Christ personally secured his salvation. A criminal was sentenced to die, but with Jesus, there was no condemnation (Rom. 8:1), only paradise!

What does this mean for us? We start with a statement and a question: "God will forgive your sins. Are you interested?" Before Jesus said, "Today shalt thou be with me in paradise," the condemned man perceived his guilt and asked the Savior for forgiveness with faith and a repentant heart. This account reminds us that salvation is a gift to be received, not a reward (Rom. 6:23). It is also immediate. The thief had no time for good deeds. He had no history of righteous living nor a future to prove he was a changed man. He could not repay his victims, help the poor, or be baptized. He could not attend a local church, give money in the offering plate, or join a discipleship class. He had no opportunity to do any of the things people mistakenly attach to salvation. All he could do was look to the Savior and ask for mercy (Luke 18:13). This salvation story perfectly illustrates that no evil is too extreme to be forgiven. The death of Jesus Christ is sufficient to pay the debt of every sin (Rom. 6:23). With very little theological knowledge and no church membership card, yet through faith, the unnamed criminal received a passport to Heaven. His prayer was prompted by what he believed about Christ. It was an expression of faith. The moment of your faith is the moment of your salvation (Rom. 10:9, Eph. 2:6). This is the lesson from a dying thief. This is the simplicity of the Gospel of Jesus Christ!

The condemned man hanging on a cross outside the walls of Jerusalem acknowledged that he deserved the sentence of crucifixion for the life he had lived while on earth. But he found mercy for his eternity that day! Zacharias, the father of John the Baptist, said, "Through the tender mercy of our God; whereby the dayspring from on high hath visited us, to give light to them that sit in darkness and the shadow of death, to guide our feet into the way of peace" (Luke 1:78-79). The "dayspring from on high" refers to Jesus, the Messiah who is the light of men (John 1:4-5, Eph. 5:14). It is a beautiful name of the coming Savior given by Zacharias when he was "filled with the Holy Ghost, and prophesied" (Luke 1:67). In that same prophecy, Zacharias also called that coming one the Lord who would "give knowledge of salvation unto his people by the remission of their sins, through the tender mercy of our God" (v 77-78). Just six months later, Jesus was born. Jesus' response to the dying man's plea tells us about heaven and our mission here on earth. The compassion of Christ toward us is no less complete. The power of the blood of Jesus to cleanse us from our sins is no less absolute!

The Greek word for *paradise* in this verse is a transliteration of a Persian word used in ancient times to refer to a king's garden, which was often a place of profound beauty. The thought of heaven as the King's Garden, where love and justice prevail and where people I love are in the very presence of God, sounds like paradise to me. The story is told of a doctor who made house calls back in the day when that was what doctors did. He took his dog with him in his horse-drawn buggy. One day, he visited a dying man, and as he went into the man's house, he left his dog on the front step. The dying man asked the doctor, "Doc, what will it be like—heaven—what will it be like?" At that moment, the doctor's dog began to scratch at the door, whimpering and whining to get in. The doctor stopped and said, "Do you hear that?" "Yes," the man replied. The doctor continued, "That's my dog. He has never been inside your house. He doesn't know what's on the other side of this door. All he knows is that his master is in here, and if his master is in here, it must be okay." Jesus told us nothing of eternity's geographical location or spatial configuration. But what little He did tell us forever draws the sting of death and the grave. What Jesus said was so simple and clear that it can never be misunderstood or misinterpreted. He said, "You shall be with Me." Make no mistake. Heaven will fulfill every desire our hearts could ever hold. Heaven will satisfy every need we possess. Heaven will complete every relationship we hold dear. Heaven will heal every wound. Heaven will quench every thirst. But above all else, Heaven will be this: We shall be with Jesus! This was all the thief needed to hear. He was still writhing in physical agony, but the misery in his soul was not gone. For the first time in his life, he was free from the guilt and consequences of his sin. The Savior at his side was bearing it all for him, and soon, the two of them would be in Paradise together.

We have sinned against a holy God and deserve His wrath. Romans 3:23 tells us, "For all have sinned, and come short of the glory of God." The wage of sin is death, but the gift of God is eternal life through Jesus Christ our Lord (Rom. 6:23). One day, we will appear for judgment (Heb. 9:27). But, as we see in Luke 23, there is hope for all who will humble themselves before God in faith and repentance. Jesus will do for you what He did for the criminal hanging next to

Him! Both men heard the words of Christ, yet they responded very differently. One dying man regarded the cross as a contradiction. He concluded that because Jesus was on the cross, he was no Savior. So he ridiculed the man on the middle cross: "If thou be Christ, save thyself and us" (v39). But the other man saw the cross as confirmation. He recognized that because Jesus was on the cross, he must be the Savior. In his final hours, he had seen and heard enough of Jesus to conclude that he was innocent of any crime. And the Holy Spirit had opened his eyes to realize that his predicament was far different from what he had formerly thought. Not only was he being punished justly, receiving the condemnation his sins deserved, but his punishment would extend into eternity if he lacked the forgiveness of which Jesus spoke. A criminal had more faith that day than anyone observing this gruesome scene. He offered nothing and asked the King for everything. We have nothing to bring to Jesus but what the criminal brought: our sin. The example of the thief on the cross is often cited as the pattern for deathbed conversions. And so it is. What a tremendous promise Jesus gives to a repentant believer! Child of God, let that knowledge be your joy and praise today!

The words of Jesus will still change lives today. He has not changed (Heb. 13:8). At some point while hanging on his cross, this man changed his mind about who Christ was - and so must we. The blood of Jesus pays for the sins of everyone who calls on the name of the Lord for salvation (Rom. 10:13). The Bible says, "Neither is there salvation in any other; for there is none other name under heaven given among men, whereby we must be saved" (Acts 4:12). This thief, who was utterly undeserving, experienced salvation by grace through faith (Eph. 2:8-9), and in a moment, even before his physical death, he received eternal life (John 17:1-11). He had already "passed from death unto life" (John 5:24). People who are rich in mere religion will tell you, "First, let us consider whether this evildoer met the qualifications for a heavenly life, which include conforming to God's moral standards and manifesting such qualities as honesty, integrity, and compassion. One must remain loyal to God until the end of their earthly course. Only by meeting those requirements can they show themselves worthy of being resurrected and qualified for the weighty responsibility awaiting them in heaven." They will say, "This man had not built a record of upright conduct and faithful endurance. Those who are given the hope of life in heaven must provide a solid basis for confidence that they will uphold God's righteous standards." This belief system is not Biblical.

In 1 John 4:15, we read, "Whosoever shall confess that Jesus is the Son of God, God dwelleth in him, and he in God." Many of us have found comfort in the honesty of the apostle Paul, who openly confessed his struggle in Romans 7 to do the right thing when his flesh pulled him toward sin. I mention the ongoing battle with sin to illustrate how incredibly wonderful the forgiveness of God is for those who accept it (John 3:16). This forgiveness is made possible because of the sacrifice of Jesus Christ on the cross. Our greatest need is to respond to His amazing grace. Jesus does more than help us. He delivers from sin. He offers more than provision. He redeems us for eternity. Jesus does more than teach positive thinking. He provides a trip to paradise. This promise of eternal life to a condemned criminal illustrates the holiness and majesty of the Lord as clearly as anything He ever said. The thief was physically helpless. He was nailed to a cross! No amount of discipline or human ability will qualify us for Heaven. The thief was also morally corrupt. He openly admitted his guilt when he rebuked the other thief for mocking Jesus. But the transformation from a dead sinner into a living child of God is beautifully portrayed in the thief's conversion experience, a conversion made possible by the mercy of our Savior Jesus Christ.

Are you striving to earn the favor of God? Rest in the finished work of Christ on the cross. His grace is enough. Serve Him. Enjoy Him. If you have been born again, having experienced a spiritual transformation that only comes from above (Titus 3:5, Acts 2:37-47), know that the pressure is off because your standing with God has never been about what you can do for Him. It has always been about what He has so graciously done for you. Do you feel you've messed up too often to receive grace? David Berkowitz, the serial killer formerly known as Son of Sam, says. "One night, I was reading Psalm 34. I came upon the sixth verse, *'This poor man cried, and the Lord heard him and saved him out of all his troubles.'* I got down on my knees and began to cry to Jesus Christ. I asked Jesus to forgive me for all my sins. In my heart, I just knew that somehow my life was going to be different." The thief on the cross lived a life of sin until his final moments, and Jesus did not refuse him. There is no sin so big that the blood of Christ cannot cover it (Eph. 1:7, Heb. 10:17). God's mercy depends not on what you do but only on His unchanging love. The incarnate God entered a guilty plea for you and me. Rest in knowing that the Lord will never let you go. Jesus Christ is the promise of paradise!

What Shall I Render?

THE WRITER OF PSALM 116:12 WAS GRATEFUL FOR GOD'S MERCY AND grace in his time of need. He was thankful for several things: an inclined ear, deliverance from death, bountiful treatment, and freedom from bondage. And to every child of God, these blessings are given! Therefore, he asks, "What shall I render unto the Lord for all his benefits towards me?" What can we give the Lord for the many blessings He has given us? What do we give when all we have is not enough? We will love and trust Him. The psalmist said he would yield the affection of his heart because God had loved his soul out of the pit of corruption. He wisely considered that God's richest blessings belong to those who trust Him (Ps. 112:1). With a life gratefully pledged, the singer declared God's majesty and faithfulness, ascribing all the glory where it was due. In Psalm 96:1-2, David said, "O sing unto the Lord a new song: sing unto the Lord, all the earth. Sing unto the Lord, bless his name; shew forth his salvation from day to day."

Psalm 116 is one of several thanksgiving psalms in which God does great things for those devoted to Him. It's a psalm that was written, some suggested by David, but the author is unknown. We don't know the nature of the difficulty that prompted the psalmist's supplication in verse one, only that he had no way to turn. So he called out to God for help and announced that salvation and restoration of life come from God alone. He reminds us that no matter how difficult our circumstances seem, there is One who hears and answers prayer.

What can a pardoned sinner render to the Lord for his mercy and forgiveness? How will we respond to God for the many blessings He has provided? Our best is unworthy of the Lord's acceptance, yet we should devote ourselves and all we have to Him. We know we could never repay Him for His goodness, yet it calls for a response. It is proper for us to reflect on how wonderfully blessed we are. The psalmist reminds us that God is the source of all blessings. Too often, we fail to recognize where our blessings originate. Emerson said that if the stars came out only once a year, everybody would stay up all night to behold them. We have seen the stars so often that we don't bother to look at them anymore. We have grown accustomed to our blessings. The Lord is the giver of every good gift. Apostle James said, "Every good gift and every perfect gift is from above, and cometh down from the Father of lights, with whom is no variableness, neither shadow of turning" (James 1:17). The air that we breathe is a gift from God. He gives us strength and health. We owe our ability to work or earn a living to Him. Our family and friends are the results of His goodness. Above all, we owe our eternal redemption entirely to God. If we are in Christ, we understand the salvation of God's grace through faith in Jesus (Eph. 2:8-9). We live in the promise that we will see our Savior and those who have gone to Heaven before us (John 14:2- 3, 1 Thess. 4:13- 18, 2 Sam. 12:23, Luke 9:28- 36). How could we ever thank God enough for His benefits?

The psalmist said, "I will take the cup of salvation and call upon the name of the Lord" (v13). This was an act of worship. He said, "I will pay my vows unto the Lord now in the presence of all his people" (v14). In other words, I will testify to the grace of God in my life with the sacrifice of praise (Heb. 13:15). The Lord is glorified when thankfulness is evident in what we say and do. We have been redeemed from sin and death so that we might live in this world as a living testimony to the goodness of the One who has redeemed us. Our Lord has bestowed so much mercy on us that we ought to look about and within us to find a way to manifest our love and appreciation. The joy of living comes from an attitude of thankfulness.

Even in death, we are blessed abundantly. In verse 15, we read, "Precious in the sight of the Lord is the death of his saints." Why? Because death removes the remaining barriers between God and his children. Charles Spurgeon said, "Death to the saints is not a penalty, it is not destruction, it is not even a loss, but the doorway to an eternity of perfect fellowship." When the Puritan minister Richard Baxter lay dying, he said to his friends who visited him: "Choose God for your portion, Heaven for your home, God's glory for your end, and His Word for your rule." Some of the last words he uttered were in response to the question, "Dear Mr. Baxter, how are you?" The minister replied, "Almost well." And so it is. Eternal life with Jesus is the greatest of all benefits. And for this promise, we will render a lifetime of thanksgiving! When considering all God has done, we should not merely wait for the following blessing. The Lord has already done enough if He doesn't do anything else. To a born-again believer, He has given deliverance, preservation, and rest. Indeed, presenting ourselves as "a living sacrifice, holy, acceptable unto God" is our reasonable service (Rom. 12:1). We give our lives, submitting ourselves to the will of God. We trade our nothing for His everything. When the psalmist takes the cup of salvation (v13), he raises it publicly for everyone to see. This was an appropriate conclusion of a song to be sung when all the people were gathered together at Jerusalem to keep the feast. God's praise is not kept in a closet or even a place of worship but in every area of life.

What shall we render? We shall obey the Word of God. Every Christian wants to respond to God's grace, and I believe any compensation other than obedience without hesitation or reservation would insult that grace. To live and love according to Scripture is to give God the praise and glory He deserves. He gave His all for us; therefore, we give our all to Him. I love the song Jesus Paid It All, written by Elvina M. Hall in 1865: *For nothing good have I whereby Thy grace to claim; I'll wash my garments white in the blood of Calvary's Lamb. And when before the throne, I stand in Him complete, 'Jesus died my soul to save,' my lips shall still repeat. Jesus paid it all; all to Him I owe; sin had left a crimson stain; He washed it white as snow.*

The Book of Micah involves a conversation between the Lord and Israel. In chapter six, God brought a complaint against His people, "O my people, what have I done unto thee? And wherein have I wearied thee? testify against me. For I brought thee up out of the land of Egypt, and redeemed thee out of the house of servants" (v3-4). He had done nothing but good to Israel and been repaid with rejection and rebellion. Then answered the prophet Micah, "Wherewith shall I come before the Lord and bow myself before the high God?" This was a question asked out of resentment. In Micah's imagined courtroom, Israel called out to God from the witness stand and said: "Just what do you want from me? Will the Lord be pleased with thousands of rams, ten thousand rivers of oil?" We can almost hear Israel shouting at God, "You ask too much. Nothing will satisfy you. You are unreasonable." Blinded to God's goodness and character, the prophet reasons with a depraved frame of reference that God must change. In verse 8, the Lord replies, "He hath showed thee, O man, what is good; and what doth the Lord require of thee, but to do justly, love mercy, and walk humbly with God." God essentially said, "You act as if what I require of you is some mystery. It is no mystery at all. I have shown you clearly what is good and what I require of you." In Micah's imagined courtroom, God has proven His case. Israel was afflicted not because of God's neglect but because of their disregard for Him. God's requirements are not mysterious or complicated (Micah 6:8). This passage from Micah points out that sacrifice, no matter how momentous, is useless without a life of justice, lovingkindness, and humility. Sometimes, we mistakenly focus on religious traditions, and our questions about them advance from lesser to greater. Christianity is not about our human abilities. Christ's followers do not paint self-portraits but create an image of God through a lifestyle.

To believe that we have earned or deserve everything is the message of Satan's domain. We deserve only the wrath of God. Salvation is by grace alone, through faith alone, in Christ alone. The gospel, meaning 'good news,' presupposes there is bad news. We must understand that we are under divine judgment, that our sins have offended a holy God, and that we are separated from Him (Isa. 59:2). There is nothing we can do in and of ourselves to remove the condemnation of that sin (Rom. 2:1-29). The wage of sin is death (Rom. 6:23), and the soul that sins shall surely die (Ezek. 18:20). "But thanks be to God, which giveth us the victory through our Lord Jesus Christ" (1 Cor. 15:57). Our hope is found in Jesus Christ, who died upon the Cross for us. There is a common human arrogance that tries to fit God into a specific theology and then professes to be more confident than a human has a right to be. The remedy for sin is not found in more numerous or increasingly painful sacrifices but in a transformed heart made possible by the power of the Holy Ghost (Acts 2). Without the indwelling of the Spirit, any religious observance is nothing more than hypocrisy (Isa. 1:14).

Our walk through life is meant to be humble, and the journey can be safely traveled only with the guidance of the Holy Spirit. Micah's message is still relevant today. No matter how elaborate our talents and abilities are, they can never compensate for a lack of love (1 Cor. 13:3) and obedience (1 Sam. 15:22). Compliance with rules is never as valuable to God as a surrendered life. So, we return to the psalmist's question, "What shall I render unto the Lord for all his benefits towards me?" To He who owns it all, what shall we give? We will lift the name of Jesus Christ. We will honor our commitments and devotion to God. We will desire justice and mercy. We will live with humility before our Lord (Micah 6:8). The Bible says God inhabits the praises of His people (Ps. 22:3). Therefore, we will render unto God the glory, praise, and honor due to Him. We will walk in liberty because we have sought to live in His precepts (Ps. 119:45). God's mercies are new every morning, and great is His faithfulness (Lam. 3:22-23). We have been saved eternally from death and hell (Rev. 20:11-15). Therefore, we will rejoice in the God of our salvation!

Christ, The Hope of Glory

THE RICHES OF GOD'S GRACE FOR HIS CHILDREN ARE DIFFICULT, IF NOT impossible, to understand (Rom. 11:33). Unfathomable riches like mercy, redemption, unconditional love, and everlasting life are too deep to be measured. Nonetheless, God chose to make known this mystery: "Christ in you, the hope of glory" (Col. 1:27). This passage is not a mere slogan of Christianity. It is a Scriptural truth, a living reality made possible by faith in the finished work of Calvary (2 Cor. 5:17-19). Those who trust in Jesus for salvation are given a new life, destined to live with God forever (1 Thess. 5:9-11). Jesus told his disciples, "And I will pray the Father, and he shall give you another Comforter, that he may abide with you forever" (John 14:16). One of the most wonderful revelations of the Bible is that God's power, wisdom, majesty, glory, and grace live in a born-again believer! The Holy Spirit within us is the "earnest of our inheritance" that seals an eternity glorious beyond all imagination (Eph. 1:13-14). The source of our joy is knowing that one day we will see our Lord and Savior, Jesus Christ (Rom. 8:29, 1 John 3:2).

The apostle Paul's suffering for the sake of Christ was difficult by any human standard (2 Cor. 11:24-31). In chapter one of 2 Corinthians, he spoke about a time when he utterly "despaired even of life" (v8). Paul's joy was relative, not to his circumstances, but to his calling. He said even the worst suffering on this earth is only a "light and momentary affliction" when weighed against the glory of our eternal life to come (2 Cor. 4:17). Paul refused to lose heart because he understood that, for a Christian, trials come with both a purpose and a reward (James 1:2-4, 12; Rom. 5:3-5). In a letter to the saints at Philippi, Paul uses words like rejoice or joy sixteen times. Incredibly, he wrote this epistle while imprisoned and apprehensive that his execution was close at hand. He had been in custody for several years, but he didn't allow dire circumstances to drive him to desperation. Paul looked forward to the glories of Heaven, and he encouraged every child of God to do the same (Phil. 2:2-5). We have a new song to sing in the face of hopelessness because hope is at the heart of God's love for us. And this hope is not a feeling of expectation for something to happen but rather a confident assurance of what shall happen according to the Word of God (Acts 1:11, Rev. 21:4).

The creator of an animated television comedy show had booked American Airlines Flight 11, but he arrived late at Logan Airport and missed his flight. A short time later, hijackers flew that very plane into the North Tower of the World Trade Center. Seth McFarlane found himself healthy and alive. When someone asked the inevitable question: "After that narrow escape, do you think of the rest of your life as a gift?" "No," said MacFarlane, "that experience didn't change me at all. It made no difference in the way I live my life. It made no difference in the way I look at things. It was just a coincidence." Oh, friend, it is right and proper that we thank God at all times and in all places (1 Thess. 5:16-18). John Calvin said, "All that Christ has done for us is of no value to us so long as we remain outside of Christ." Eternal hope will be ours only as we throw ourselves upon the mercy of God to free us from the grip of sin (Gal. 2:20). All sovereignty and sufficiency are in Jesus, for He is the image of the invisible God (Col. 1:15).

The early Christians were amazingly different from their non-believing neighbors. They were more thankful, compassionate, and forgiving. Were they just more excellent people? Not at all. Their behavior resulted from what they believed their future to be. It always does. When we live in the hope of the Word of God, thankfulness and godly conduct will follow. Knowledge of Scripture will affect how we interpret this world and make us long for the world to come. Of all the mysteries God has revealed in the New Testament, I believe the most profound is this: "Christ in you, the hope of glory" (Col. 1:17). Since the beginning of time, people have looked beyond this world to find hope in crisis. But Hope has arrived! It is a blessed hope, a visible hope, and a glorious hope. Freedom is for you. Jesus Christ is the deliverance from the bondage that is griping your life. Eternal hope begins in a relationship with God through faith in Christ, and the hope of glory is available to everyone! Paul writes to the believers in Rome, "Therefore being justified by faith, we have peace with God through our Lord Jesus Christ" (Rom. 5:1). We who are born from above (John 3:1-21) are no longer the object of God's wrath. We have peace with God now and forever. So, when Paul uses the word 'hope' in Romans, he is not talking about a desire that something will happen. He is speaking of the Holy Spirit's indwelling that has already appeared in our hearts (Titus 2:11). God incarnate came from Heaven to live among us, and we are complete in Him! I love the song inspired by John 1:14 and written by William E. Booth-Clibborn, Down From His Glory:

> Without reluctance, flesh, and blood, His substance
> He took the form of man, revealed the hidden plan.
> O glorious mystery, Sacrifice of Calvary,
> And now I know Thou art the great "I AM."
>
> Oh, how I love Him! How I adore Him!
> My breath, my sunshine, my all in all!
> The great Creator became my Savior,
> And all God's fulness dwelleth in Him.

As followers of Christ, we are not our own (1 Cor. 6:20). We are His. Romans 14:8 says, "For whether we live, we live unto the Lord; and whether we die, we die unto the Lord; whether we live therefore, or die, we are the Lord's." Jesus gave Himself for us, and Paul proclaimed that Christ alone is enough. No other person, knowledge, or system is needed (Col. 1:15,18). The reason Paul and Timothy could continually give thanks to God (Col. 1:3) is explained as "the hope which is laid up for you in heaven..." (v5). The Greek term is translated here as "laid up" or "reserved." The folks Paul wrote to had already accepted the gospel, so their reservation had been made (v7-8). Now, if you doubt the eternality of salvation from the moment you are born again, please consider this question: "Since the validation of heaven had already been made for these people, how could a reservation kept by God in eternity ever be removed in time?" It is a question worth considering. And the answer is clear: It cannot. Christ in us, the hope of glory, is the Creator entering His creation. The Spirit's presence in our hearts guarantees our ultimate salvation (Eph. 1:13, 4:30).

When we meet some people, we immediately know that they are different. It is not that they have affixed a name tag to themselves and proclaimed themselves the advocate of a particular religion or ideology. It is that they know Jesus Christ and that He is a living reality to them. They dwell in Him, and He dwells in them. He is the source of their life, and it shows in everything they do. To use Biblical expressions, "The peace of Christ rules in their hearts" (Col. 3:15), "the power of Christ is made perfect in their weakness" (2 Cor. 12:9), and "the life of Christ is made manifest in their mortal flesh" (2 Cor. 4:11). But let me give you an example of one who spoke of his inner turmoil and conflict. Veteran broadcaster Sir Paul Holmes (1950-2013) was interviewed shortly after his knighthood was announced and again just before his death. Near the end of the second interview, he was asked, "Are you frightened?" "Yes, I'm frightened," he said. "I plan to increase my peace with God. I am worried about what's over there, far away and over the hill. I wonder what there is." He said, "The hardest thing is closing my eyes and night and not knowing whether I will ever wake up." I pray that someone told this good man that Jesus Christ is the hope of earth and joy of Heaven!

Florence May Chadwick (1918-1995) was the first woman to swim across the English Channel in both directions, setting a time record each time. In 1952, young Florence stepped into the waters of the Pacific Ocean off Catalina Island, determined to swim to the shore of mainland California. The weather was foggy and chilly, and she could hardly see the boats accompanying her. She swam for 15 hours. When she begged to be taken out of the water, her mother, who was in one of the boats accompanying her, said, "You're so close; don't give up; you can make it." Extremely exhausted, she demanded to be taken out. It wasn't until she was on the boat that she discovered the shore was less than half a mile away. The next day, she said at a news conference, "All I could see was the fog. I think if I could have seen the shore, I would have made it." Can you relate to those words? We sometimes live in a fog that blinds us from a peaceful shore. We allow troubles, worry, doubt, depression, health problems, finances, uncertainties about the future, and remorse over the past to exhaust us. Our focus is clouded, and we feel like giving up, forgetting that Heaven is just in sight. But soon, we shall finally see the One whom our soul loves. If the saints presently in Heaven were allowed to speak to us, as Miss Chadwick's mother was, I'm sure they would say something like, "Oh dear Saint, press on, don't turn back, don't give up, if you could only see what's waiting for you."

God's people of all ages endured hardship because they had their hearts set on everlasting life with Him. They knew that to be absent from the body was to be present with the Lord. Heaven was the reference point by which they could navigate their lives. So today, let us put aside every weight and the sins that so easily beset us and let us run with patience to the goal set before us (Heb. 12:1). Consider Florence Chadwick's words once again: "I think if I could have seen the shore, I would have made it." For the child of God, that shore is Jesus and a place called Heaven. Satan's strategy is to divert our attention from the only Person where reconciliation with God is accomplished (Rom. 5:10). I am always blessed by the words of Isaac Watts: 'O God, our Help in ages past, our Hope for years to come, our Shelter from the stormy blast, and our eternal Home. O God, our Help in ages past, our Hope for years to come, be Thou our Guard while life shall last, and our eternal Home.' May I encourage you today? Set your affections on things above (Col. 3:2). Entrust your life to the God who will reign with perfect justice in an eternity that awaits all who have received Jesus. For indeed, in Christ alone, our hope is found!

Living In Christ

IN THE FIRST TWO CHAPTERS OF HIS LETTER TO THE EPHESIANS, APOSTLE Paul uses the phrase "in Christ" or "in Him" repeatedly. In verse 13 of chapter two, he writes, "But now in Christ Jesus ye who sometimes were far off are made nigh by the blood of Christ." It seems the concept "in Christ" or "living in Christ" is a little vague nowadays and is often used as just another label for Christianity. So, according to Scripture, what does it mean to live in Christ? First, understand that Jesus Christ, the Son of God, who was born in Bethlehem, died on the cross and rose from the dead, lives by His Spirit in the soul of every believer. Living in Christ means having a relationship with Him in such a way that His resources and sufficiency belong to us. The term "in Christ" is a New Testament expression that describes the closeness of the personal union where God's character becomes our experience and possession (1 John 2:5, Gal. 5:22-23). Jesus emphasized the value of this union in John 15:5, when He said, "I am the vine, ye are the branches." Before Paul's conversion in Acts 9, he was actively persecuting followers of Jesus. He even consented to Stephen's death in Acts 7. But, on the road to Damascus, God stopped Paul (formerly named Saul) with a bright light and a question. The question was not, "Saul, why are you persecuting these Christians?" but "Why do you persecute me?" (Acts 9:4). This was because Stephen, being "full of the Holy Ghost" (Acts 7:55), was so identified with Jesus, and Jesus was so identified with him that when Saul laid a finger on Stephen, he was, in effect laying a finger on Jesus. Stephen was "living in" or "abiding in" Christ.

Galatians 3:26-27 gives us insight into the phrase and what it means: "For ye are the children of God by faith in Jesus Christ. For as many of you as have been baptized into Christ, have put on Christ." We who have trusted in Christ for salvation are sons and daughters of God with all the rights and privileges that come with that eternal position. Romans 8:17 says we are "joint heirs with Christ." The Greek term translated as 'heirs' refers to those who receive their allotted possession by right of sonship. In other words, we are His beneficiaries (Matt. 25:34, Gal. 3:29). To be "baptized into Christ" means we are identified with Christ, having left our old sinful lives and fully embracing the new life in Him (Mark 8:34, Luke 9:23). Colossians 3:3 says, "For ye are dead, and your life is hidden with Christ in God," meaning we have accepted His sacrifice as payment for our sins. To those born of the Spirit, washed in the blood of Christ, the distance and barriers that separated us from God have been removed (Col. 1:12-21). It is purely the mercy of God that has pronounced us children of God through faith in Christ. Our everlasting position in Christ is entirely founded on God's grace towards us. The Bible says that, while we were yet sinners, Christ died for us (Rom. 5:8). To be in Christ means that God no longer sees our sin but the righteousness of His Son (Eph. 2:13, Heb. 8:12). Only in Jesus is our sin debt canceled, our relationship with God restored, and our eternity secured (John 3:16-18, 20:31). Clothed in the righteousness of Christ (Rom. 13:14, Gal. 3:27), our minds become so identified with Christ that our requests are made in harmony with His will (1 John 5:14). He becomes the source of our life that is manifest in everything we do.

The expressions "in Christ," "in the Lord," and "in him" occur 164 times in the letters of Paul alone. The word "Christian" occurs only three times in the Bible. What is often mistakenly called "Christianity" is, in essence, neither a religion nor a belief system. It is the person of Jesus Christ. God becomes our reality when His peace rules in our hearts (Col. 3:15), when His power is made perfect in our weakness (2 Cor. 12:9), and when the way Jesus lived is seen in us (2 Cor. 4:11). Paul said, "For me to live is Christ" (Phil. 1:21). The apostle is saying that everything he has tried to be, everything he is, and everything he looked forward to being pointed to Christ. It means Christ is the center of our mind, heart, body, and soul. New life in Christ leads to a new lifestyle where we share the gospel, impact society, and, above all else, bring honor and glory to the name of Jesus. To be "in Christ" is to be fulfilled in Him. The Gospel of Jesus, the good news of the indwelling Christ, means we are never alone. At your lowest moment, when you feel isolated, abandoned, and lonely, you can say, "He is at my right hand; I shall not be moved" (Ps. 16:8). When you know that Christ lives within, you will say with David, "The Lord is my light, and my salvation; whom shall I fear? The Lord is the strength of my life; of whom shall I be afraid?" (Ps. 27:1). You will say with Paul, "If God be for me, who can be against me?" (Rom. 8:31). You will say with John, "Greater is he that is in me than he that is in the world" (1 John 4:4). Christ has a real-time awareness of every trial and every temptation you face.

My wife Marjorie passed from this life on August 19, 2020. She enjoyed watching Downton Abbey, an English drama from the early 20th century set in a home where the servants live, eat, and work downstairs while the earl and his family enjoy their stately home upstairs. One distinguishing feature of the house is a system of little bells that ring in the kitchen with a pull cord in every room. The earl and his family can call for anything, and the servants immediately respond. Christ has installed a bell system that connects your heart with heaven. This is a bell system in reverse where we can ring a bell in heaven for the help of the Master (Heb. 4:16). Jesus Christ, God on heaven's throne, understands all that you face and fear. Why? Because He understands basement living (Matt. 4:1-11). He was tempted and tested in every respect when He lived downstairs for 33 years!

Throughout Paul's epistle to the Romans, we learn that in Christ, we are free from the bondage of sin (Rom. 6:11). We are no longer condemned (Rom. 8:1). We are united with God and each other, working towards a common cause (Rom. 12:5). The phrase "in Christ" refers to the redeemed state of believers who have declared a decision to follow Jesus. As a practical matter, living in Christ means recognizing that how we respond to circumstances can serve the eternal purpose of advancing the Gospel and encouraging others. In Philippians 1:12, God was glorified in Paul's imprisonment because he understood true freedom is in Christ. Living in Christ is pursuing the knowledge of Scripture and surrendering anything that would prevent us from hearing Him say, "Well done, thou good and faithful servant" (Matt.

25:21). Paul reminded the church at Colossae, "And whatsoever ye do in word or deed, do all in the name of the Lord Jesus, giving thanks to God and the Father by him" (Col. 3:17).

To abide in Christ is not a mystical experience but a defined knowledge. It is allowing God's Word to fill our minds, direct our wills, and transform our affections. Simply put, our relationship to Christ is connected to what we do with our Bibles. Obedience to the teachings of Christ is the evidence of our love for God (John 15:10-14). Jesus said, "Abide in me, and I in you" (John 15:4). Nothing is uniquely religious about the word 'abide.' In Scripture, it is the ordinary word for "stay," "continue," or sometimes "dwell." Our Lord says, "As a branch cannot bear fruit by itself, neither can you." Power flows from the energy of staying connected to the fruit-producing vine, namely Jesus Christ. If you abide, you bear fruit. William Carey spent thirty-five years in India before he saw one convert. Some people think he led a fruitless life. But almost every convert in India to this day is the fruit of his branch because he translated the New Testament into many different Indian dialects. In this life, he did not reap directly what he had sown, but his eternal legacy bore much fruit.

Our relationship with Christ is unlike anything else in the human realm. The writers of Scripture often used metaphors to describe it: He is the King, and we are the subjects (Phil. 2:10); He is the Shepherd, and we are the sheep (John 10:11-18); He is the Head, and we are the body (Col. 1:18). Fruit is a metaphor that is used many times in the Bible, appearing in nearly every book of the New Testament. Yet, it is often misunderstood. Fruit is neither outward success nor sensationalism. It is not merely compelling others to be enthusiastic about a church program. Spiritual fruit is Christlike character as defined in Galatians 5:22-23: Love, joy, peace, longsuffering, gentleness, goodness, meekness, faith, and temperance. A true believer will demonstrate these attributes of Jesus. Biblical fruit is not behavior produced by self-effort but grows naturally from a relationship with God.

In Christ, we have a life-giving, joy-producing communion with God (John 15:11, 1 John 1:3), and we should desire this intimate relationship more than anything. When in the wilderness of Judah, the Psalmist David prayed, "O God, thou art my God; early will I seek thee: my soul thirsts for thee, my flesh longs for thee, in a dry and thirsty land." He told God, "Because thy lovingkindness is better than life, my lips shall praise thee" (Ps. 63:1-3). When we live in Christ, the love of God is perfected. Abiding in Him is something we do. It is walking by faith, spending time in prayer, and the reading of Scripture. It is engaging in intentional actions that glorify God. It is a daily, hour-by-hour confidence in Him. J.C. Ryle explains, "To abide in Christ means to keep up a habit of constant close communion with Him; to be always leaning on Him, resting on Him, pouring out our hearts to Him, and using Him as our Fountain of life and strength." He said, "To have His words abiding in us is to keep His sayings and precepts continually before our memories and minds and to make them the guide of our actions."

Heavenly Father, help us to treasure Christ Jesus above all else (Phil. 3:8). May we forget what is behind us and run this race of faith with endurance (2 Tim. 4:7-8). We want to press toward that which You have called us. We have made mistakes and have fallen short of Your glory (Rom. 3:23). Thank you for mercy and grace. Help us to experience the power of Your resurrection in our lives and share that gospel with others. We ask for guidance and wisdom to discern what is true, noble, correct, pure, lovely, and of good reputation (Phil. 4:8). May we experience "the depth of the riches both of the wisdom and knowledge of God" (Rom. 11:33) that are reached when we live in Christ.

Giving God's Way

FROM EARLY CHILDHOOD, MY PARENTS TAUGHT ME THE DISCIPLINE OF giving. At the age of eleven, I got my first job – delivering newspapers. My first delivery route was quite a distance from my home. A few months later, I was given a different bicycle route that included our house. Whenever I brought the collections home, Mom would tell me to put at least ten percent in the church offering plate. She called it the tithe. I usually did this, but not always with a cheerful disposition. It seemed there was always something I wanted to buy. After all, I'm the one who made the money… right? Well, yes and no. In time, I learned that everything I have, including my finances, comes from God. I found that He will bless someone who understands the joy of giving. John 3:16 says, "For God so loved the world that he gave…" The Kingdom of God is not one of coercion; His government is not oppressive, and we are most like God when we give.

In 2 Corinthians 9:7, the apostle Paul writes, "Every man according as he purposes in his heart, so let him give; not grudgingly, or of necessity: for God loves a cheerful giver." In my mind, I see a 'cheerful giver' as a generally cheerful person – who is also a giver. The Bible offers ways to focus our giving. First, we are to give to those who cannot give back to us. Through giving to the poor (feeding the hungry, clothing the naked), we store up "a treasure in the heavens" (Luke 12:32-34). We give to the local church (1 Tim. 3:1-7) and provide for others who spread the Gospel of Christ (1 Cor. 9:14). God uses our generosity in current circumstances to prepare us for great things later. Many years ago, I was acquainted with a man who had done very well in the financial markets. He also made a lot of money restoring antique cars. Gene was a practical man who lived a very simple life, and I enjoyed our conversations. I recall the week of his wife's passing. I happened to stop by his place of business, not knowing that she had died. But this day was different. I noticed a sadness in his eyes, and I didn't know why. As I had done before, I remember telling him that I appreciated his giving heart and how he shared his wealth with those less fortunate. I'll never forget the pause in his voice when he said to me, "Yes, but what good is money if you don't have someone you love to spend it on?" I found out a few days later that he was speaking of his great loss. To this day, his words have influenced the way I handle money.

I want to be known as a generous person. I want my children and grandchildren to learn what it means to surrender their desire to elevate themselves and serve the Lord. We are all characteristically broken by a disease called selfishness. It is the core problem of every marital difficulty or parenting struggle. The same is true of our refusal to become cheerful givers as instructed in Scripture (2 Cor. 9:6-7). Sadly, the area of tithing is one of the last spiritual disciplines that believers put into practice. According to a recent survey by a respected polling firm on the subject of generosity within the local church, just 21 percent of Christians set their giving at 10 percent or more of their income, while one-quarter (25%) do not give to their church at all. Parents who want to raise generous teens must understand and practice cheerful giving before they can pass it along. Young adults are good at sniffing out hypocrisy. Parents must lead with integrity in this area. We generally dislike hearing messages on the subject of money. But the reality is that the Bible contains more than two thousand verses about money — far more than subjects like heaven, hell, or love. Giving is a heart issue. A proper understanding of lordship means we are no longer the supreme commander of our lives. We surrender control of our lives to the One who both created us and redeemed us. Apostle Paul said Christ died for us so we may no longer live for ourselves (2 Cor. 5:14-15). Opposition to cheerful giving often flows out of a selfish, corrupt heart. When we offer partial surrender to God while trying to hold onto "our" money, our worship is tainted, and our devotion is half-hearted.

Giving God's way goes deeper than just the amount of money we are willing to donate. Biblical generosity is tangible and indiscriminate (Matt. 25:31-46). The Bible says, "And God is able to make all grace abound towards you; that ye, always having all sufficiency in all things, may abound to every good work" (2 Cor. 9:8). Parents and grandparents, our highest aim is to train the next generation to place their hope in the Lord and build their lives on the unshakable foundation of God's Word. Jesus referred to a contented life when he said, "It is more blessed to give than to receive" (Acts 20:35). In God's perfect design, joy and generosity are linked. When fully surrendered to Jesus Christ (Rom. 12:1), we will cease to worry about the semantics of tithing. We will respond to the generosity of God's grace in our lives by supporting gospel ministries, extending help to the poor, and making a difference where we live, work, and play. Jesus said, "For where your treasure is, there will your heart be also" (Matt. 6:21). The issue is about demonstrating the Lordship of Christ by giving back a portion of what already belongs to God. Once you have established your ministry of giving, it will naturally grow into a lifestyle of love and gratitude toward God.

I have known Christians who are flagbearers for every discipline of the Bible except financial giving. You know them, too. These folks pride themselves on being champions for the deep theological doctrines of the Word, but generous giving is not a priority with them. In Proverbs 3:9, we read, "Honor the Lord with thy substance, and with the first fruits of thine increase." Giving is vital to our spiritual development because it is the remedy for selfishness and greed. Financial giving is a spiritual obligation. The Bible says the righteous consider the cause of the poor, but the wicked have no such concern (Prov. 29:7). Moreover, Scripture does not exempt anyone from the responsibility of giving. Even those with modest means are commended for assisting with their meager resources. Jesus himself was impressed by a small donation from an impoverished woman. He was so impressed that He used her example to teach the disciples an important lesson (Luke 21:1-4). Only when we grasp the sacrifice of Christ can we find the joy of cheerful giving. Just this week, I saw a television program that showed a class of elementary school children who raised money to help those less fortunate. The story moved me emotionally. When interviewed, several children wept with joy over what they had experienced. One young girl with tears in her eyes said, "We gave them a gift - and their joy is our gift." As believers, when we give sacrificially with a spirit of thankfulness and compassion, we will affect the lives of those around us while carrying out our Christ-given mission. If we listen closely to what the Holy Spirit is leading us to do, we can make a difference for God by living with open hands. Oh, what a joy to live this way!

Paul told Timothy, "Charge them that are rich in this world, that they be not high-minded, nor trust in uncertain riches, but in the living God, who giveth us richly all things to enjoy; that they do good, that they be rich in good works, ready to distribute, willing to communicate" (1 Tim. 6:17-18). One of the most challenging aspects of the Christian life is choosing not to depend on money for security and happiness. Many of us feel pressure to keep up appearances through material goods, but the Bible looks at money differently. Hebrews 13:5 says, "Let your conversation be without covetousness, and be content with such things as ye have: for he hath said, I will never leave thee, nor forsake thee." Are you trusting in your paycheck more than you are relying on Christ? Think of something you could sacrifice and trust God to provide. After all, we brought nothing into the world and can take nothing out of it (1 Tim. 6:6-8). Scripture connects giving with God's worship and love for others. So, what kind of giving honors God? It is generosity from a heart that longs to see His purposes accomplished. God loves a cheerful giver.

Cheerful giving begins by recognizing that everything comes from God, everything exists by his power, and everything is intended for his glory (Rom. 11:36). As a result, we bless God in times of plenty and times of want (Job 1:21; Phil. 4:11-13). Our hearts always overflow with generosity out of love for God and others. Like the widow who gave all she had (Mark 12:41-44) or the believers in the Macedonian churches who gave lavishly amid their poverty (2 Cor. 8:1-5), cheerful givers sow generously, not sparingly. They are like Barnabas, who sold a field and brought the money to the apostles. Cheerful givers give willingly, even joyously – not grudgingly or under compulsion. Their giving flows out of the joy of their relationship with Jesus (Luke 19:1-9). Generous givers do not leave giving to chance. They prioritize it. They understand the importance of putting the work of God first (Prov. 3:9). As a result, they are prepared when an opportunity to give arrives. In his first letter to the Corinthian church, Paul advised them to prepare their gift for the saints in Jerusalem by setting aside money each week in proportion to their income (1 Cor. 16:1-2). So when he came, the gift would be given joyfully – not grudgingly or as an afterthought.

Cheerful givers experience the abundant blessings of God. Sometimes, those blessings are material. Other times, they are not. But one thing is sure: cheerful givers have all that they need at all times (Phil. 4:19). This abundance comes from their sense of gratitude and their realization that God owns all things and is the source of every good gift (James 1:17). Cheerful givers experience God's riches in every way – spiritually, relationally, and materially. God blesses them so they can abound in every good work and be generous on every occasion (2 Cor. 9:1-15). Like Abraham, they are blessed to be a blessing. They sow generously – but God provides the seed that they sow. Sharing our lives and possessions is a profession of the Gospel and a testimony of our salvation. It's a witness to sinners, an encouragement to saints. It is evidence of the grace of God. Generosity reflects the image of God, who gave His Son to meet the greatest need of all time.

Be Still and Know

SOMETHING ABOUT PSALM 46:10 CAUSES US TO PAY CLOSE ATTENTION. God speaks: "Be still, and know that I am God: I will be exalted among the heathen; I will be exalted in the earth." This verse should help us step back from the frantic activity of life and remember that, regardless of what happens to us, God is in control. The Psalm begins with, "God is our refuge and strength, a very present help in trouble. Therefore, will not we fear…" It is wonderful to understand that "be still" is the same thing Jesus said to the wind and waves in Mark 4:39. The tone of both passages is that we stop stressing over the circumstance. God is saying, "Let me be God. Don't try to do my job. Be patient, be still, and let me go to work on your behalf." Too often, we reach out to people in our lives to say or do something that will heal the pain of our situation. We look for someone to fix our problems. We get upset when they can't. Good friends are wonderful, and I thank the Lord for them all. But answers will be found only in the One who can meet the needs of the human heart. God will protect his people from evil (Ps. 91) and bring them everlasting peace (Rev. 21:4). Seek the Lord in prayer. Turn off the distracting noises of your world and experience God's presence. Silence the internal disturbances and know that God has secured the souls of believers through Jesus Christ. Be still and know that He is God, for indeed, He is exalted!

The demands of life can pull us in many directions, even as we strive to serve the Lord. But through all, we must embrace the reality that God is ever-present, and He alone is the remedy for a troubled soul. Amid the clamor, seek the stillness. Quiet moments with God will serve as a wellspring of grace from which we draw strength and understanding. More remarkable, we become a beacon of hope for others seeking refuge. Listening for the Spirit's guidance is difficult when loud, persistent voices clamor for our attention. Moses, Samuel, and Elijah intentionally positioned themselves to hear God. Moses was curious and investigated the burning bush (Ex. 3). Samuel paid attention to patterns and repetition (1 Sam. 3). Elijah came out of the cave of fear (1 Kings 19). In Exodus 14:14, God tells his people, "The Lord shall fight for you, and ye shall hold your peace." Holding our peace suggests a calm surrender to His will. When we are silent before God, He often brings to mind a passage of Scripture that is just what we need to calm our spirit. (John 14:26). David said, "He only is my rock and my salvation, and my refuge is in God" (Ps. 62:7). In Philippians 4:6, the apostle Paul says, "Be careful for nothing; but in everything by prayer and supplication with thanksgiving let your requests be made known unto God." These are great and precious promises for those determined to allow Jesus Christ to be their all in all!

The Psalmist tells us to "Rest in the Lord and wait patiently for him" (Ps. 37:7). What does it mean to rest in the Lord? God's sabbath plays a vital role in this idea of relaxing, where we stop, step back from the intense pace of life, and focus on Him. We set aside the chaos of our circumstances, and through prayer and the reading of the Word, we allow the peace of God to fill our hearts. God often speaks in a still, small voice (1 Kings 19:11-13), and we must be near Him to hear Him. What does it mean to wait on the Lord? The idea of waiting implies an end goal, something we expect to happen. There's an active anticipation, all on God's timeline and according to His purpose, not ours. A wonderful lady in my church responds to all of life with this: "I'm rejoicing in the Lord." When her grown children are physically distant from her, she has a positive outlook on life. When her faith is tested, she's still rejoicing. Oh, what a joy it is to be around people like her!

My grandmother was removed from her biological family at a very young age. She and her sister were taken from the house in separate police cars, never to be together again. She was placed into several foster homes through the years, and life was difficult. Yet, she remained strong in spirit. Grandma Nonie passed from this life in her mid-eighties, and her legacy was cheerfulness and encouragement. She spent the last twenty-three years as a widow and died a painful death caused by cancer. But not one time did I hear her complain. She was the person everyone loved. Why? Because when you visited her, you always walked away refreshed. And when she spoke of heartache, it was always in the context of how God accomplished His purpose. During the Great Depression, her three-year-old boy died, having suffered from spinal meningitis. On one occasion, little Donald Wayne told his mother there were two Teddy Bears at the foot of his bed, but there was only one. The disease had caused pressure on his optical nerve, and his eyes had crossed. He died a few days later. Grandma would tell the story, only to say that it was through this suffering that she surrendered her heart to God. Glorifying Jesus Christ was her greatest desire, and people loved to hear what she had to say! How is it in our lives today? Are we content or discontented? And if we are discontented, are we partly to blame? And, if we are partly to blame, have we done what we can to improve the situation, or do we go through life justifying our poor attitude? Be still and know that He is God! Regardless of how difficult our circumstances are, we can still find reasons to praise Him.

We are told in Colossians 3:15 to be thankful. Some things happen in our lives that we are truly grateful for. We are thankful for birthdays, weddings, love, and family. But some things that happen are really difficult. We might have an illness, the death of a loved one, divorce, separation from family members, or some other sad event. What is our response to these things? Many are preoccupied with telling others how disgruntled they are... wherever they are. But let's look closely at 1 Thessalonians 5:18. Some have said this verse tells us to be thankful for all situations. But the verse says to be thankful IN all situations. The original word for IN here means "in the middle of" or "during." Apostle Paul's various ministry experiences offered him times of plenty and times of need, but he had a grateful attitude. Contentment is not automatic, nor is it a natural disposition. Rather, it is a learned skill, and Paul learned he could do all things through the strength of Jesus Christ (Phil. 4:13).

A university undergraduate was impressed with a Christian man who addressed his class calmly and peacefully. Said the college student, "I suppose he spends most of his time in prayer and preparation in his study, apart from the chaos and noise of ordinary life." Smiling rather knowingly, his older friend said, "Would you like to meet him?" The young man said he would, and they arranged to meet the following day. Pushing his way through the swinging doors of a large manufacturing company, the old friend introduced his young companion to the man with a beautiful message and calm countenance. He was sitting at his desk immersed in business, a business that was not without daily challenges. "My young friend is very anxious about your occupation," said the older man. The Christian businessman responded, "My occupation? My boy, my occupation is to wait for Jesus Christ to return from heaven... and meanwhile, I make buttons." There will always be another cause for anxiety just around the corner. This is life. But, as we learn to release all outcomes to God, our hearts and minds will rest — even in turbulence (Psalm 52:8). Contentment is the inward expression of a relationship with Jesus Christ.

Some years ago, we had a celebration of life for my wife's mother. She was ninety-four years of age at her passing. This wonderful Christian lady would say, "In any situation, you can laugh or cry. I choose to laugh because it makes me feel better." She seemed to find something positive in every unpleasant situation. How? She found it because she was looking for it! She would tell us, "When sadness comes, I choose to busy myself and think about the good things." Frances Ashurst was content despite her circumstances because her faith in God was strong. How do we declare our satisfaction in God? By acknowledging His wisdom, justice, and goodness – and then obeying His commands. Many Christians are dissatisfied, not because they aren't doing well, but because others are doing better. But our circumstances are the arrangement of the providence of God, and hope in Christ is the secret of our joy. Thankfulness is a state of mind. We are not obliged to say, "I like these circumstances," to be satisfied in the Lord. And when we are content in Christ, we become useful. Paul learned to be patient with his surroundings in all circumstances and was used mightily by God. Joy is found in our Lord's promise, "I will never leave thee, nor forsake thee" (Heb. 13:5). A contented spirit is a cheerful, thankful, and quiet spirit. Be still, and know that He is God!

As we mature in the faith, we will remember the enormous sacrifice the Lord Jesus made for us on the Cross. Individuals saved by grace will develop an attitude of grateful praise and ceaseless thanksgiving for all the Lord has done for them. Gratitude is no companion of dissatisfaction or murmuring. Contentment comes through an understanding of the Almighty God that transcends whatever we face in life. Therefore, let us give thanks in everything, knowing His grace is sufficient (2 Cor. 12:9). Are you content? The question is not whether there are circumstances in your life that you would like to change. There are certainly at least some. The question is whether or not we can be content with them. Is that possible? God says it is.

Heavenly Father, may we grow in grace with an attitude of thanksgiving for all you have done for us in Christ Jesus. Indeed, we desire to be useful in your Kingdom on earth, and we want your will to be done in our lives. Please forgive our murmuring and help us always to give thanks with a sweet spirit, for this will be our testimony to those around us who need you in their lives. We pray that you will develop and refine the grace of thanksgiving in our hearts today. This we ask in Jesus' name. Amen.

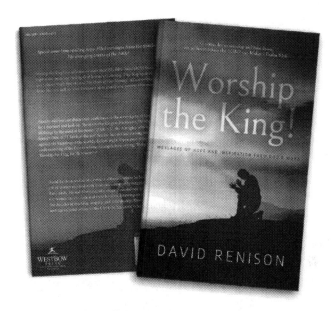

WORSHIP THE KING!
A 260-page collection of Bible-based devotionals

LIGHT FOR OUR WAY
A 545-page collection of Bible-based devotionals

Printed in the United States
by Baker & Taylor Publisher Services